OMAKE
OUR TEACHERS ARE DATING

HAYAMA ASUKA

TERANO SAKI

HEALTH AND PE

DATING

BIOLOGY

♪ OBSERVES

TEASES ♪

BANDOU RUI

MIYAZAWA ELENA

JAPAN-ESE

EN-GLISH

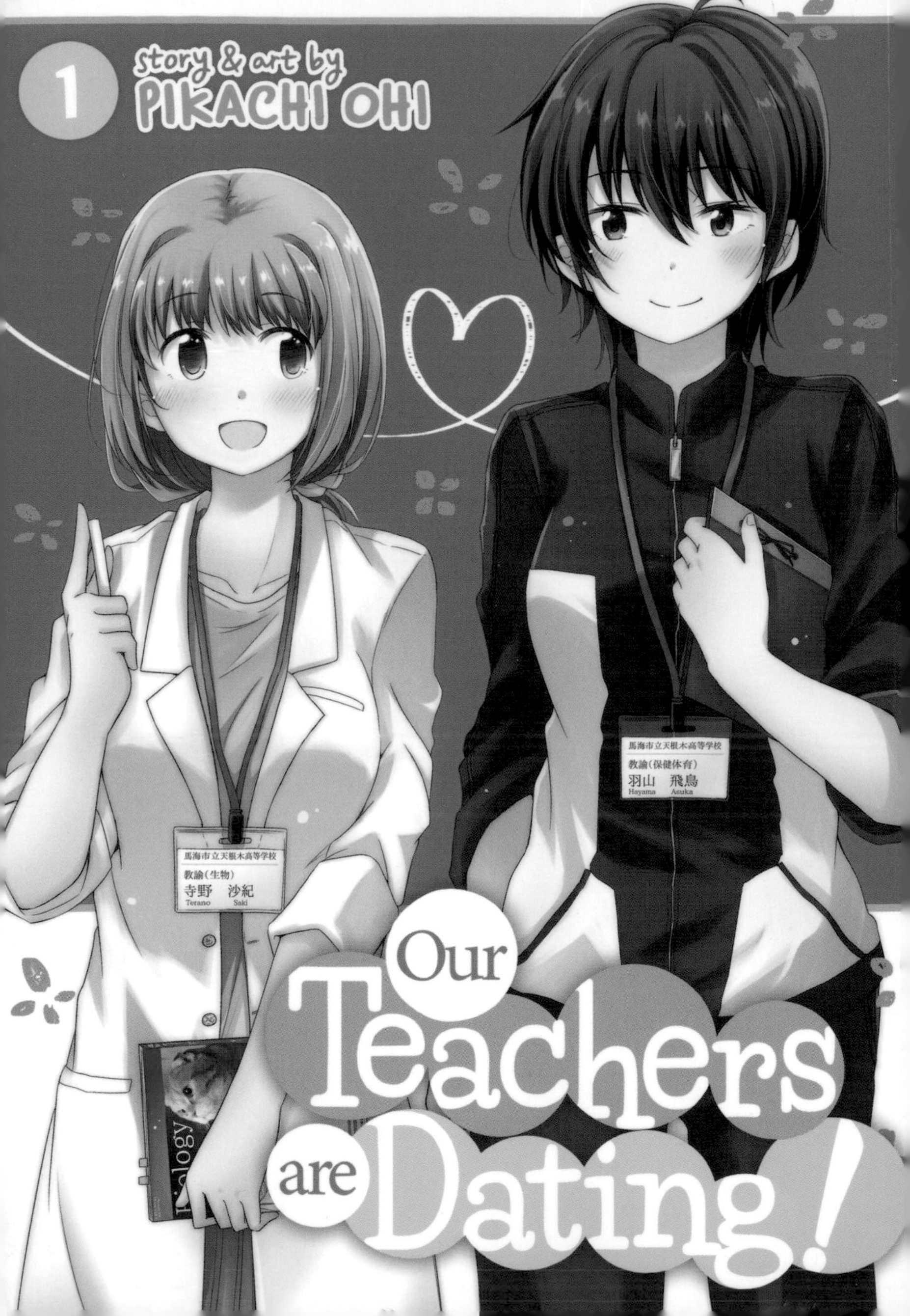
1
story & art by
PIKACHI OHI
馬海市立天根木高等学校
教諭（保健体育）
羽山　飛鳥
Hayama　Asuka
馬海市立天根木高等学校
教諭（生物）
寺野　沙紀
Terano　Saki
Our Teachers are Dating!

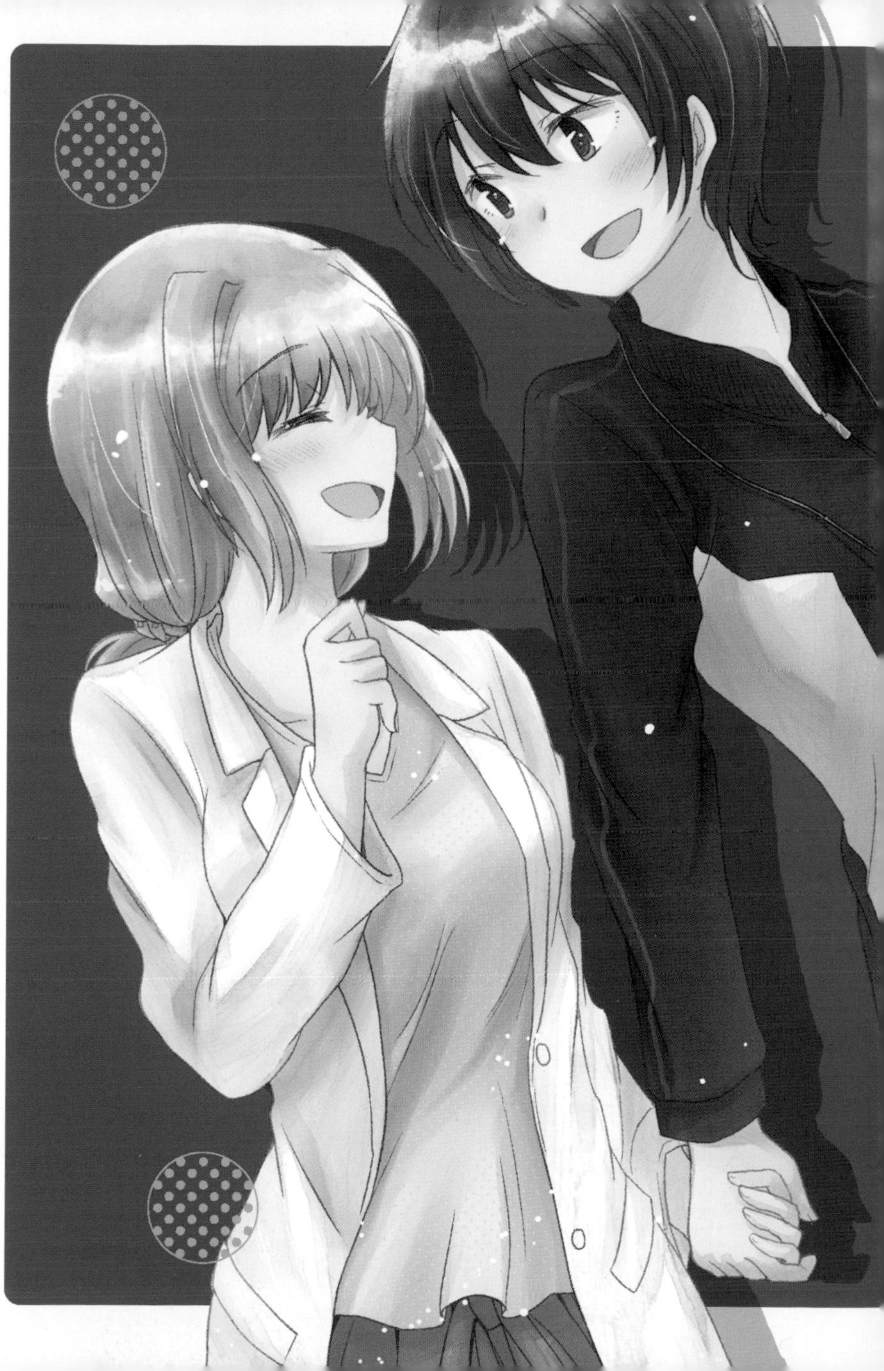

No.

Date / /

Our Teachers are Dating!

TIMETABLE

1

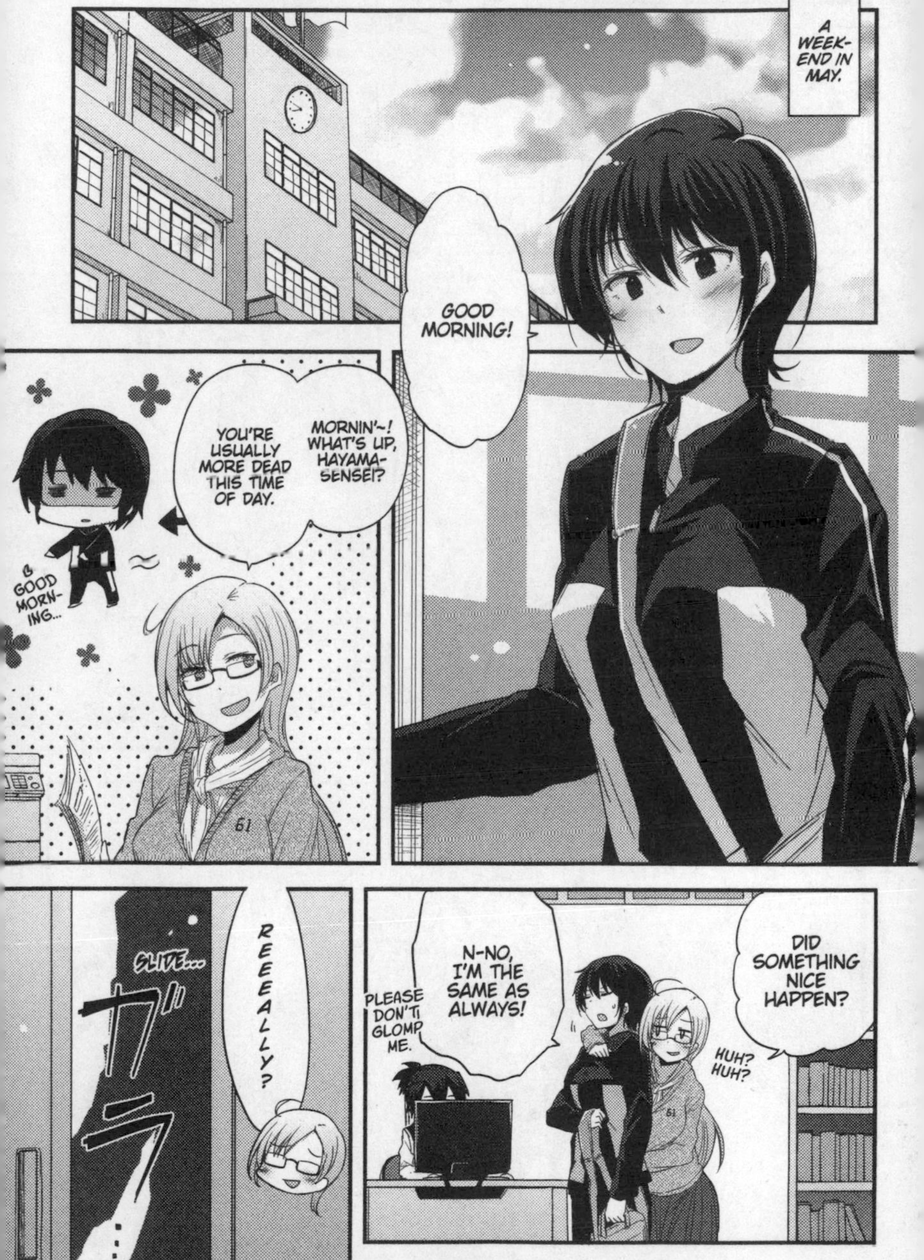
A WEEK-END IN MAY.
GOOD MORNING!
MORNIN'~! WHAT'S UP, HAYAMA-SENSEI?
YOU'RE USUALLY MORE DEAD THIS TIME OF DAY.
GOOD MORN-ING...
DID SOMETHING NICE HAPPEN?
HUH? HUH?
N-NO, I'M THE SAME AS ALWAYS!
PLEASE DON'T GLOMP ME.
REEEEALLY?
SLIDE...

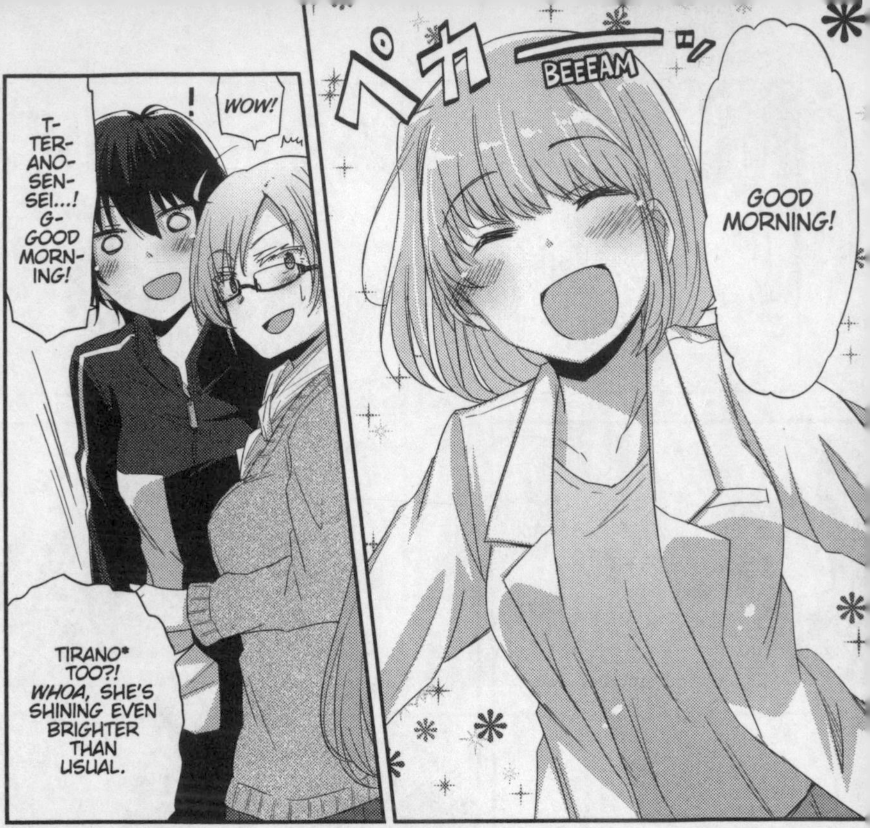
ペカ
BEEEAM
GOOD MORNING!
WOW!
!
T-TERANO-SENSEI...! G-GOOD MORNING!
TIRANO* TOO?! *WHOA*, SHE'S SHINING EVEN BRIGHTER THAN USUAL.

**A nickname.*

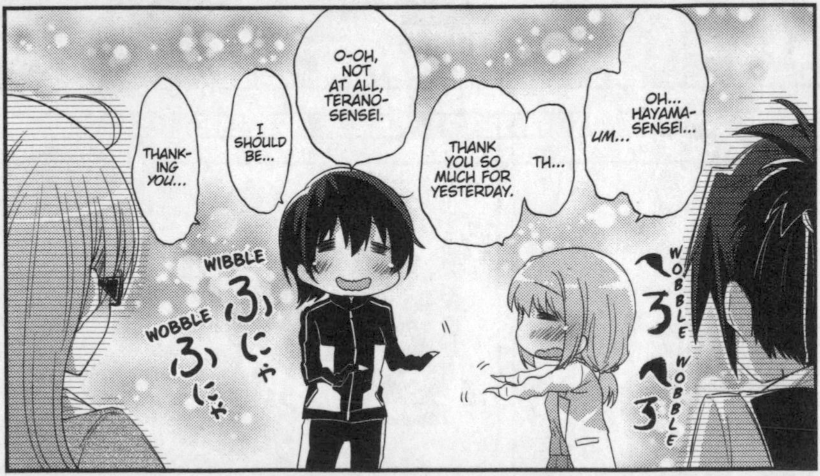
OH... HAYAMA-SENSEI...
UM...
TH...
THANK YOU SO MUCH FOR YESTERDAY.
O-OH, NOT AT ALL, TERANO-SENSEI.
I SHOULD BE...
THANKING YOU...
へろ WOBBLE
へろ WOBBLE
WIBBLE ふにゃ
WOBBLE ふにゃ

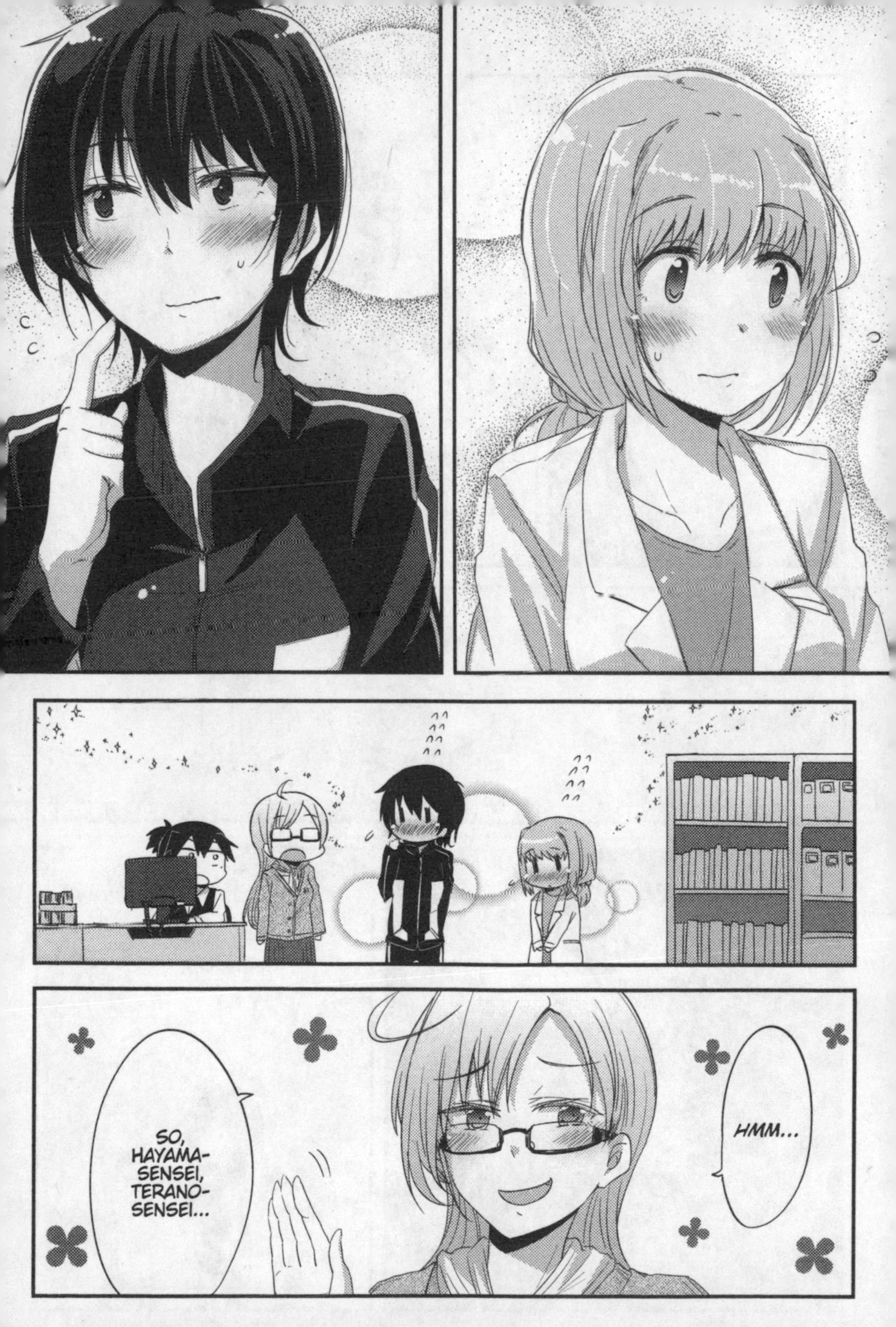
HMM...
SO, HAYAMA-SENSEI, TERANO-SENSEI...

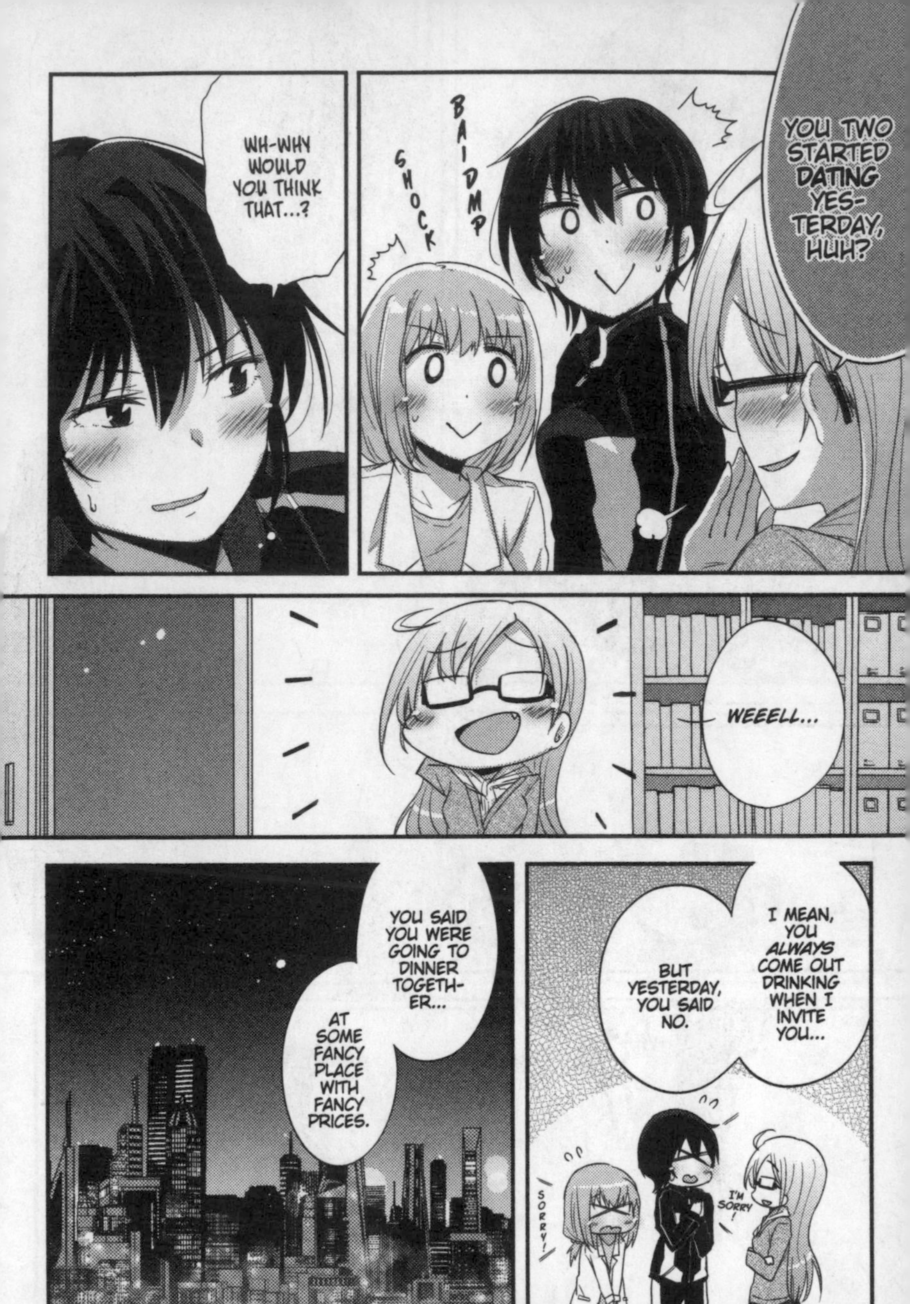
YOU TWO STARTED DATING YES-TERDAY, HUH?
BA-DMP
SHOCK
WH-WHY WOULD YOU THINK THAT...?
WEEELL...
I MEAN, YOU *ALWAYS* COME OUT DRINKING WHEN I INVITE YOU...
BUT YESTERDAY, YOU SAID NO.
I'M SORRY!
SORRY!
YOU SAID YOU WERE GOING TO DINNER TOGETH-ER...
AT SOME FANCY PLACE WITH FANCY PRICES.

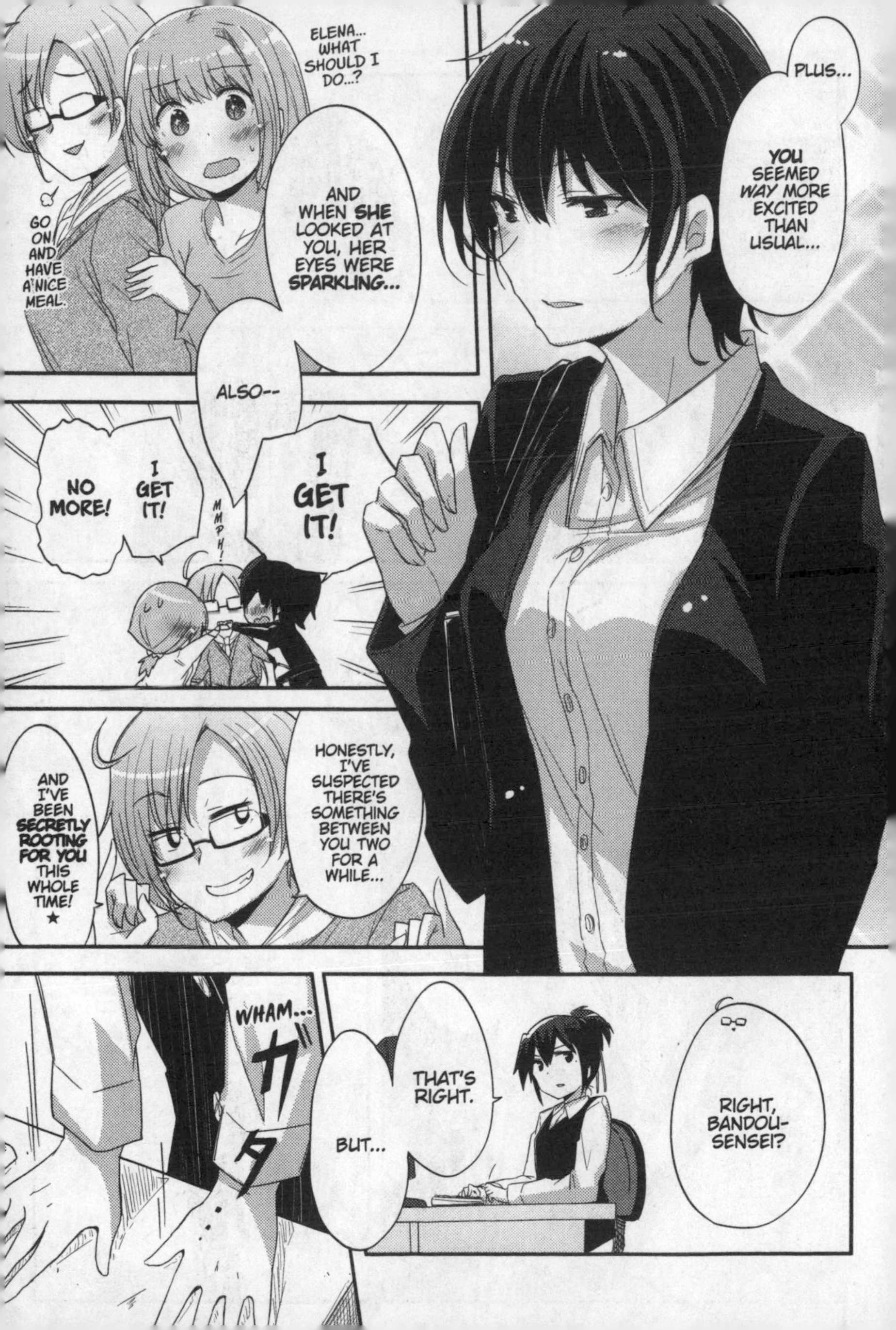
PLUS...
YOU SEEMED WAY MORE EXCITED THAN USUAL...
AND WHEN SHE LOOKED AT YOU, HER EYES WERE SPARKLING...
ALSO--
ELENA... WHAT SHOULD I DO...?
GO ON AND HAVE A NICE MEAL.
I GET IT!
MMPH!
I GET IT!
NO MORE!
HONESTLY, I'VE SUSPECTED THERE'S SOMETHING BETWEEN YOU TWO FOR A WHILE...
AND I'VE BEEN SECRETLY ROOTING FOR YOU THIS WHOLE TIME! ★
RIGHT, BANDOU-SENSEI?
THAT'S RIGHT.
BUT...
WHAM...
カタ

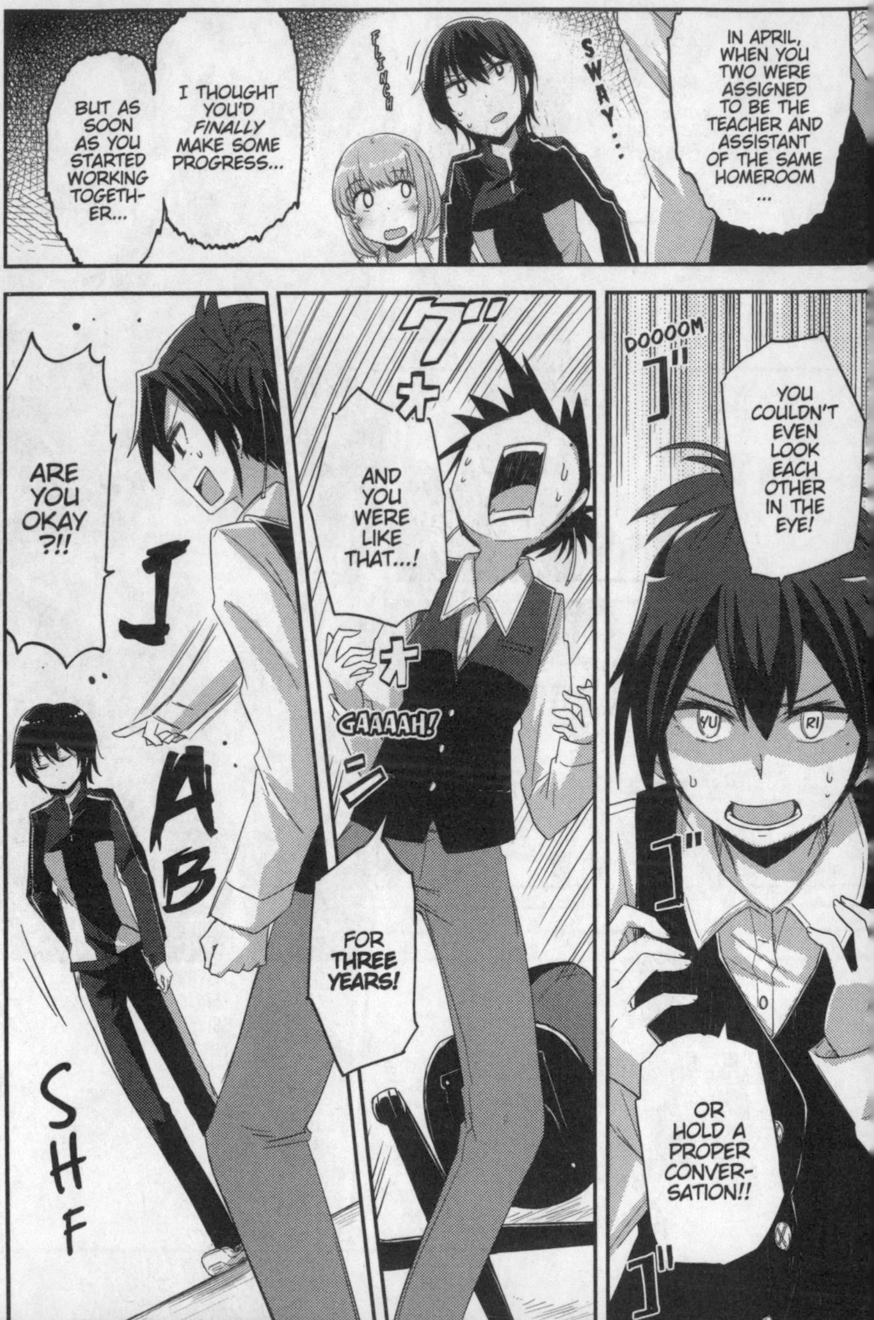
IN APRIL, WHEN YOU TWO WERE ASSIGNED TO BE THE TEACHER AND ASSISTANT OF THE SAME HOMEROOM ...
SWAY...
FLINCH
I THOUGHT YOU'D *FINALLY* MAKE SOME PROGRESS...
BUT AS SOON AS YOU STARTED WORKING TOGETH-ER...
DOOOOM
YOU COULDN'T EVEN LOOK EACH OTHER IN THE EYE!
YU
RI
OR HOLD A PROPER CONVER-SATION!!
AND YOU WERE LIKE THAT...!
GAAAAH!
FOR THREE YEARS!
ARE YOU OKAY ?!!
JAB
SHF

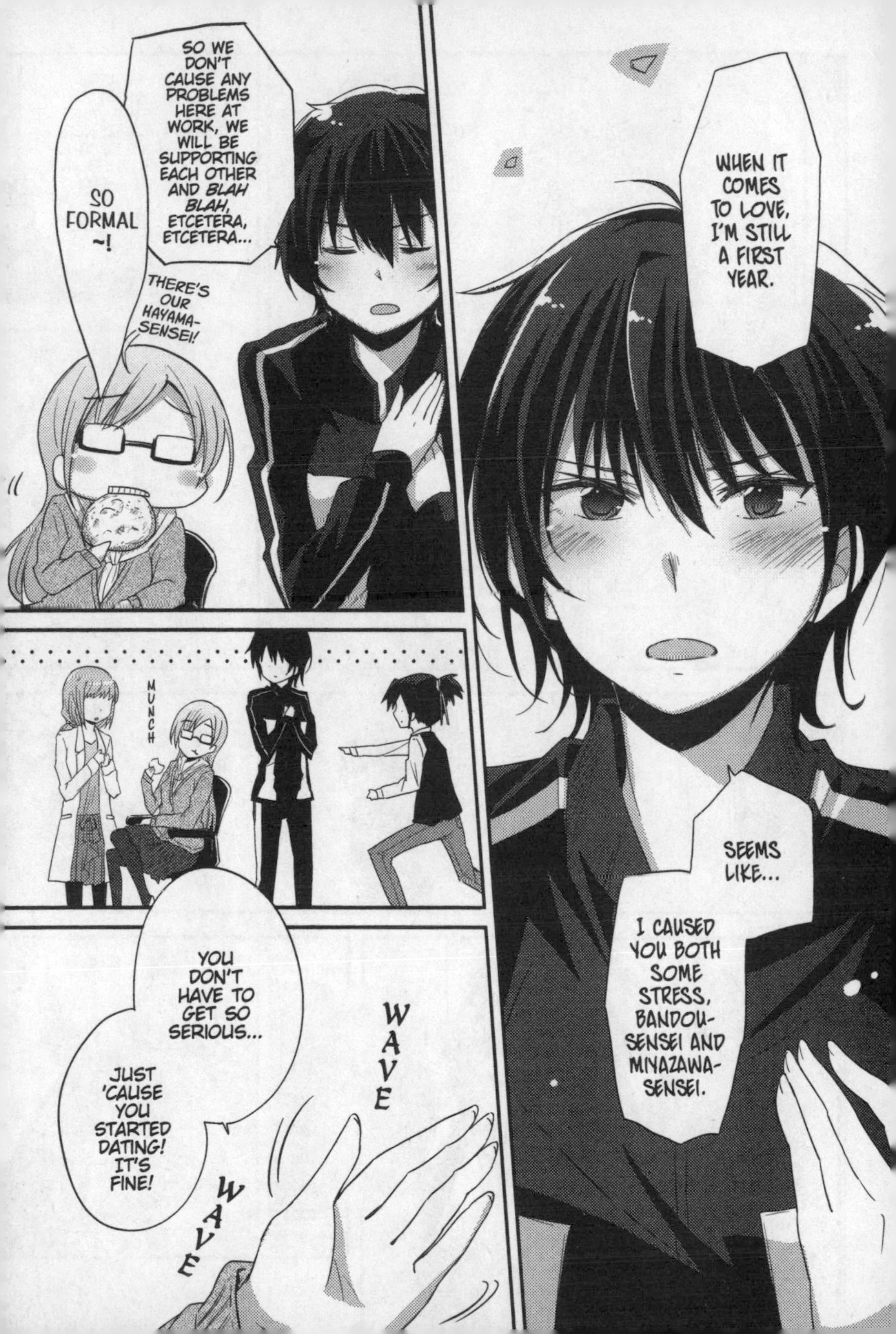
WHEN IT COMES TO LOVE, I'M STILL A FIRST YEAR.
SEEMS LIKE...
I CAUSED YOU BOTH SOME STRESS, BANDOU-SENSEI AND MIYAZAWA-SENSEI.
SO WE DON'T CAUSE ANY PROBLEMS HERE AT WORK, WE WILL BE SUPPORTING EACH OTHER AND BLAH BLAH, ETCETERA, ETCETERA...
SO FORMAL ~!
THERE'S OUR HAYAMA-SENSEI!
MUNCH
WAVE
WAVE
YOU DON'T HAVE TO GET SO SERIOUS...
JUST 'CAUSE YOU STARTED DATING! IT'S FINE!

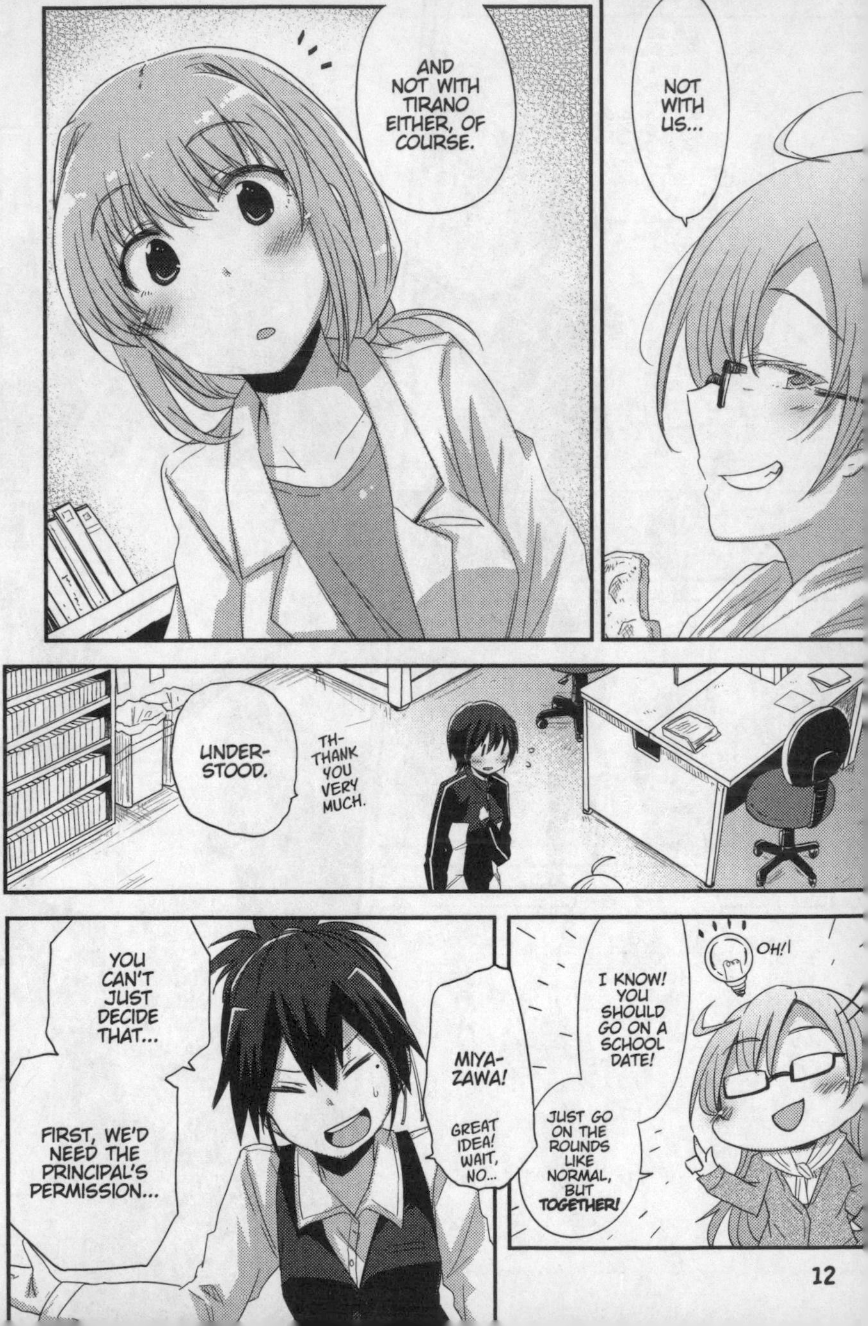
NOT WITH US...
AND NOT WITH TIRANO EITHER, OF COURSE.
TH-THANK YOU VERY MUCH.
UNDER-STOOD.
OH!
I KNOW! YOU SHOULD GO ON A SCHOOL DATE!
JUST GO ON THE ROUNDS LIKE NORMAL, BUT **TOGETHER!**
MIYA-ZAWA!
GREAT IDEA! WAIT, NO...
YOU CAN'T JUST DECIDE THAT...
FIRST, WE'D NEED THE PRINCIPAL'S PERMISSION...

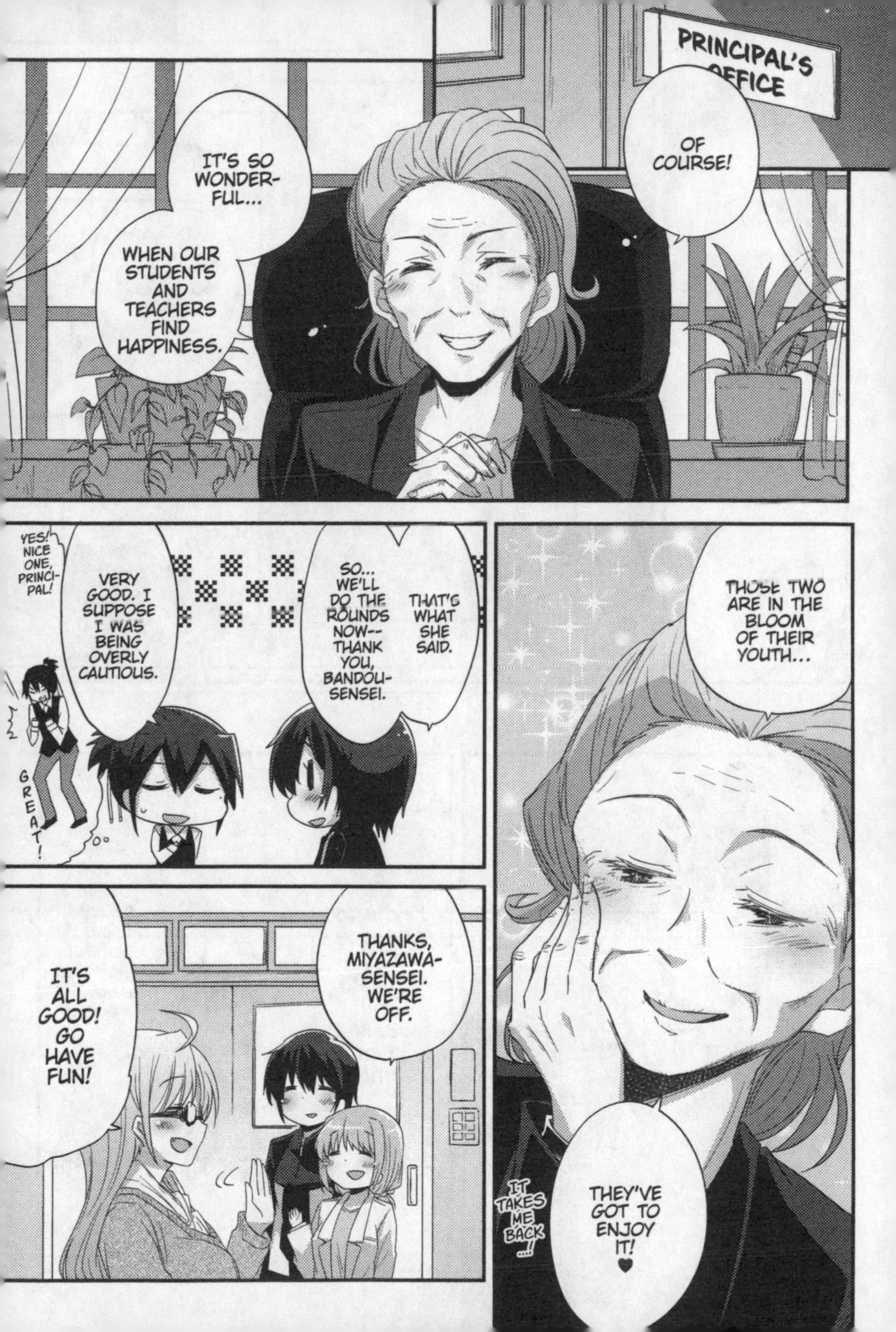
PRINCIPAL'S OFFICE
OF COURSE!
IT'S SO WONDERFUL...
WHEN OUR STUDENTS AND TEACHERS FIND HAPPINESS.
THOSE TWO ARE IN THE BLOOM OF THEIR YOUTH...
THEY'VE GOT TO ENJOY IT! ♥
IT TAKES ME BACK...!
SO... WE'LL DO THE ROUNDS NOW--THANK YOU, BANDOU-SENSEI.
THAT'S WHAT SHE SAID.
VERY GOOD. I SUPPOSE I WAS BEING OVERLY CAUTIOUS.
YES! NICE ONE, PRINCIPAL!
GREAT!
THANKS, MIYAZAWA-SENSEI. WE'RE OFF.
IT'S ALL GOOD! GO HAVE FUN!

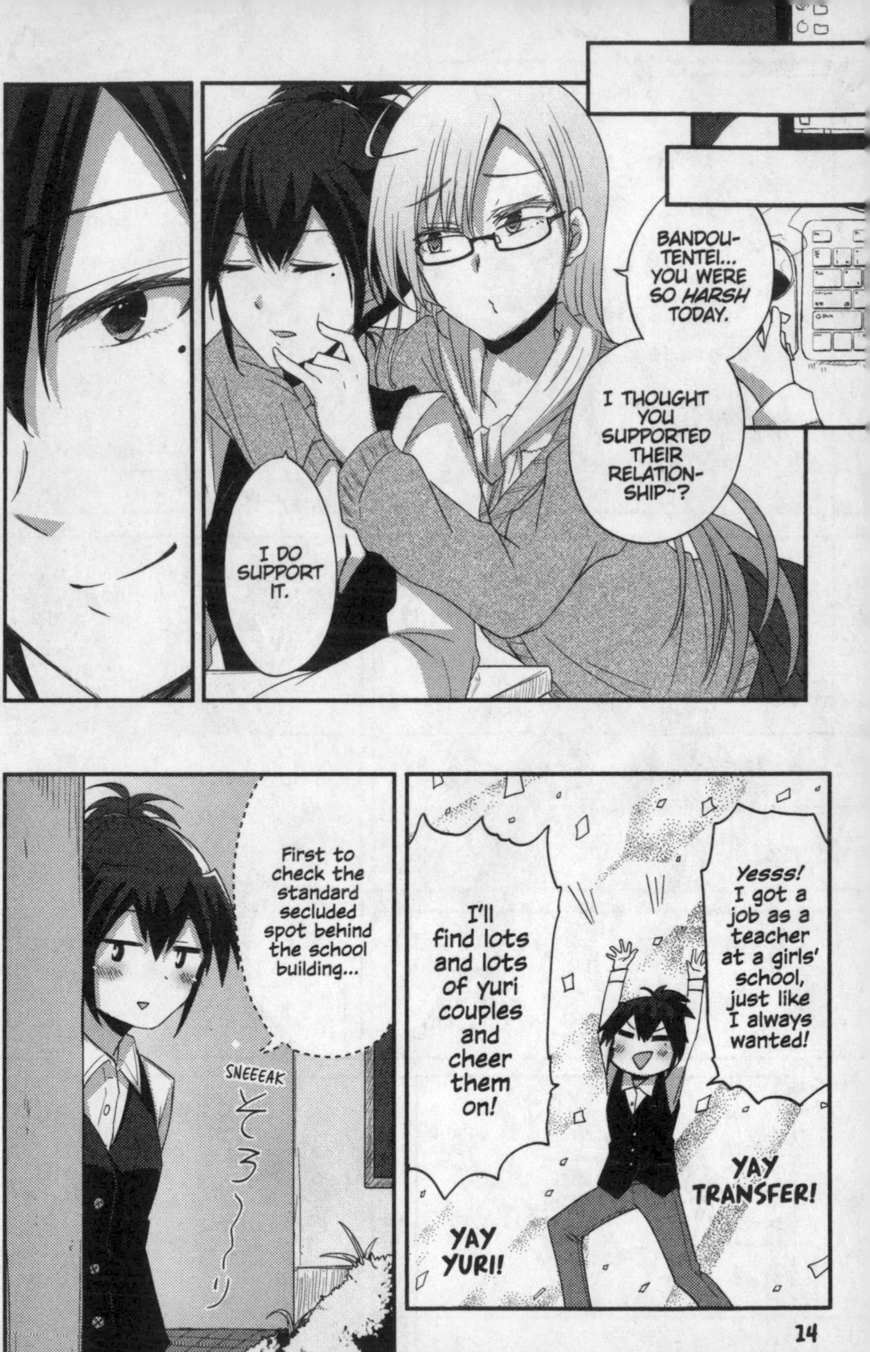
BANDOU-TENTEI... YOU WERE SO *HARSH* TODAY.
I THOUGHT YOU SUPPORTED THEIR RELATIONSHIP~?
I DO SUPPORT IT.
Yesss! I got a job as a teacher at a girls' school, just like I always wanted!
I'll find lots and lots of yuri couples and cheer them on!
YAY TRANSFER!
YAY YURI!
First to check the standard secluded spot behind the school building...
SNEEEAK
そろ～～～り

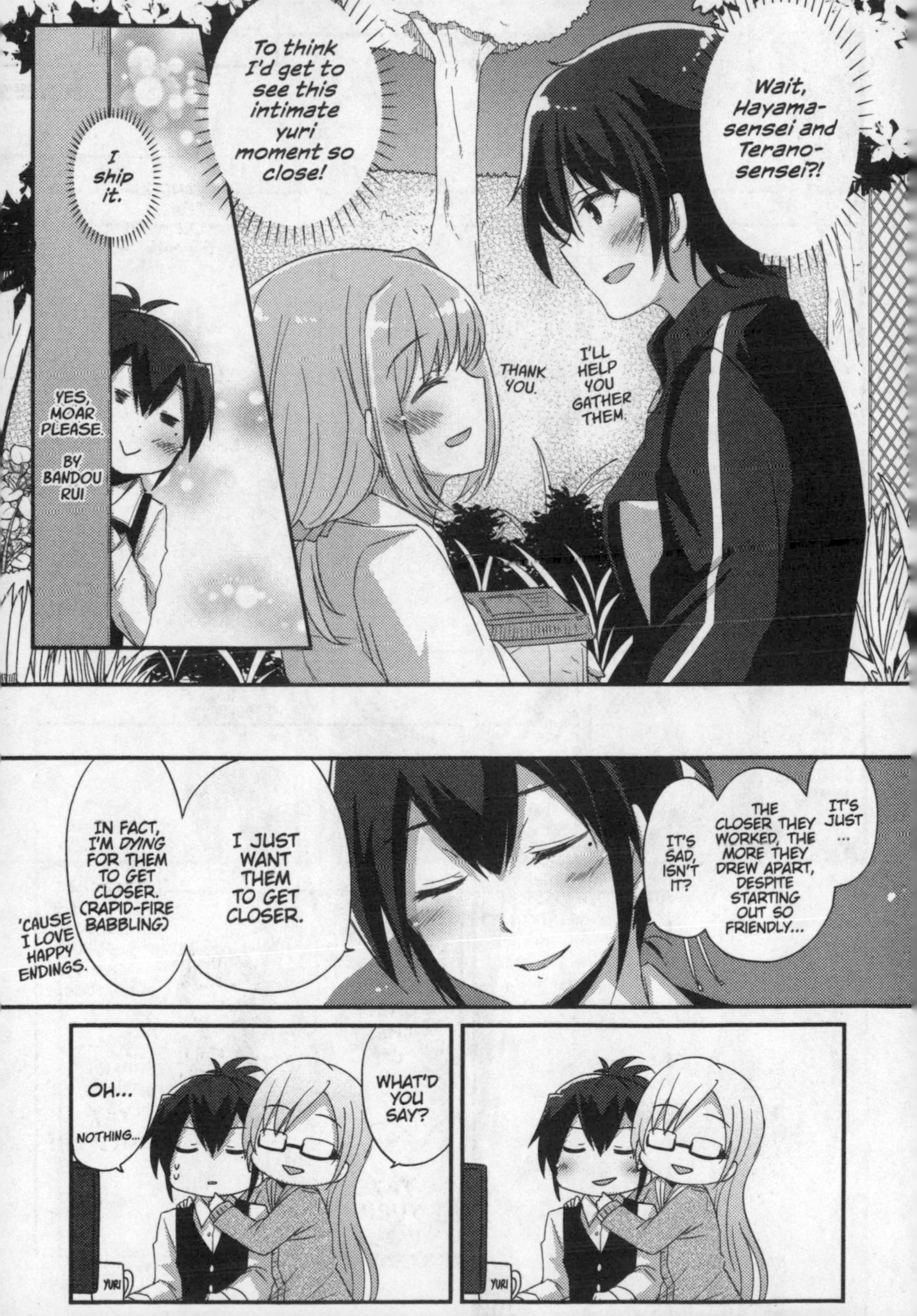
Wait, Hayama-sensei and Terano-sensei?!
I'LL HELP YOU GATHER THEM.
THANK YOU.
To think I'd get to see this intimate yuri moment so close!
I ship it.
YES, MOAR PLEASE.
BY BANDOU RUI
IT'S JUST ...
THE CLOSER THEY WORKED, THE MORE THEY DREW APART, DESPITE STARTING OUT SO FRIENDLY...
IT'S SAD, ISN'T IT?
I JUST WANT THEM TO GET CLOSER.
IN FACT, I'M *DYING* FOR THEM TO GET CLOSER. (RAPID-FIRE BABBLING)
'CAUSE I LOVE HAPPY ENDINGS.
YURI
WHAT'D YOU SAY?
OH...
NOTHING...
YURI

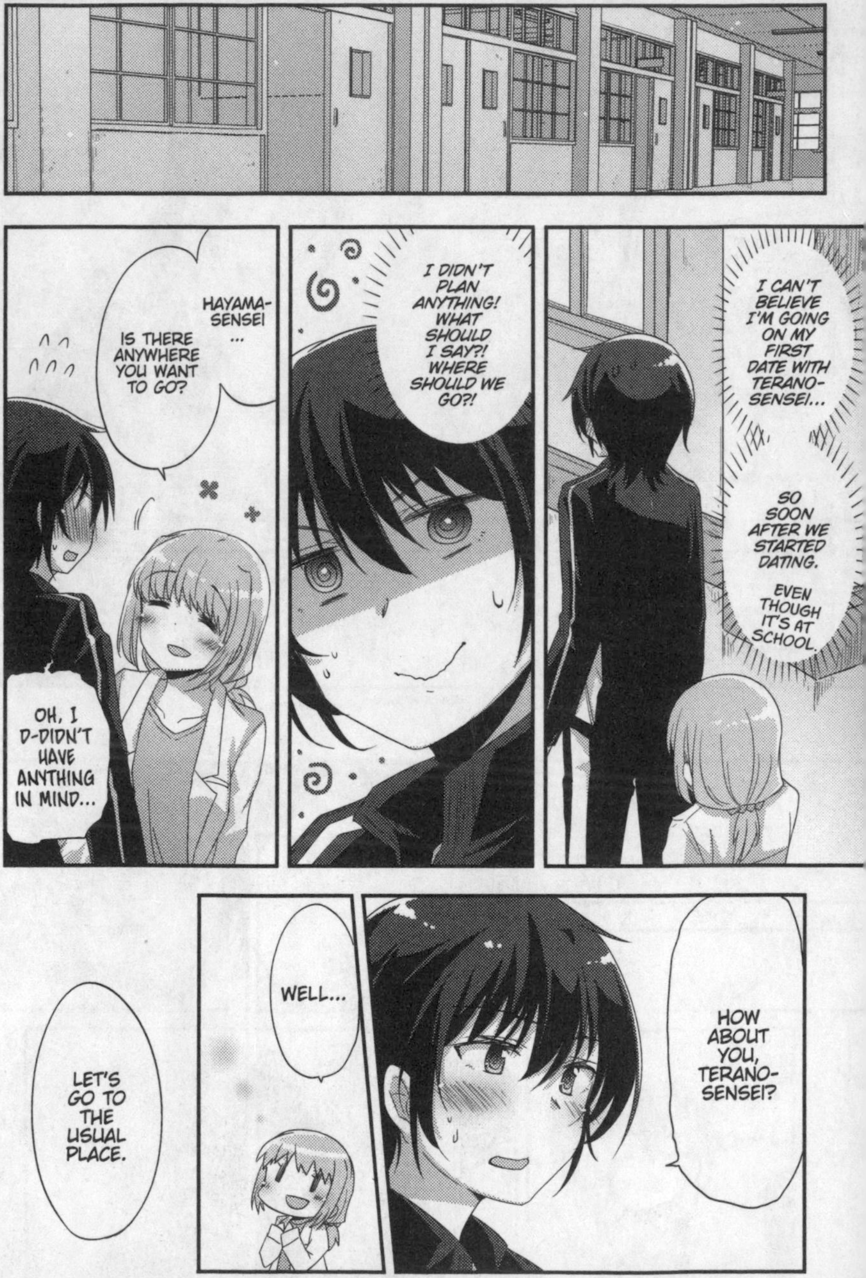
I CAN'T BELIEVE I'M GOING ON MY FIRST DATE WITH TERANO-SENSEI...
SO SOON AFTER WE STARTED DATING.
EVEN THOUGH IT'S AT SCHOOL.
I DIDN'T PLAN ANYTHING! WHAT SHOULD I SAY?! WHERE SHOULD WE GO?!
HAYAMA-SENSEI ...
IS THERE ANYWHERE YOU WANT TO GO?
OH, I D-DIDN'T HAVE ANYTHING IN MIND...
HOW ABOUT YOU, TERANO-SENSEI?
WELL...
LET'S GO TO THE USUAL PLACE.

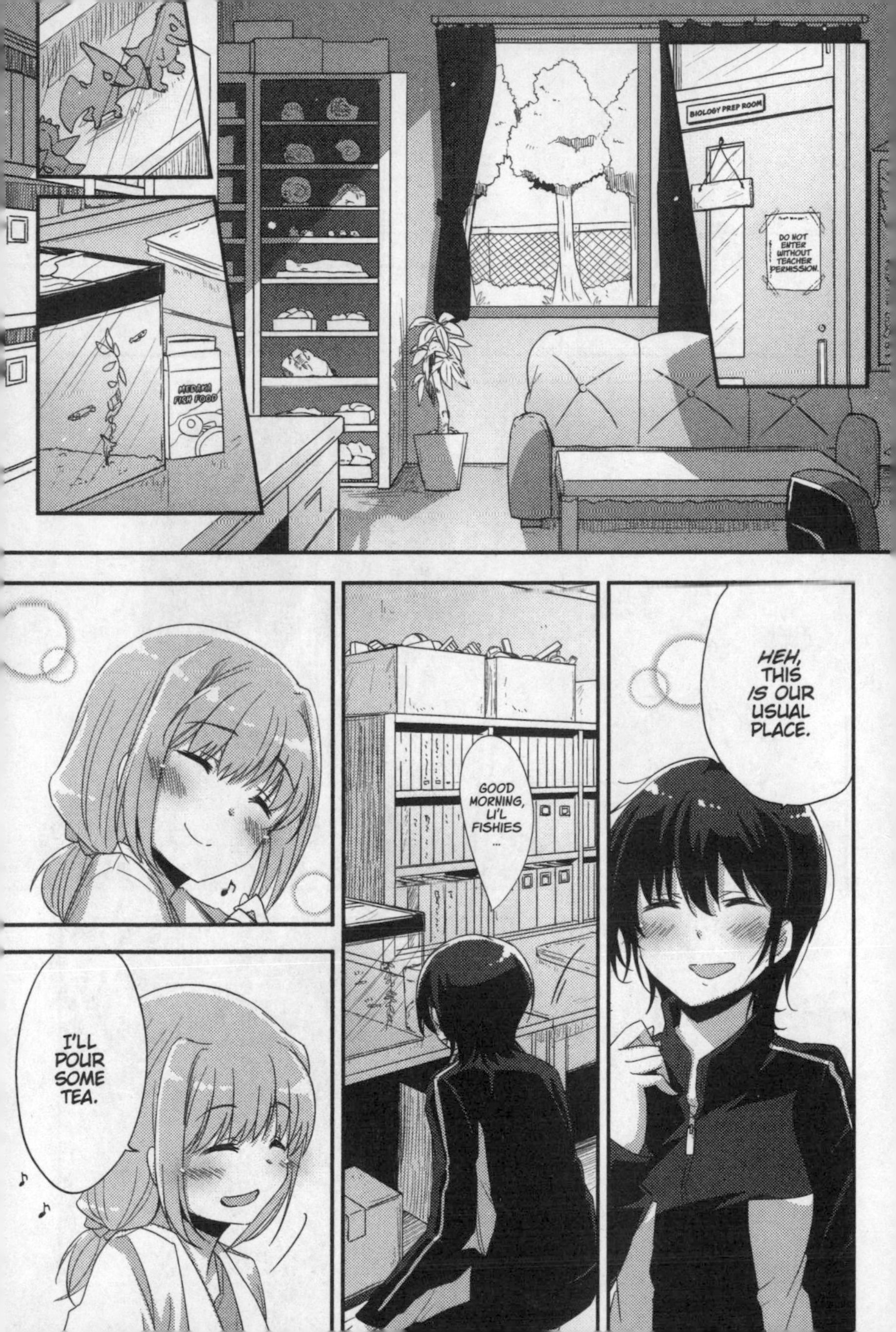
BIOLOGY PREP ROOM
DO NOT ENTER WITHOUT TEACHER PERMISSION.
MEDAKA FISH FOOD
HEH, THIS IS OUR USUAL PLACE.
GOOD MORNING, LI'L FISHIES ...
I'LL POUR SOME TEA.

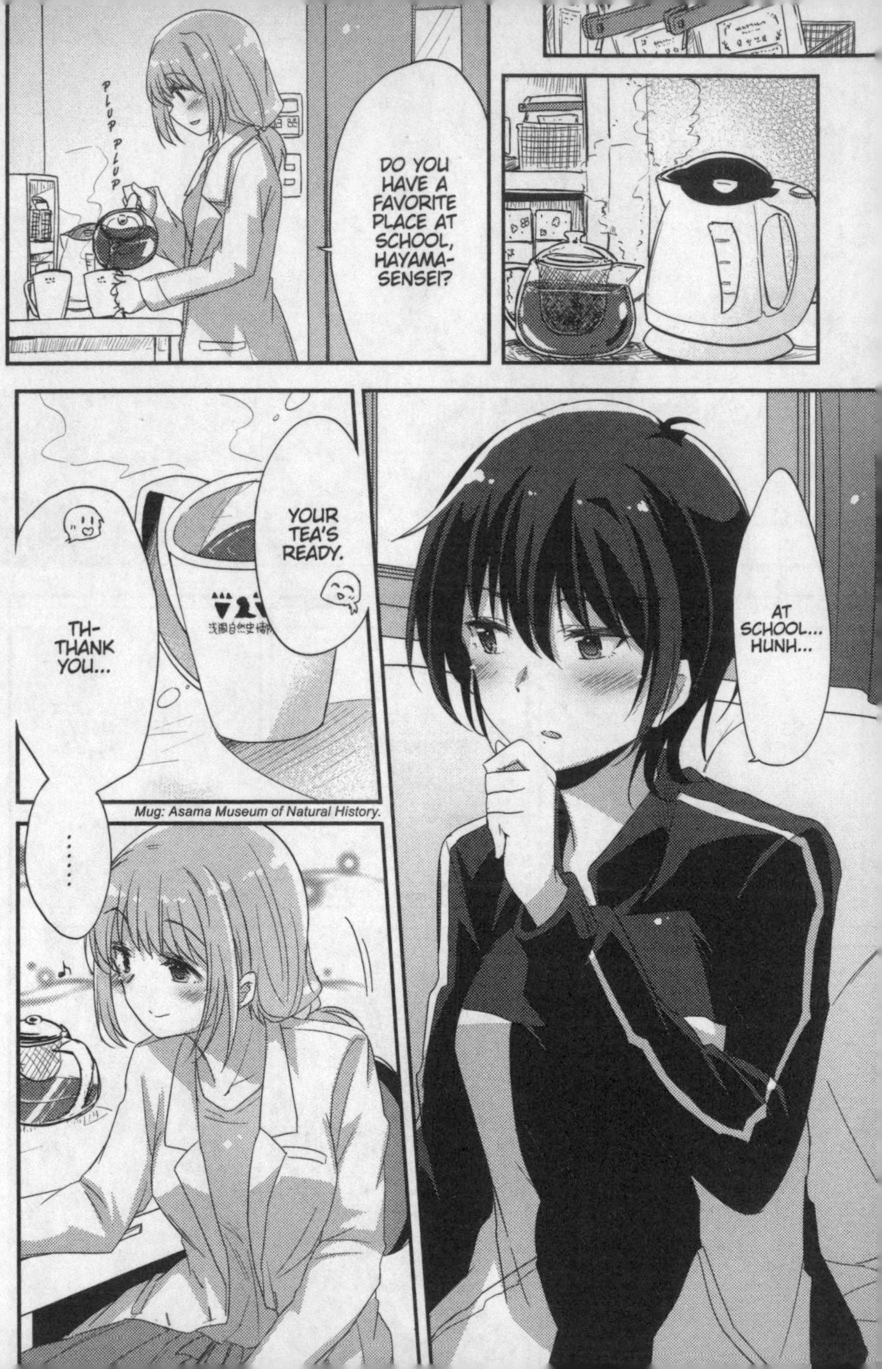
PLUP PLUP
DO YOU HAVE A FAVORITE PLACE AT SCHOOL, HAYAMA-SENSEI?
AT SCHOOL... HUNH...
YOUR TEA'S READY.
TH-THANK YOU...
......
Mug: Asama Museum of Natural History.

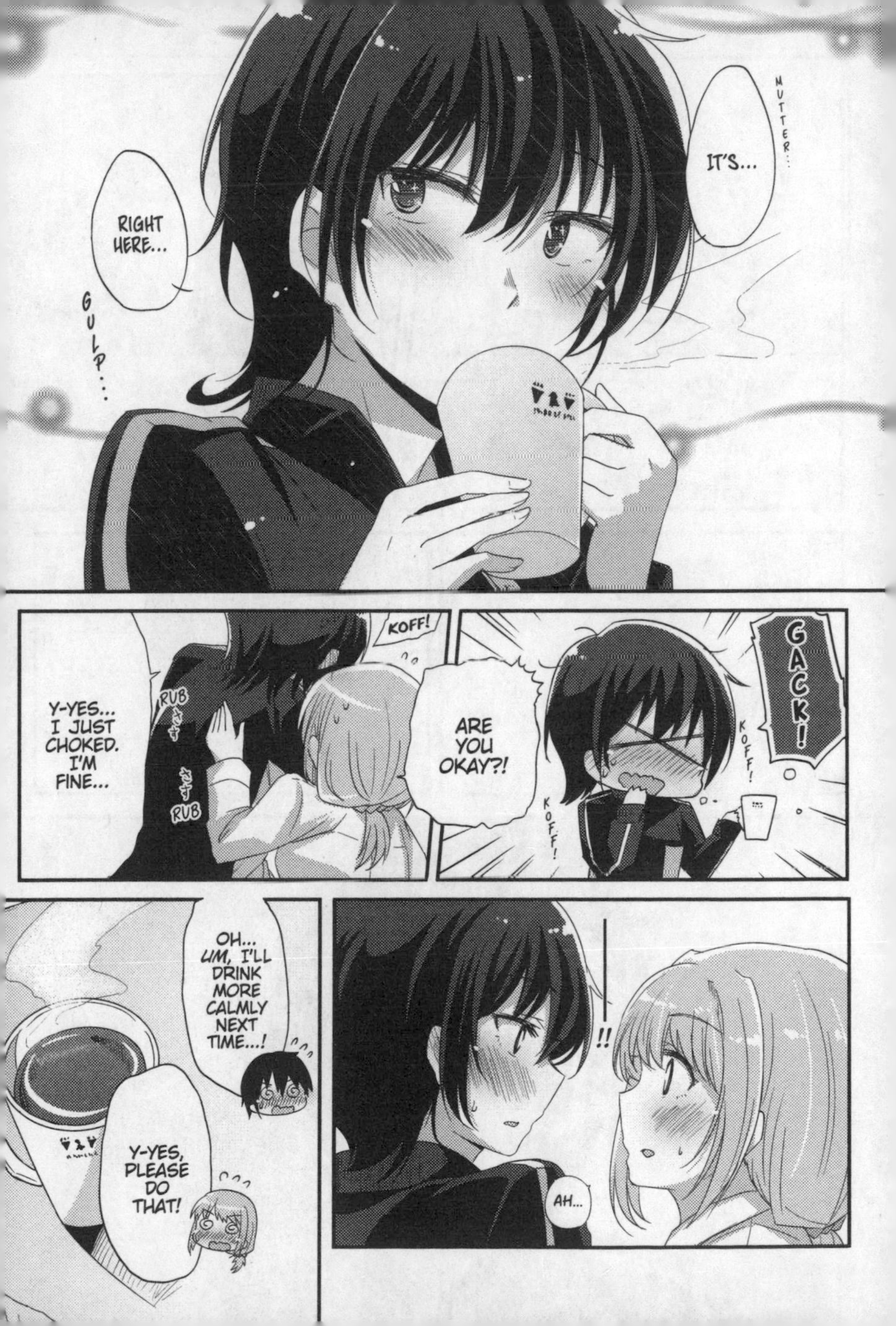
MUTTER...
IT'S...
RIGHT HERE...
GULP...
GACK!
KOFF!
KOFF!
ARE YOU OKAY?!
KOFF!
RUB さす
さす RUB
Y-YES... I JUST CHOKED. I'M FINE...
!!
AH...
OH... UM, I'LL DRINK MORE CALMLY NEXT TIME...!
Y-YES, PLEASE DO THAT!

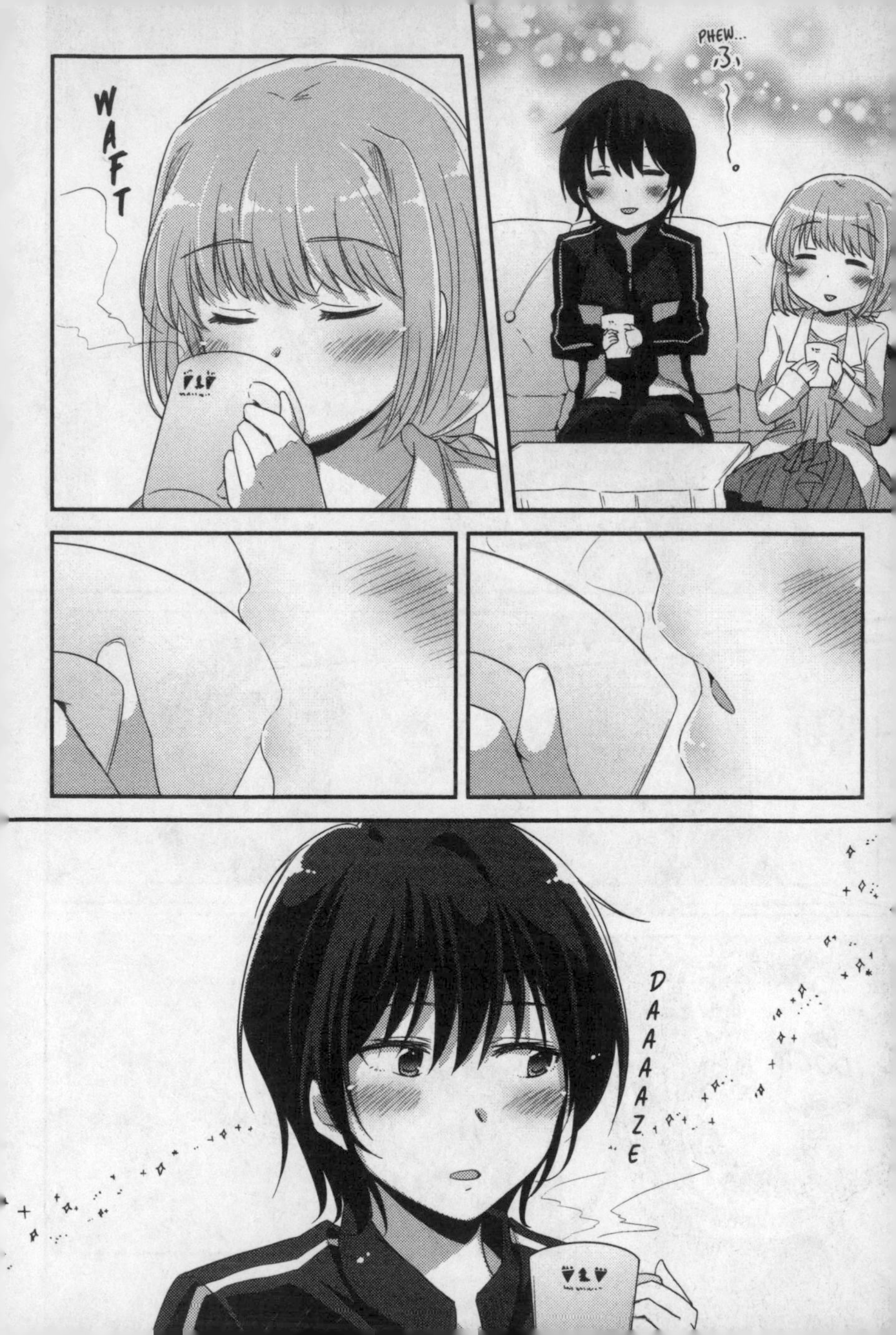
PHEW...
WAFT
DAAAAAZE

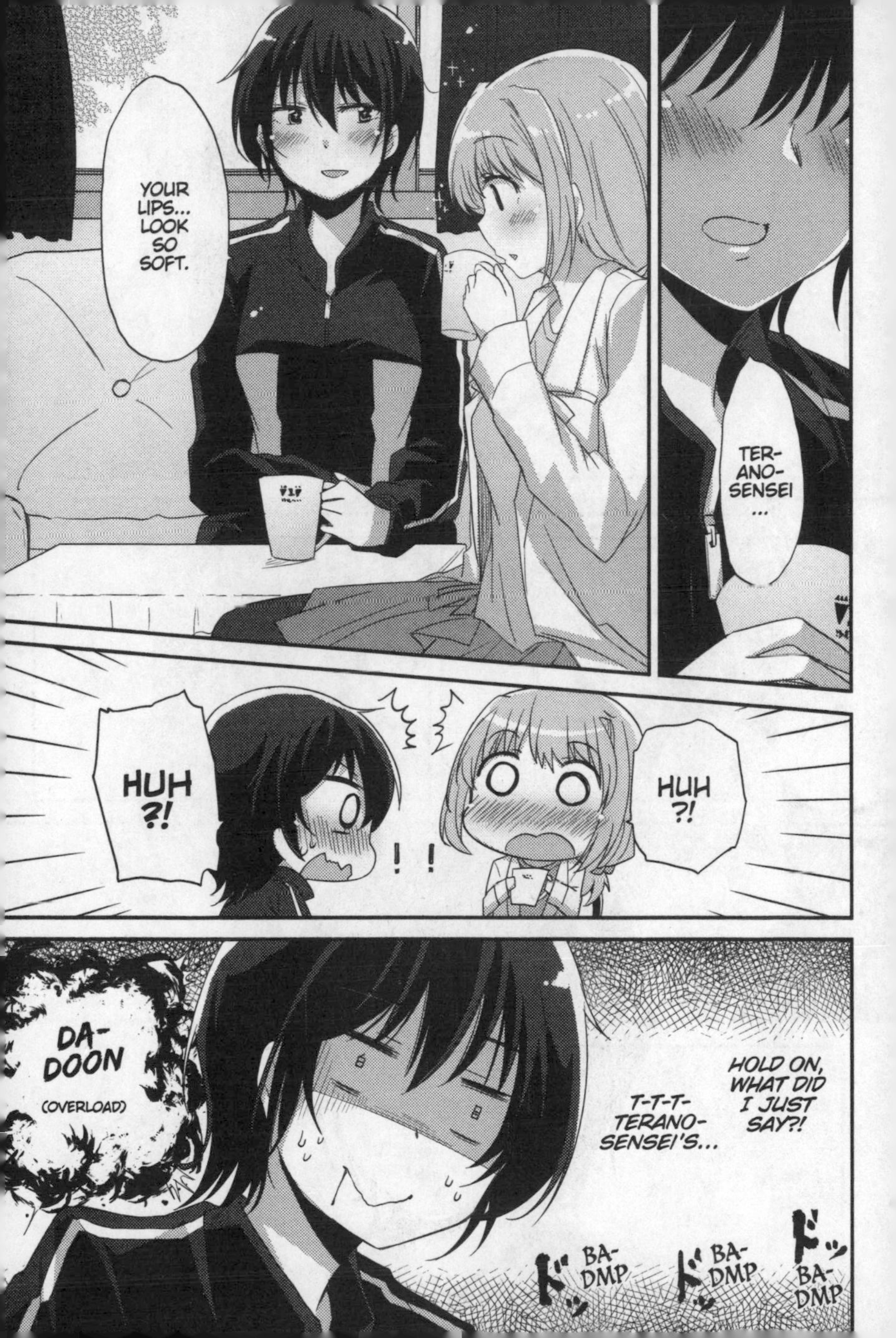
TER-ANO-SENSEI...
YOUR LIPS... LOOK SO SOFT.
HUH ?!
! !
HUH ?!
HOLD ON, WHAT DID I JUST SAY?!
T-T-T-TERANO-SENSEI'S...
DA-DOON
(OVERLOAD)
ドッ
BA-DMP
ドッ
BA-DMP
ドッ
BA-DMP

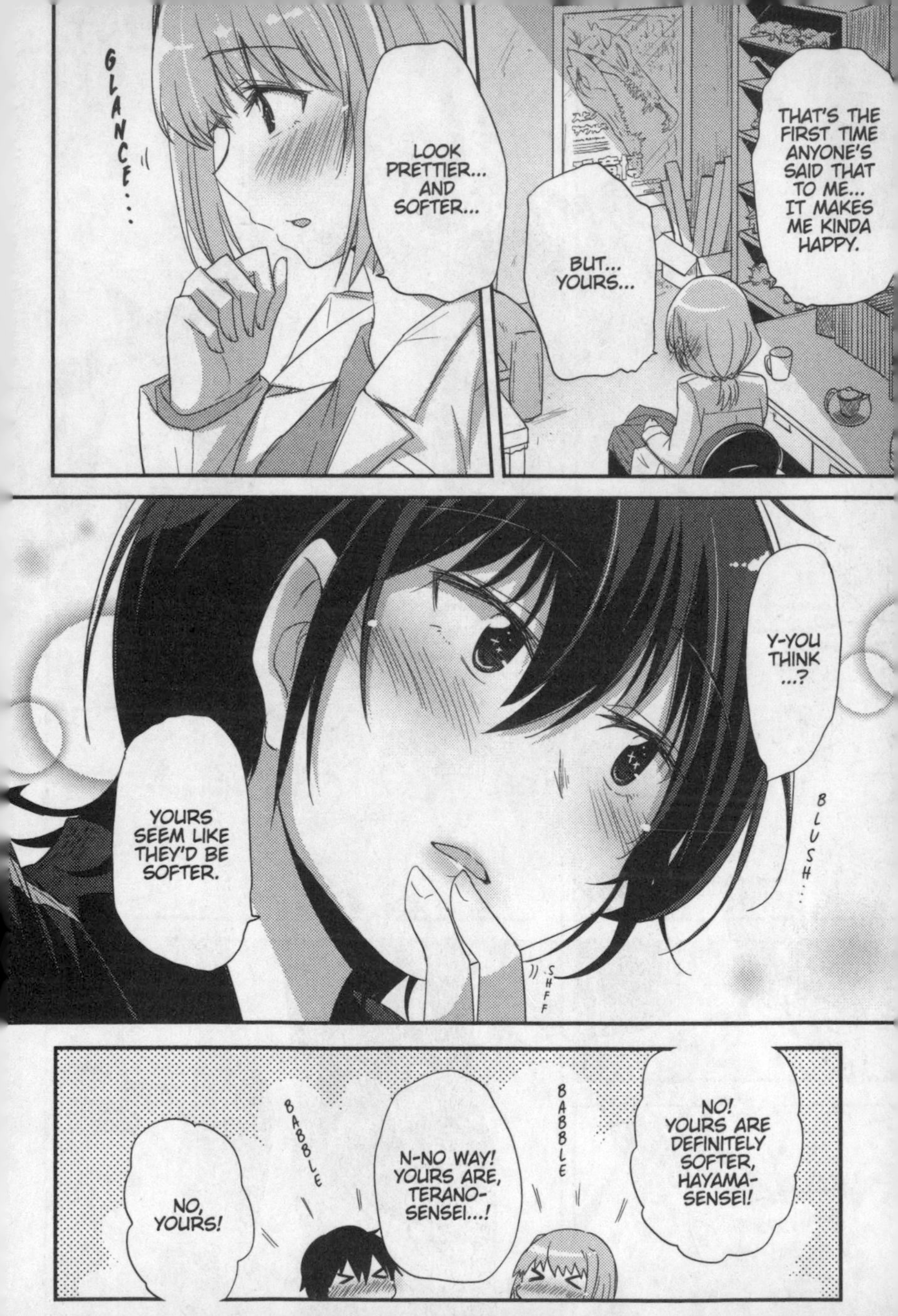
THAT'S THE FIRST TIME ANYONE'S SAID THAT TO ME... IT MAKES ME KINDA HAPPY.
BUT... YOURS...
LOOK PRETTIER... AND SOFTER...
GLANCE...
Y-YOU THINK ...?
BLUSH...
YOURS SEEM LIKE THEY'D BE SOFTER.
SHFF
NO! YOURS ARE DEFINITELY SOFTER, HAYAMA-SENSEI!
BABBLE
N-NO WAY! YOURS ARE, TERANO-SENSEI...!
BABBLE
NO, YOURS!

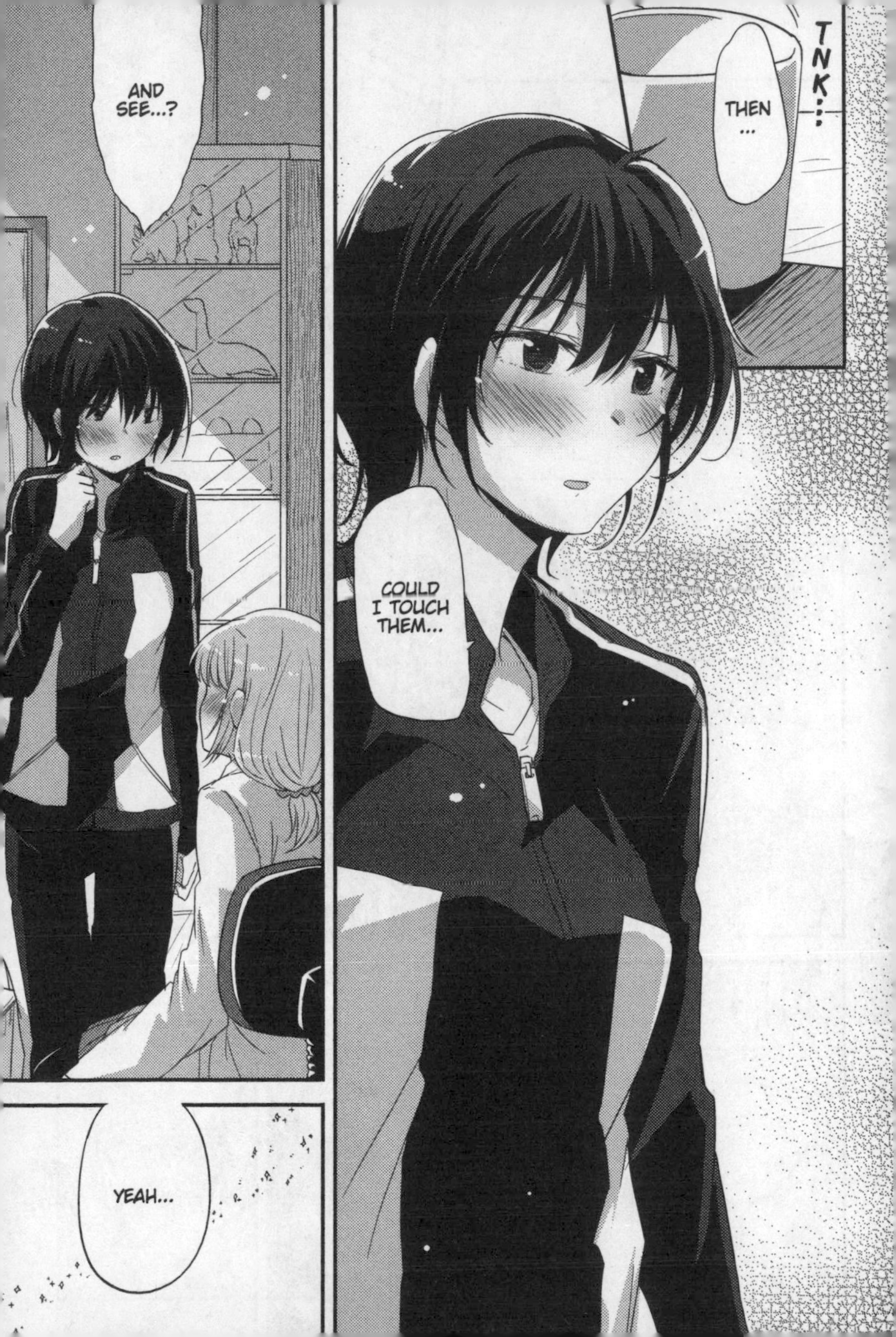
TNK...
THEN ...
COULD I TOUCH THEM...
AND SEE...?
YEAH...

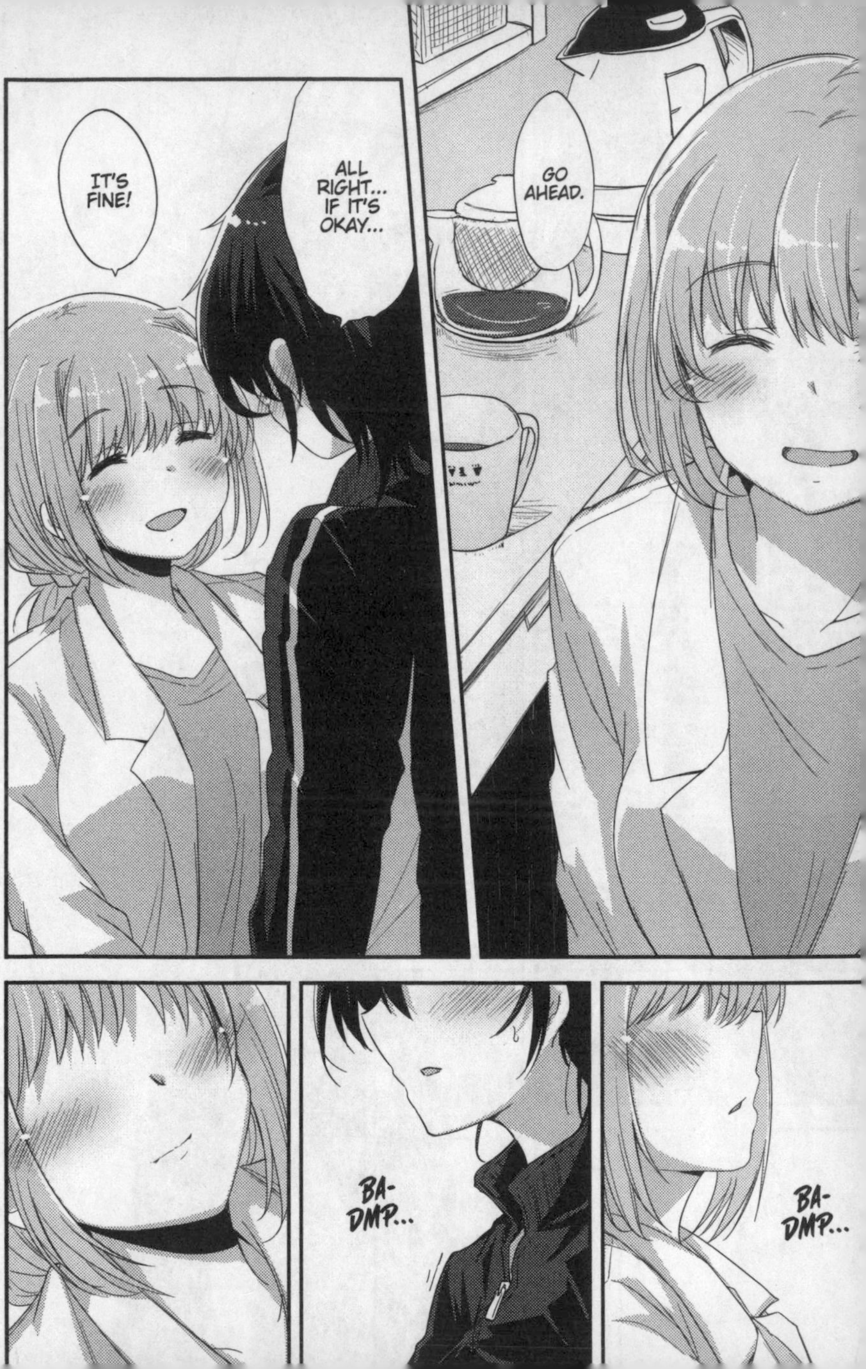
GO AHEAD.
ALL RIGHT... IF IT'S OKAY...
IT'S FINE!
BA-DMP...
BA-DMP...

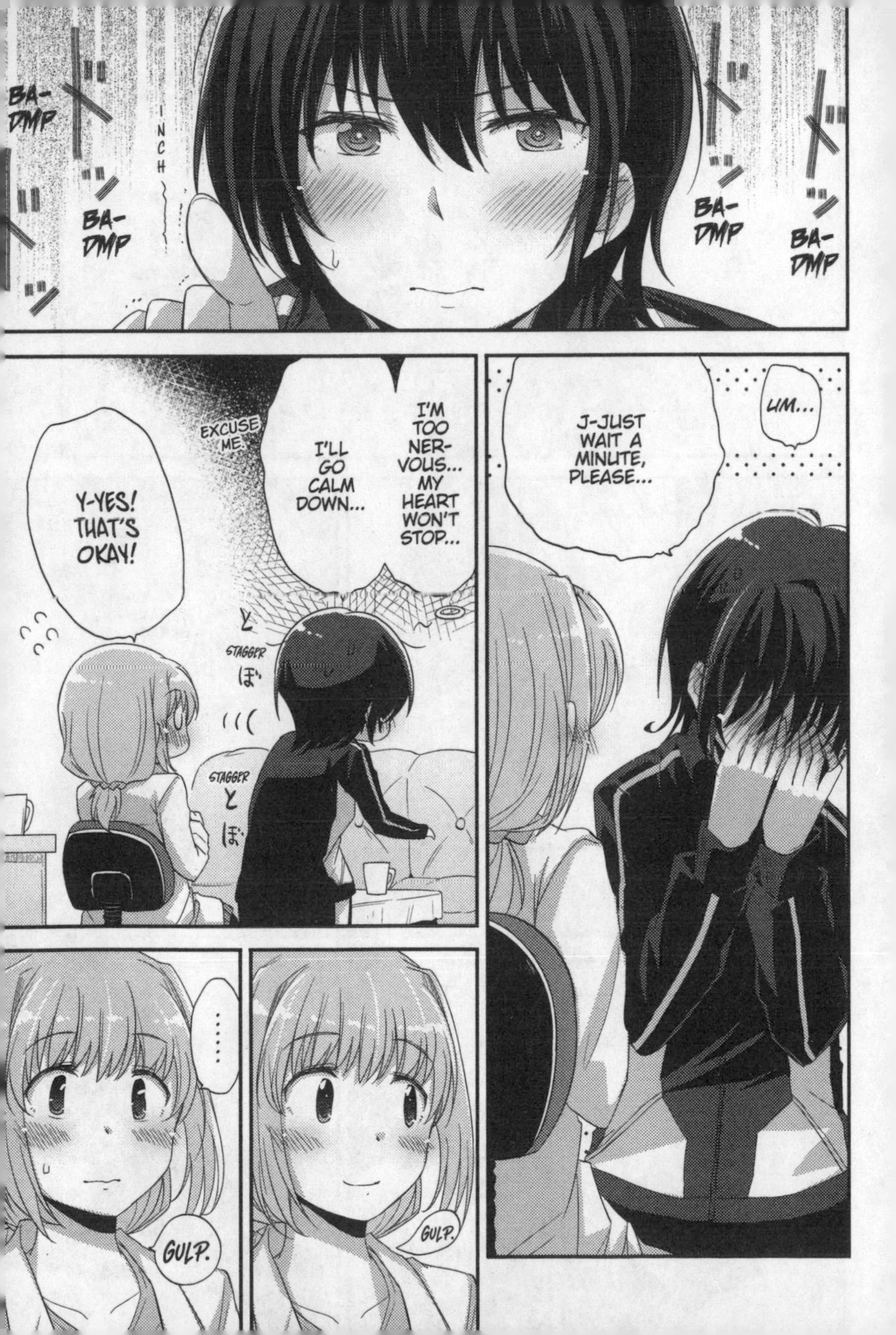
BA-DMP
BA-DMP
BA-DMP
INCH
BA-DMP
UM...
J-JUST WAIT A MINUTE, PLEASE...
I'M TOO NER-VOUS... MY HEART WON'T STOP...
I'LL GO CALM DOWN...
EXCUSE ME.
Y-YES! THAT'S OKAY!
STAGGER
STAGGER
GULP.
......
GULP.

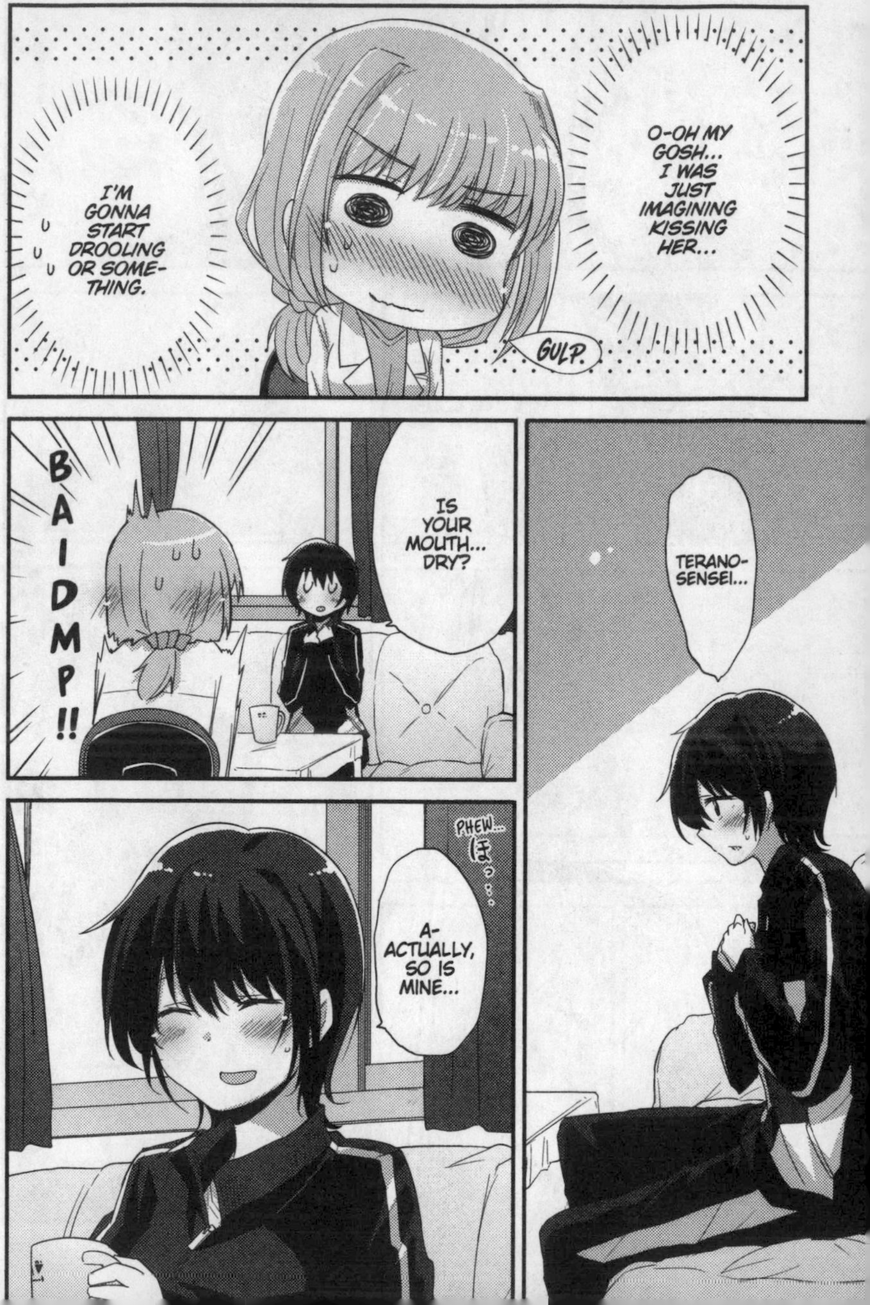
O-OH MY GOSH... I WAS JUST IMAGINING KISSING HER...
GULP.
I'M GONNA START DROOLING OR SOME-THING.
TERANO-SENSEI...
IS YOUR MOUTH... DRY?
BA-DMP!!
PHEW...
ほっ...
A-ACTUALLY, SO IS MINE...

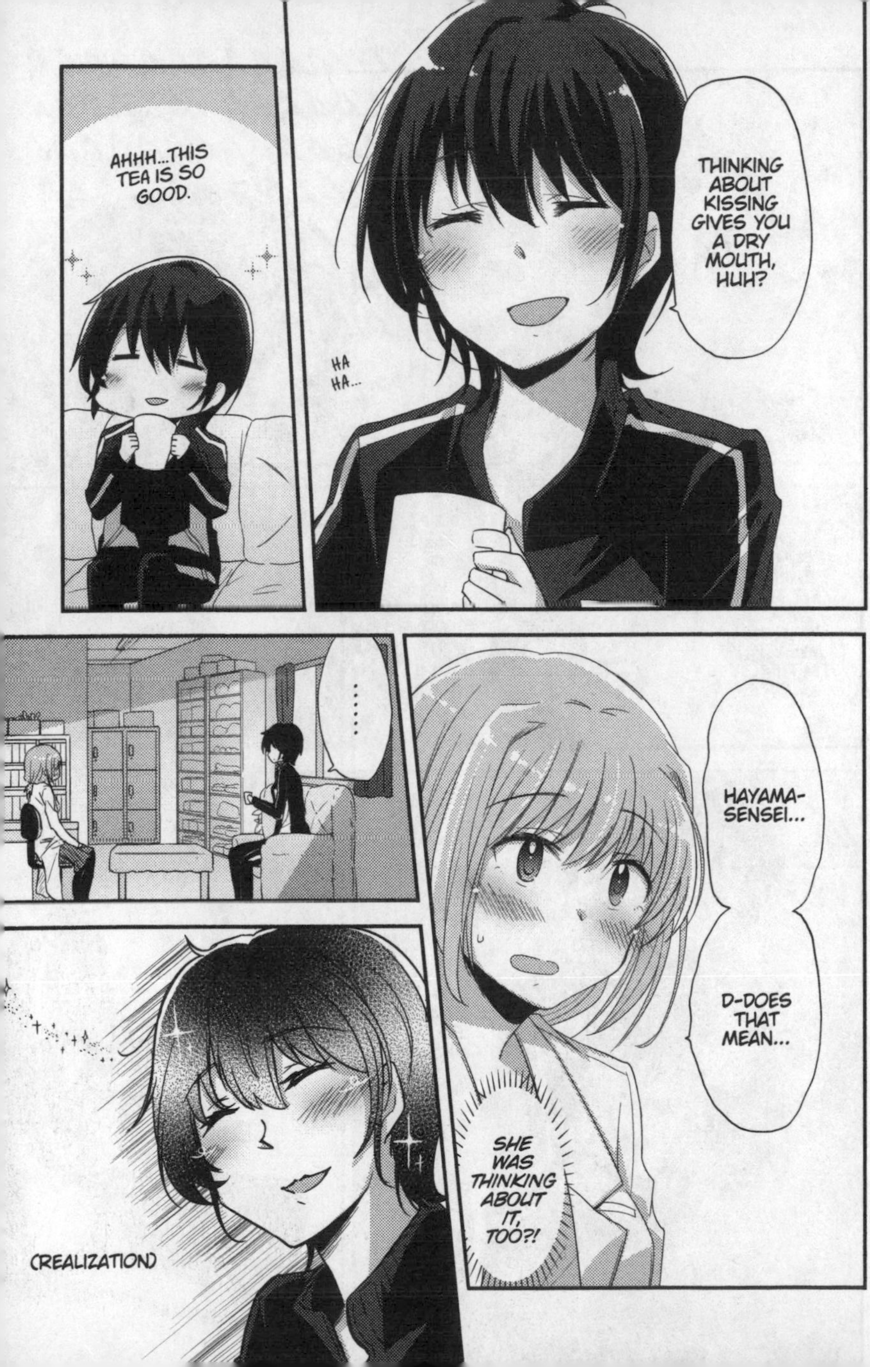
THINKING ABOUT KISSING GIVES YOU A DRY MOUTH, HUH?
HA HA...
AHHH...THIS TEA IS SO GOOD.
HAYAMA-SENSEI...
D-DOES THAT MEAN...
SHE WAS THINKING ABOUT IT, TOO?!
......
(REALIZATION)

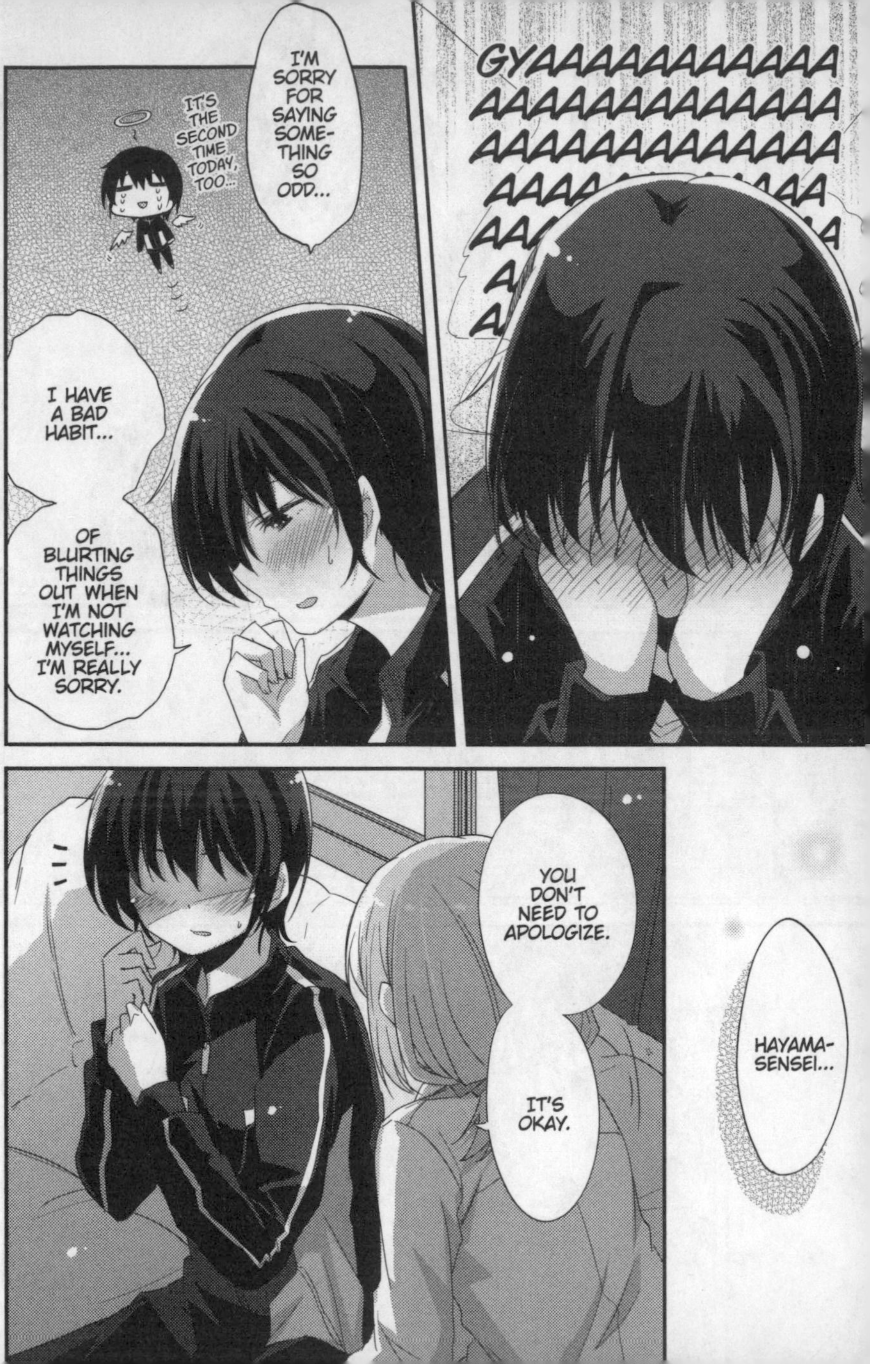
GYAAAAAAAAAAAA
AAAAAAAAAAAAAA
AAAAAAAAAAAAAA
I'M SORRY FOR SAYING SOME-THING SO ODD...
IT'S THE SECOND TIME TODAY, TOO...
I HAVE A BAD HABIT...
OF BLURTING THINGS OUT WHEN I'M NOT WATCHING MYSELF... I'M REALLY SORRY.
HAYAMA-SENSEI...
YOU DON'T NEED TO APOLOGIZE.
IT'S OKAY.

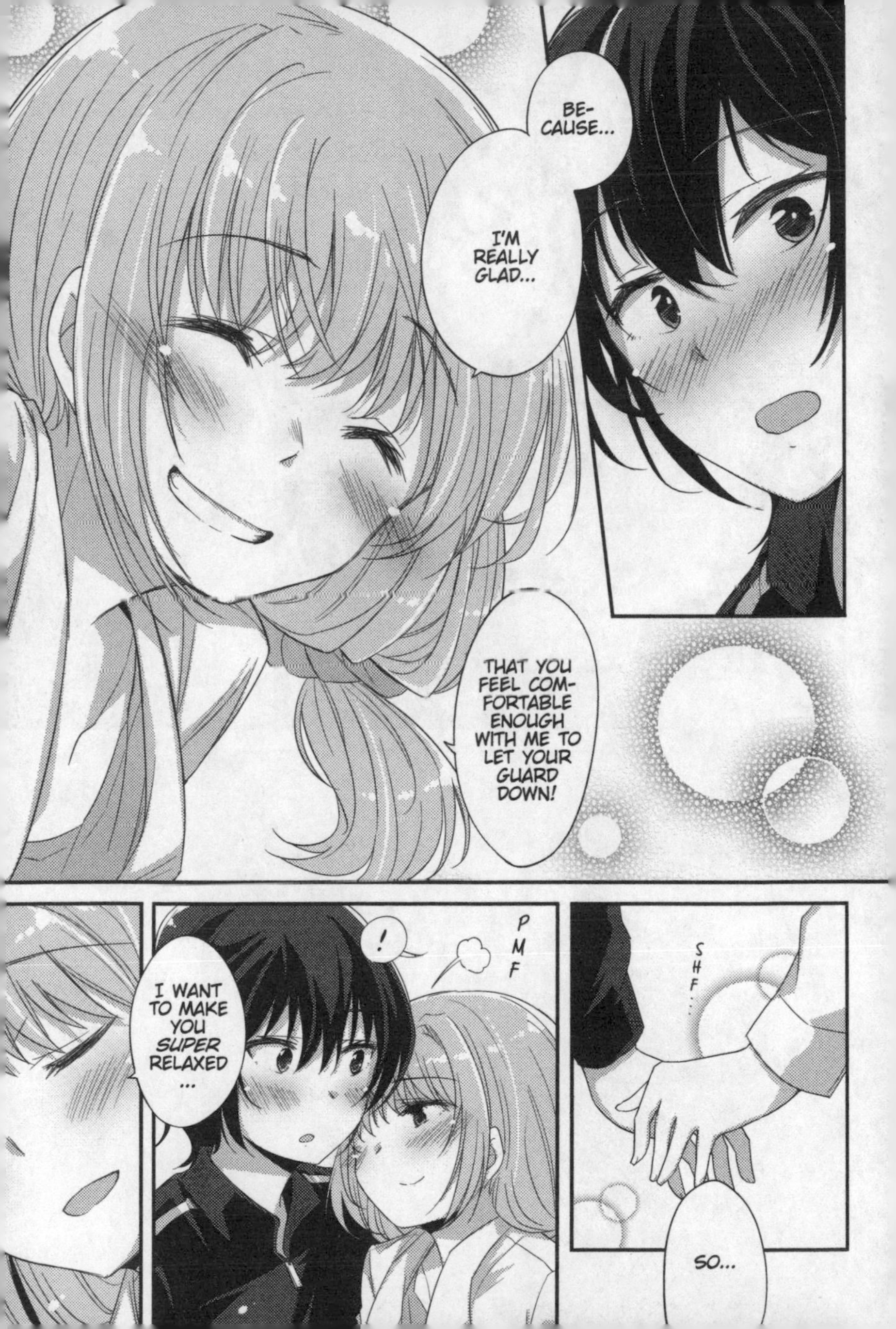
BE-
CAUSE...
I'M REALLY GLAD...
THAT YOU FEEL COM-
FORTABLE ENOUGH WITH ME TO LET YOUR GUARD DOWN!
SHF...
SO...
!
PMF
I WANT TO MAKE YOU *SUPER* RELAXED ...

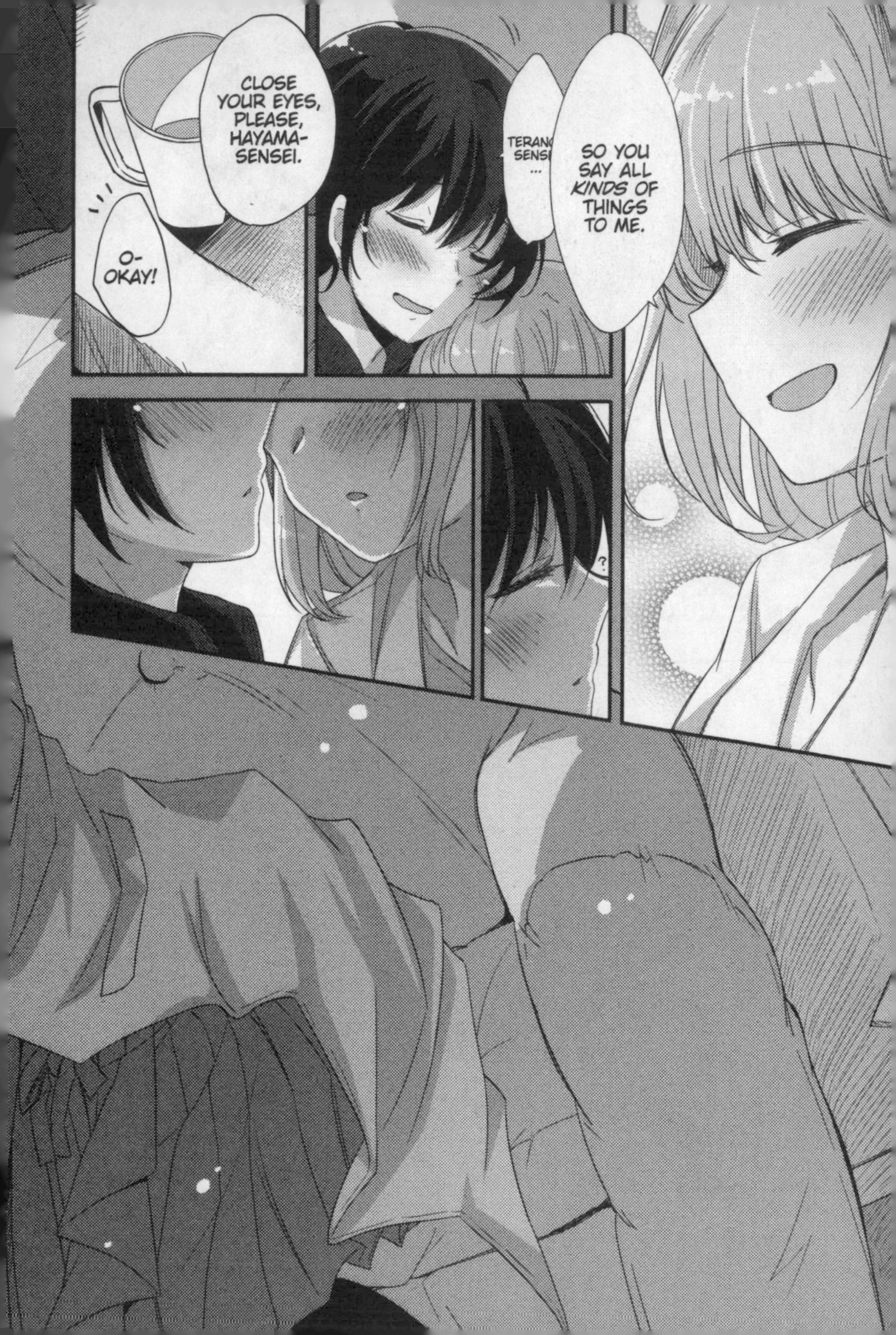
TERAN SENS ...
SO YOU SAY ALL KINDS OF THINGS TO ME.
CLOSE YOUR EYES, PLEASE, HAYAMA-SENSEI.
O-OKAY!
?

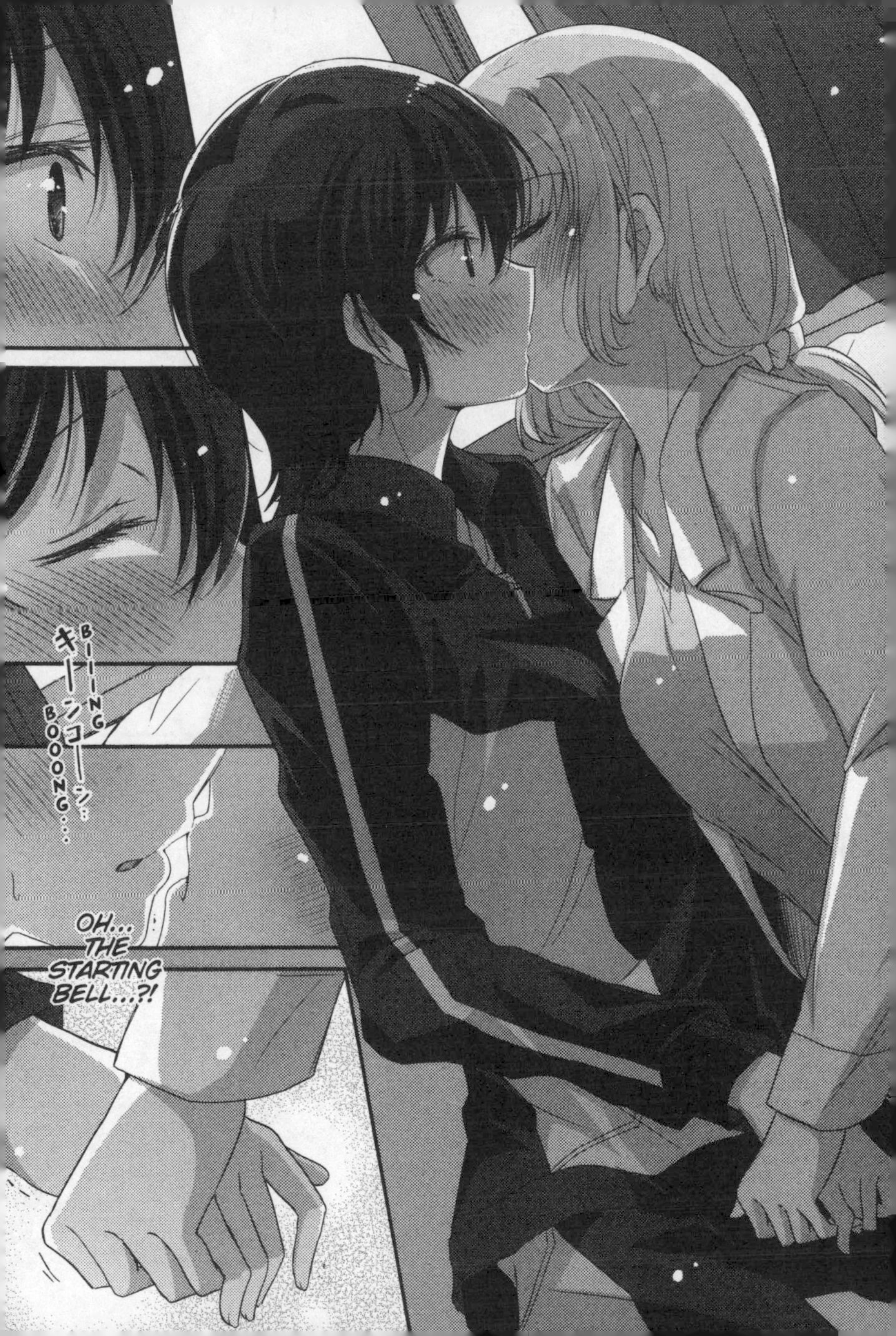
キーンコーン…
BIIING BOOONG...
OH... THE STARTING BELL...?!

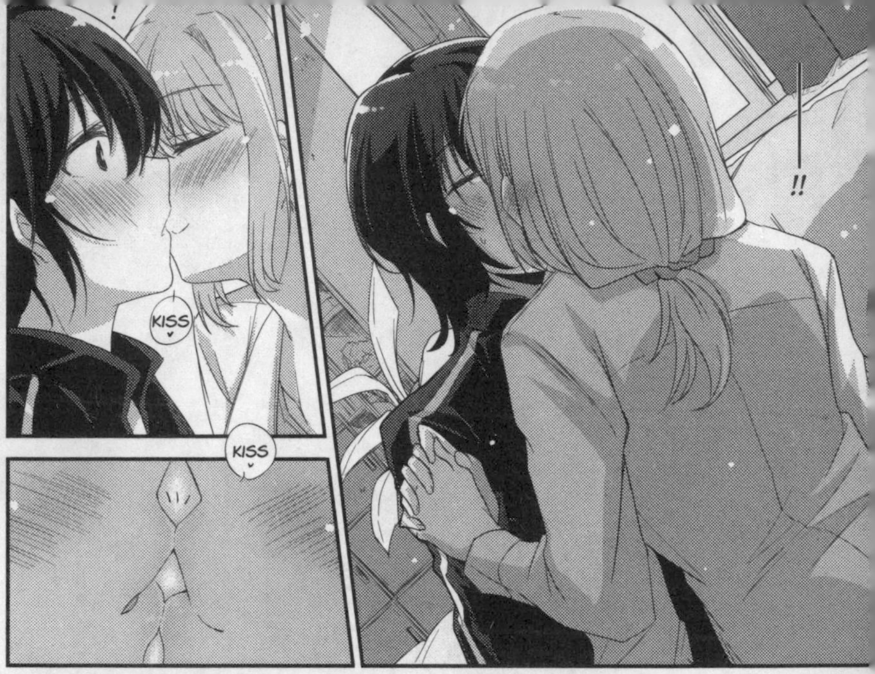
!!
!
KISS
KISS

Poster: Dinosaur Expo.

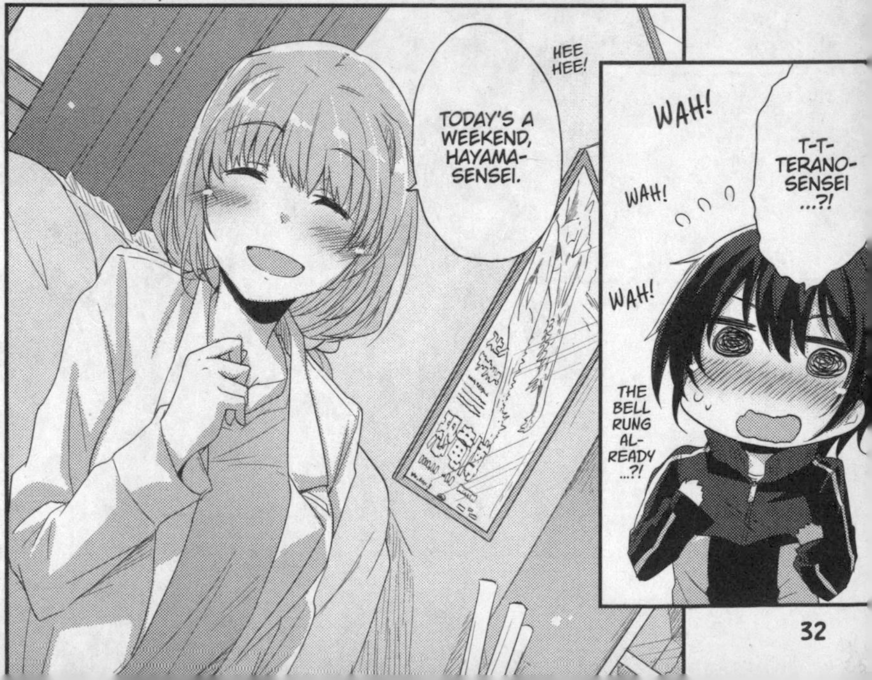
WAH!
T-T-TERANO-SENSEI ...?!
WAH!
WAH!
THE BELL RUNG AL-READY ...?!
HEE HEE!
TODAY'S A WEEKEND, HAYAMA-SENSEI.

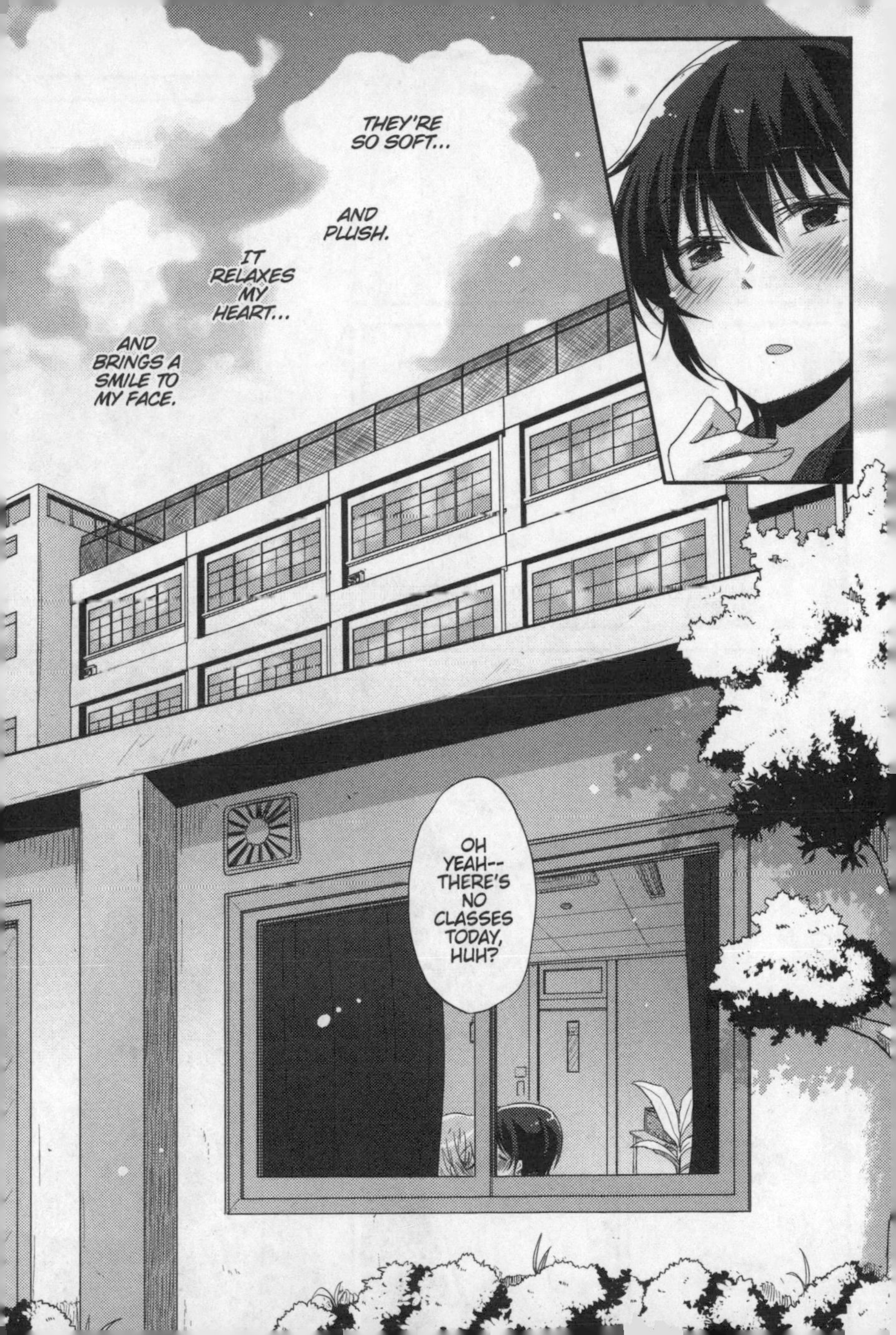
THEY'RE SO SOFT...
AND PLUSH.
IT RELAXES MY HEART...
AND BRINGS A SMILE TO MY FACE.
OH YEAH--THERE'S NO CLASSES TODAY, HUH?

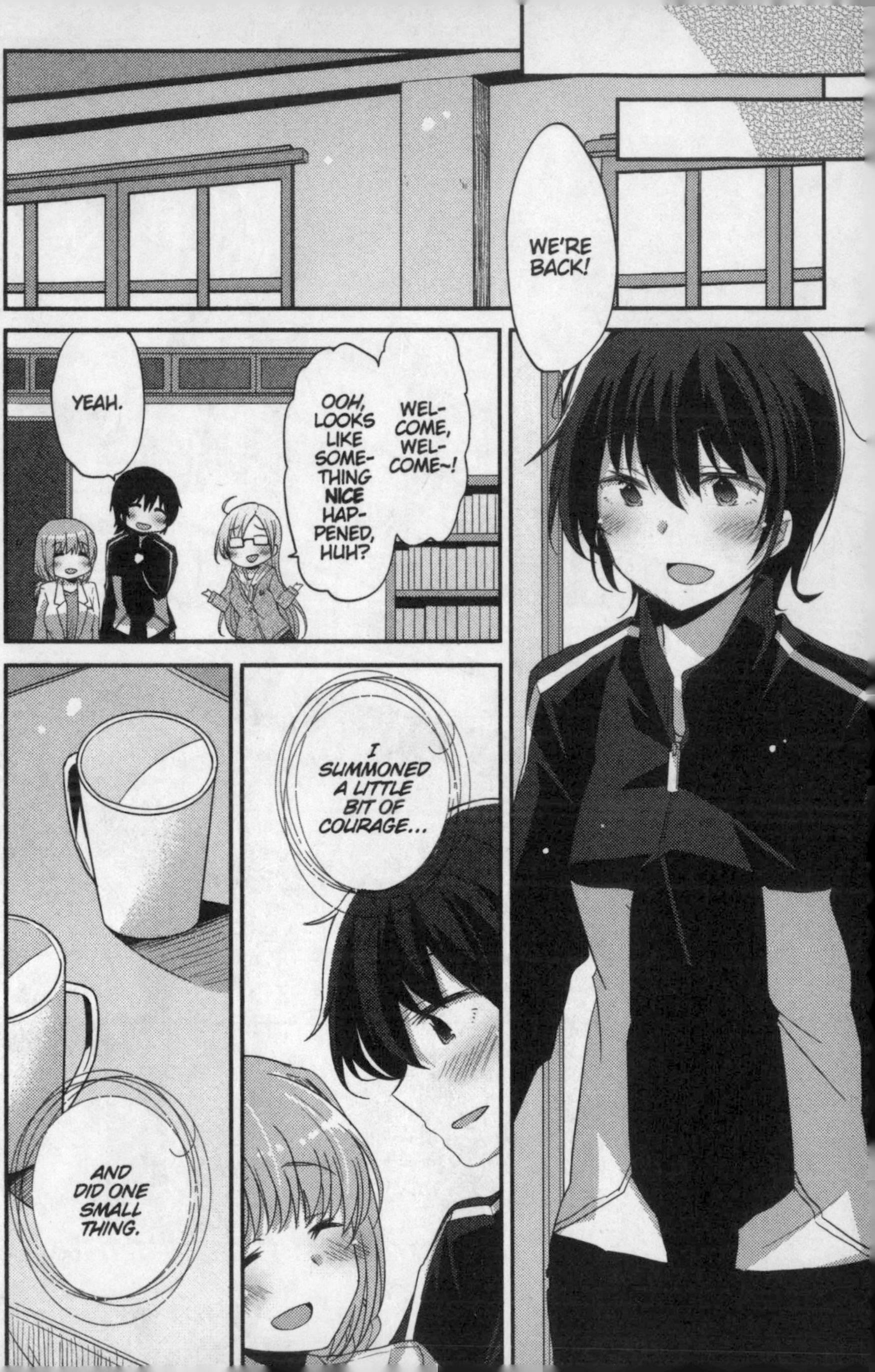
WE'RE BACK!
WEL-COME, WEL-COME~!
OOH, LOOKS LIKE SOME-THING NICE HAP-PENED, HUH?
YEAH.
I SUMMONED A LITTLE BIT OF COURAGE...
AND DID ONE SMALL THING.

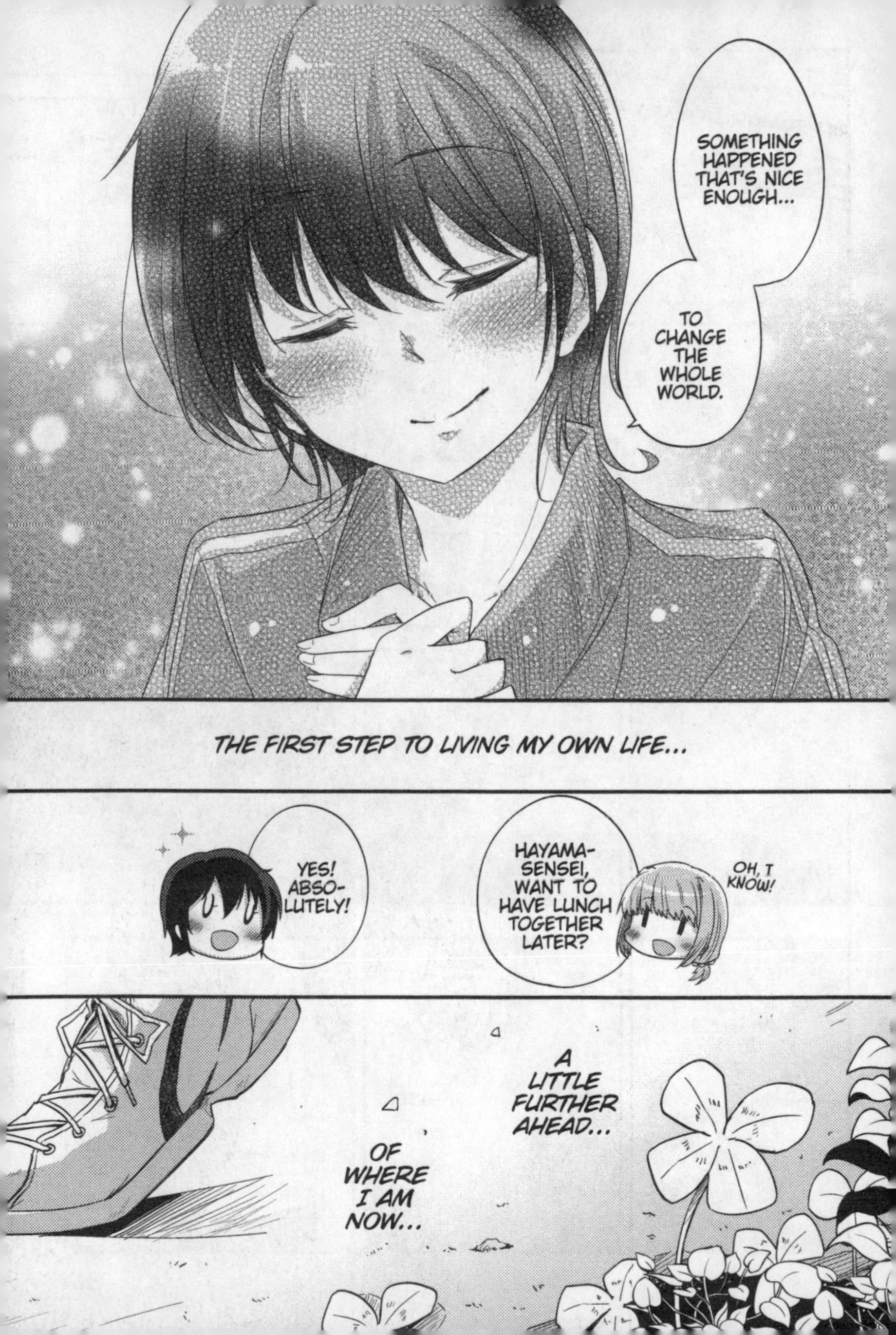
SOMETHING HAPPENED THAT'S NICE ENOUGH...
TO CHANGE THE WHOLE WORLD.
THE FIRST STEP TO LIVING MY OWN LIFE...
OH, I KNOW!
HAYAMA-SENSEI, WANT TO HAVE LUNCH TOGETHER LATER?
YES! ABSO-LUTELY!
A LITTLE FURTHER AHEAD...
OF WHERE I AM NOW...

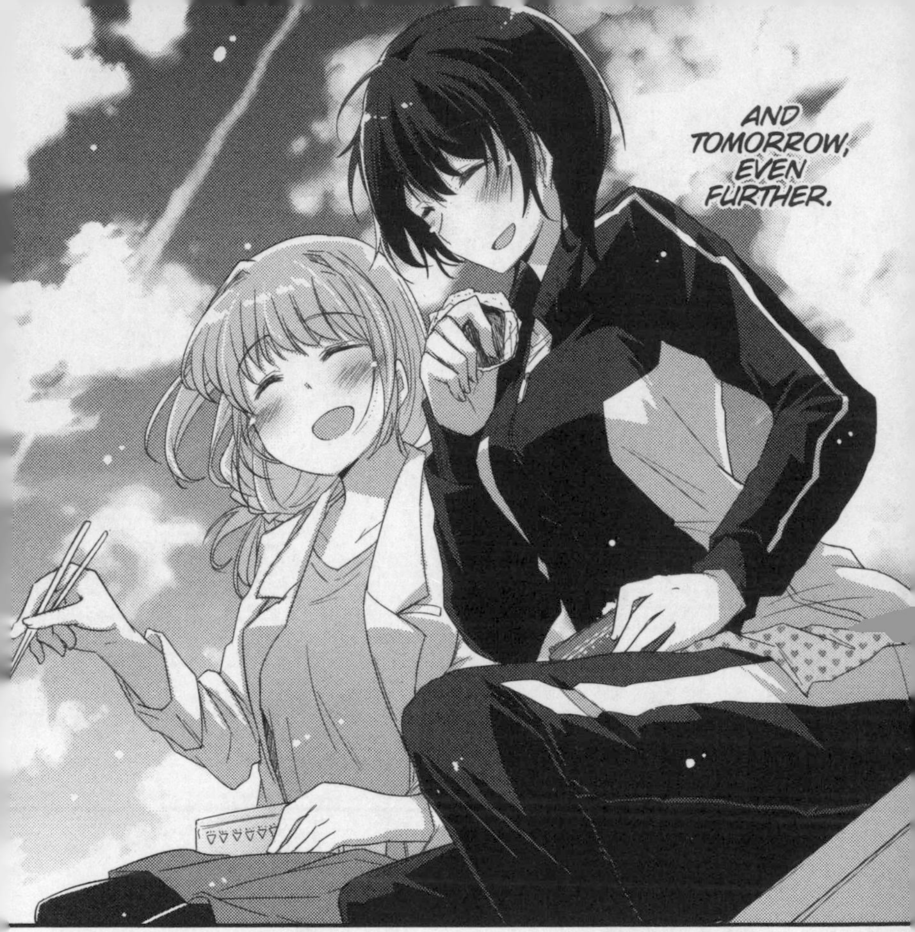
AND TOMORROW, EVEN FURTHER.
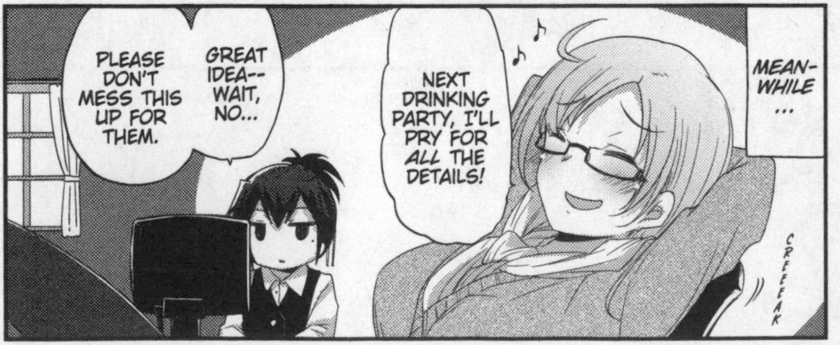
MEAN-WHILE ...
NEXT DRINKING PARTY, I'LL PRY FOR ALL THE DETAILS!
CREEEAK
GREAT IDEA--WAIT, NO...
PLEASE DON'T MESS THIS UP FOR THEM.

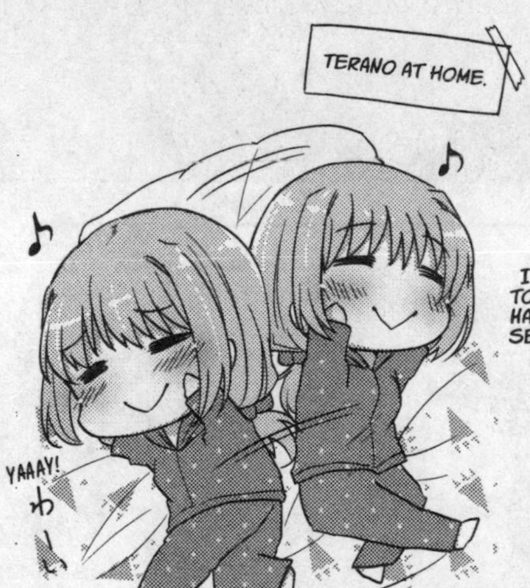
TERANO AT HOME.
I GOT TO KISS HAYAMA-SENSEI!
YAAAY!

OUR TEACHERS ARE DATING

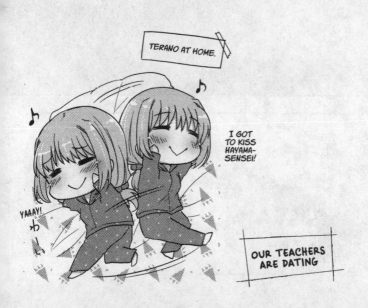

Our Teachers are Dating!

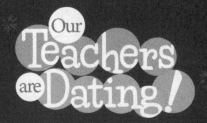

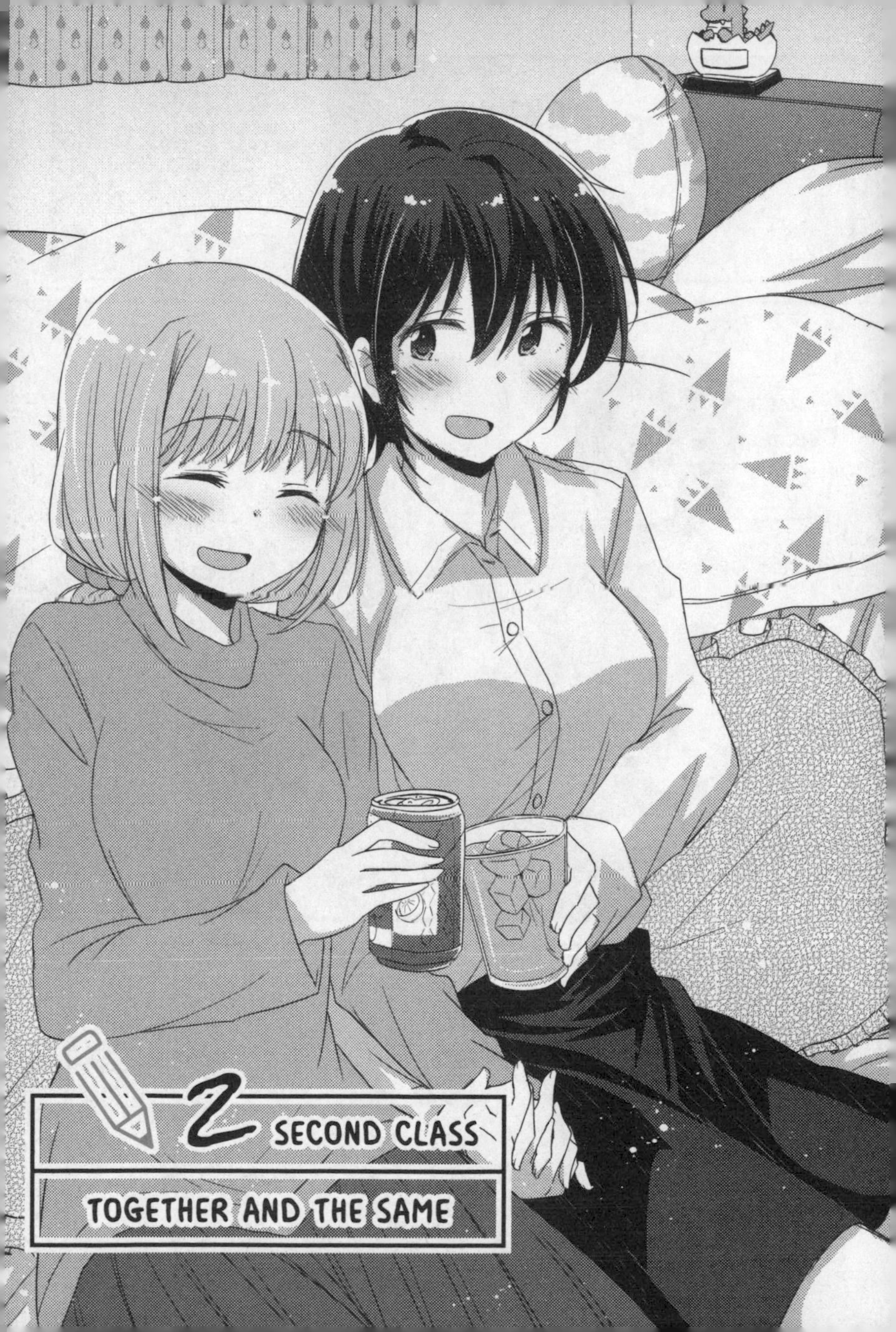
2 SECOND CLASS
TOGETHER AND THE SAME

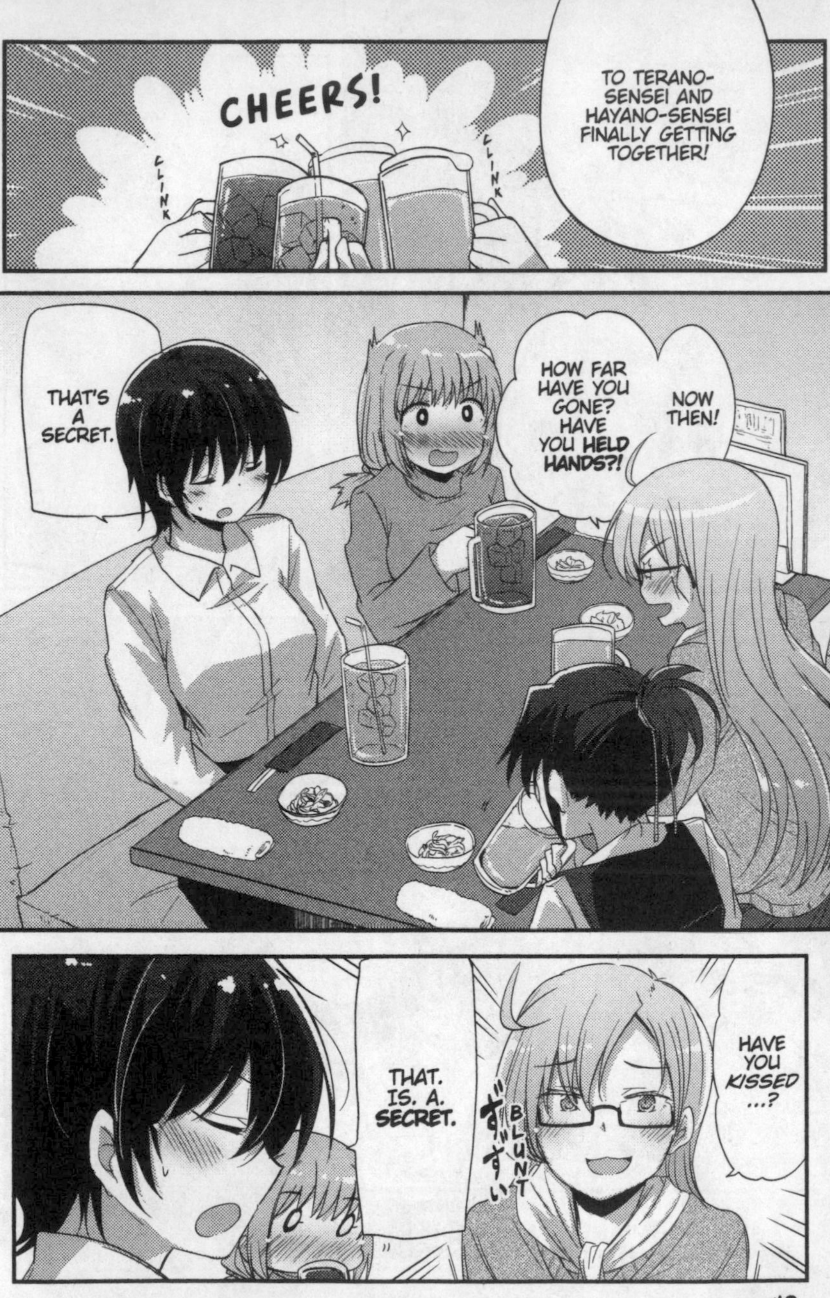
TO TERANO-SENSEI AND HAYANO-SENSEI FINALLY GETTING TOGETHER!
CHEERS!
CLINK
CLINK
NOW THEN!
HOW FAR HAVE YOU GONE? HAVE YOU **HELD HANDS**?!
THAT'S A SECRET.
HAVE YOU *KISSED* ...?
ずずい
BLUNT
THAT. IS. A. **SECRET.**

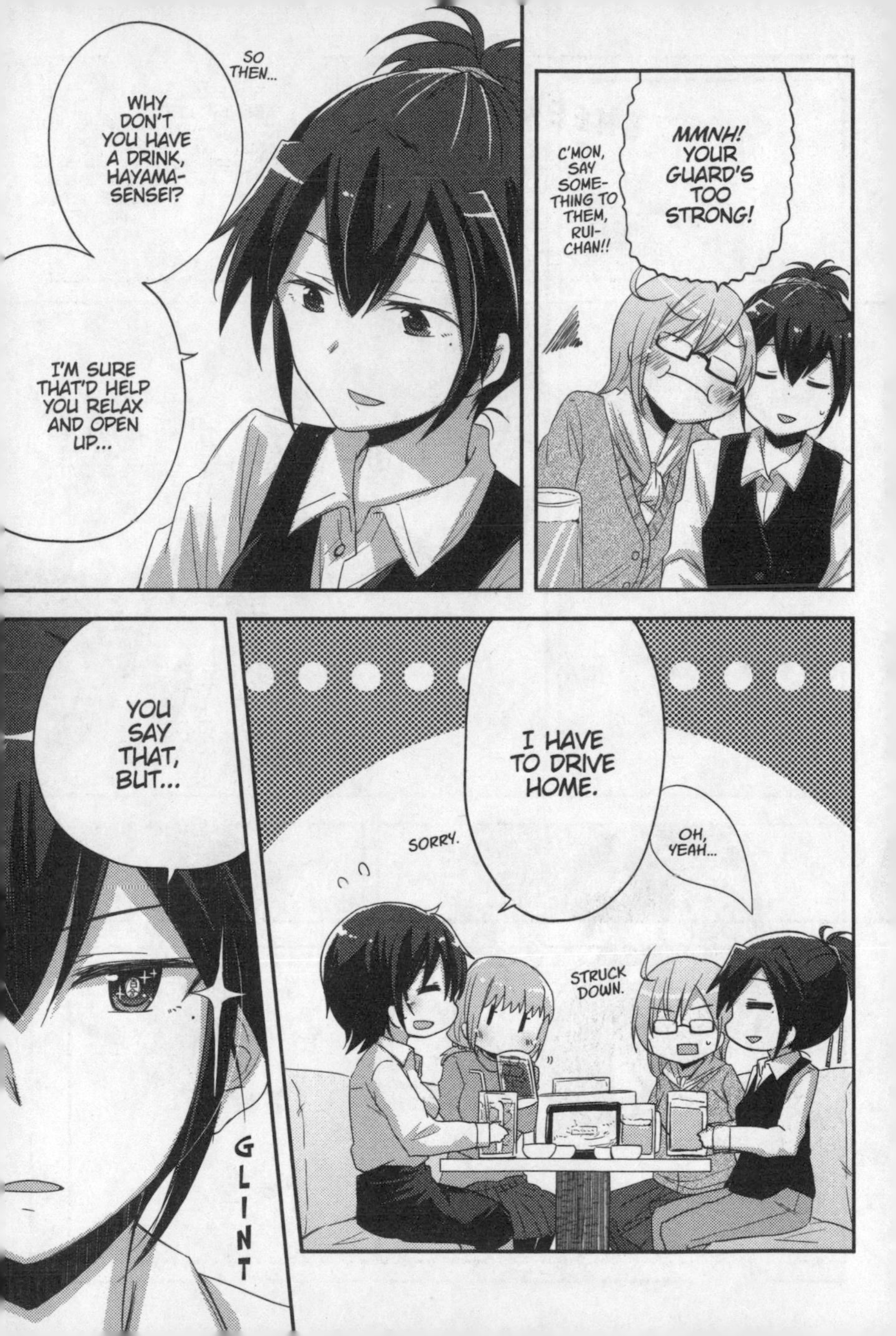
MMNH! YOUR GUARD'S TOO STRONG!
C'MON, SAY SOME-THING TO THEM, RUI-CHAN!!
SO THEN...
WHY DON'T YOU HAVE A DRINK, HAYAMA-SENSEI?
I'M SURE THAT'D HELP YOU RELAX AND OPEN UP...
I HAVE TO DRIVE HOME.
OH, YEAH...
SORRY.
STRUCK DOWN.
YOU SAY THAT, BUT...
GLINT

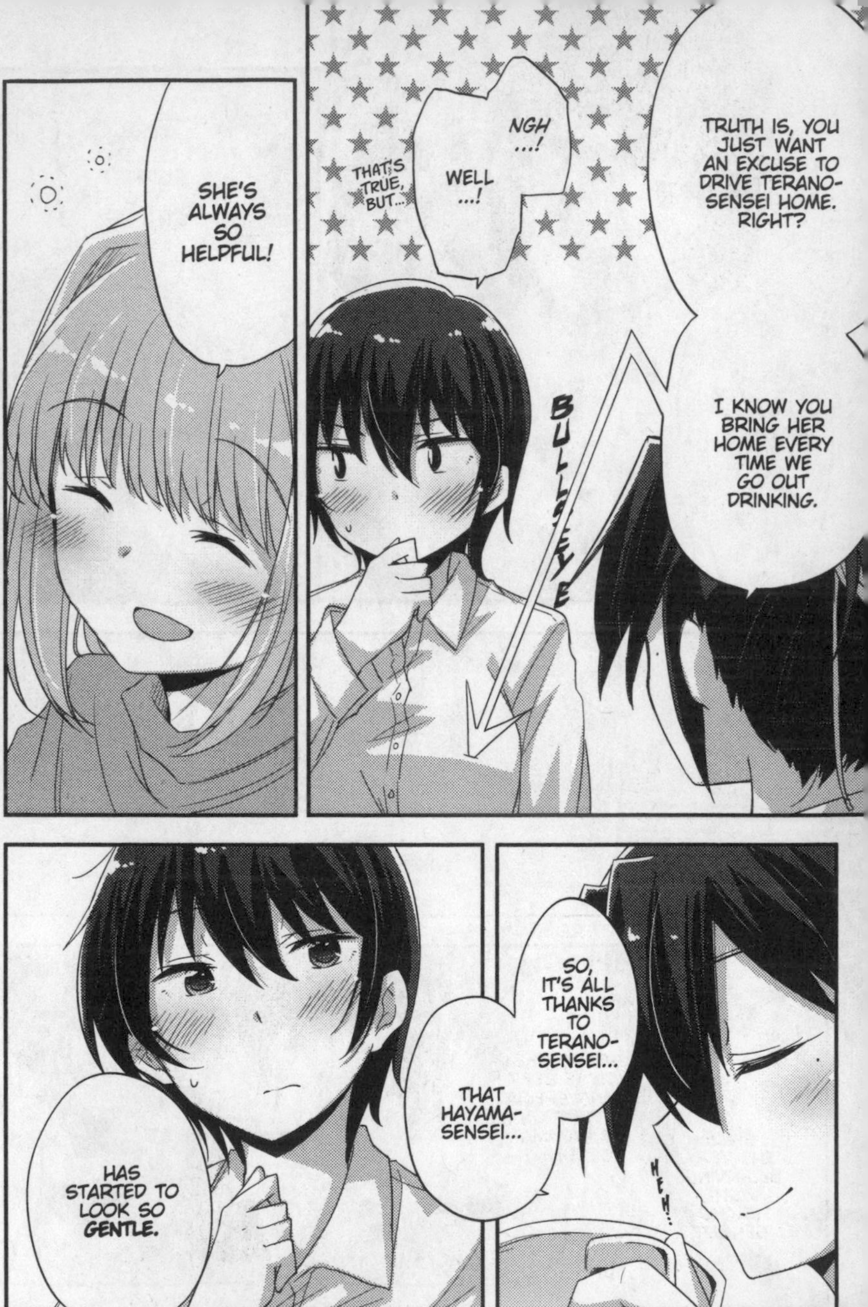
TRUTH IS, YOU JUST WANT AN EXCUSE TO DRIVE TERANO-SENSEI HOME. RIGHT?
I KNOW YOU BRING HER HOME EVERY TIME WE GO OUT DRINKING.
BULLSEYE
NGH ...!
WELL ...!
THAT'S TRUE, BUT...
SHE'S ALWAYS SO HELPFUL!
SO, IT'S ALL THANKS TO TERANO-SENSEI...
THAT HAYAMA-SENSEI...
HEH...
HAS STARTED TO LOOK SO GENTLE.

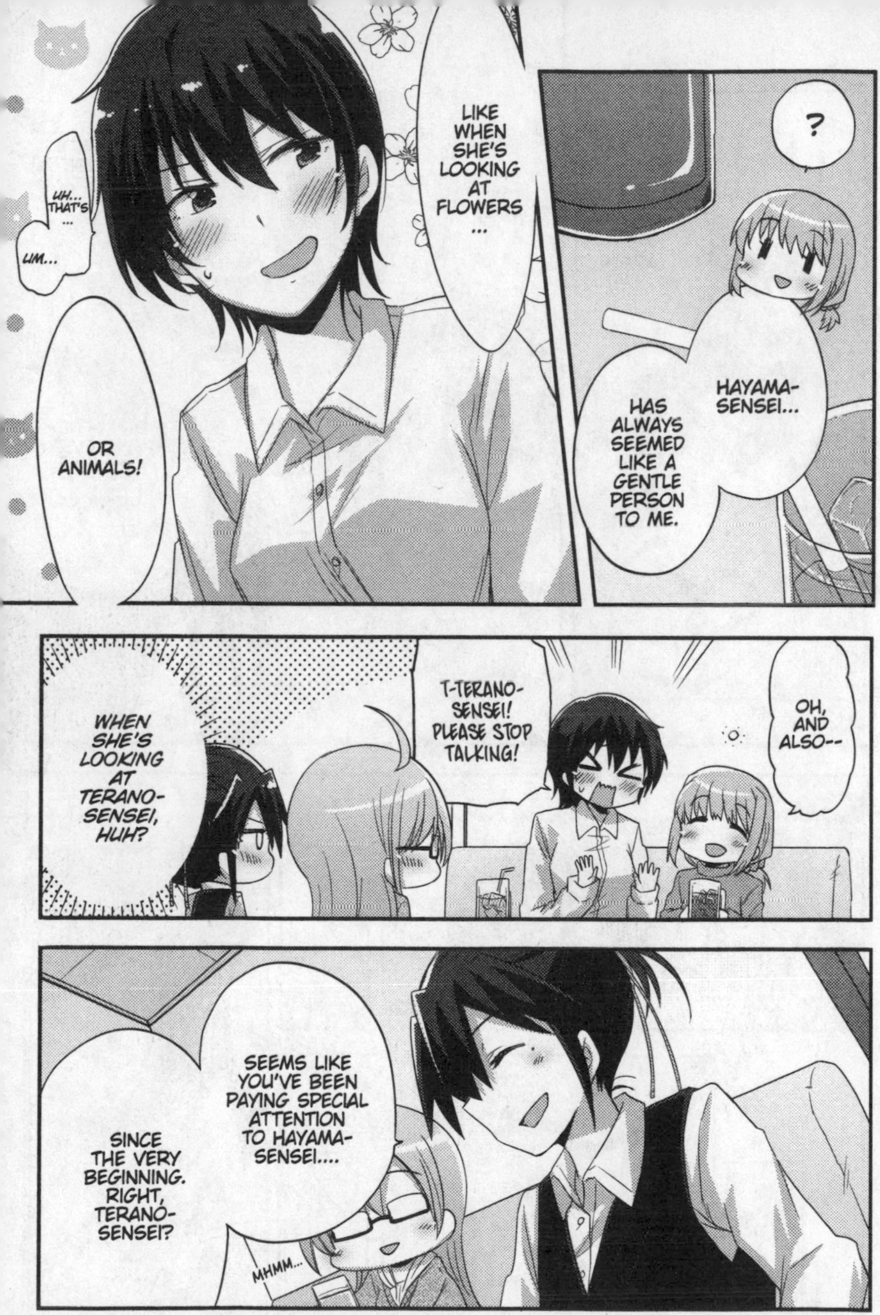
?
HAYAMA-SENSEI... HAS ALWAYS SEEMED LIKE A GENTLE PERSON TO ME.
LIKE WHEN SHE'S LOOKING AT FLOWERS...
UH... THAT'S...
UM...
OR ANIMALS!
OH, AND ALSO--
T-TERANO-SENSEI! PLEASE STOP TALKING!
WHEN SHE'S LOOKING AT TERANO-SENSEI, HUH?
SEEMS LIKE YOU'VE BEEN PAYING SPECIAL ATTENTION TO HAYAMA-SENSEI....
SINCE THE VERY BEGINNING. RIGHT, TERANO-SENSEI?
MHMM...

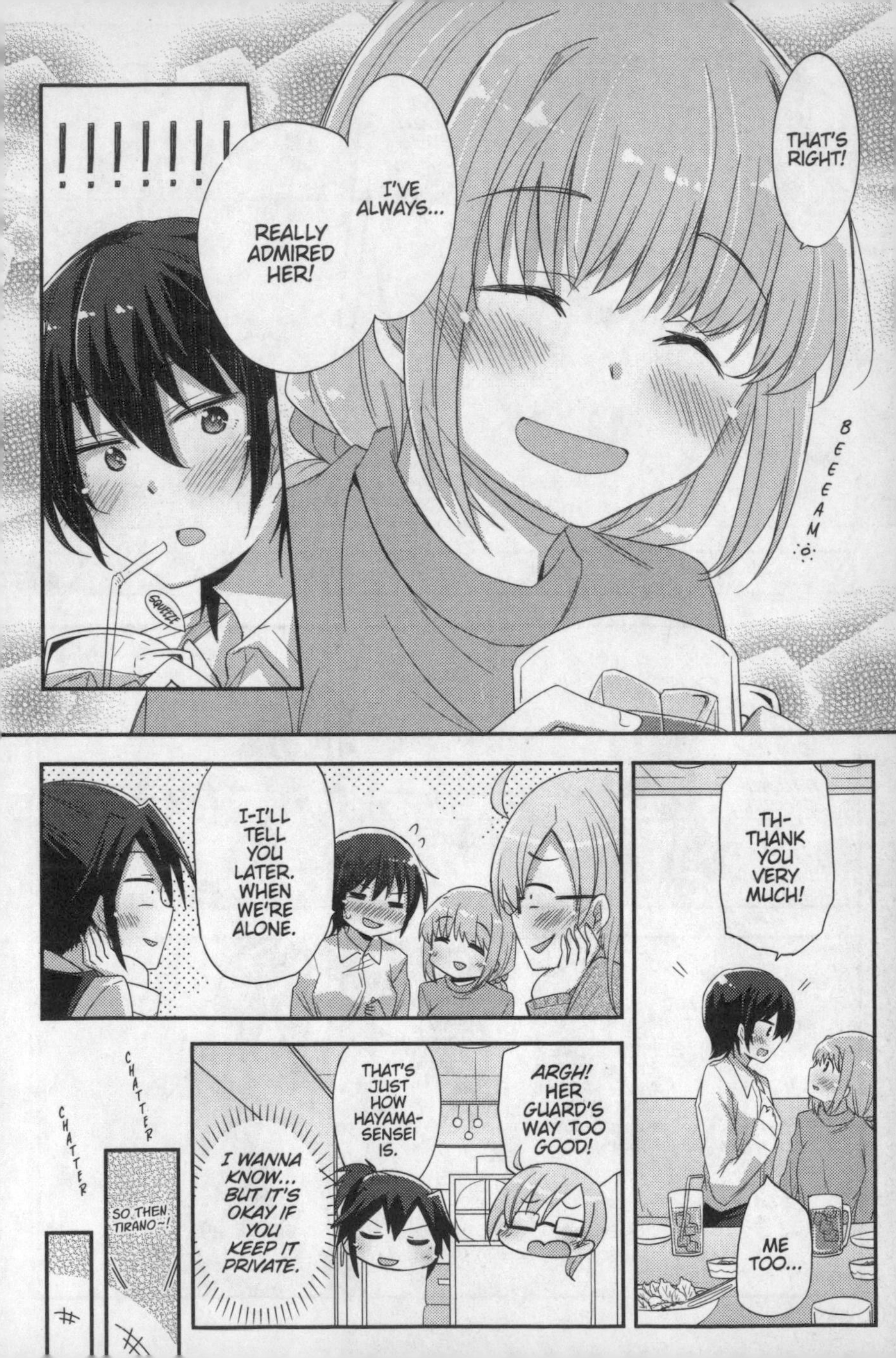
THAT'S RIGHT!
I'VE ALWAYS...
REALLY ADMIRED HER!
BEEEEAM
SQUEEZE
!!!!!!!
TH-THANK YOU VERY MUCH!
ME TOO...
I-I'LL TELL YOU LATER. WHEN WE'RE ALONE.
ARGH! HER GUARD'S WAY TOO GOOD!
THAT'S JUST HOW HAYAMA-SENSEI IS.
I WANNA KNOW... BUT IT'S OKAY IF YOU KEEP IT PRIVATE.
CHATTER
CHATTER
SO THEN TIRANO~!

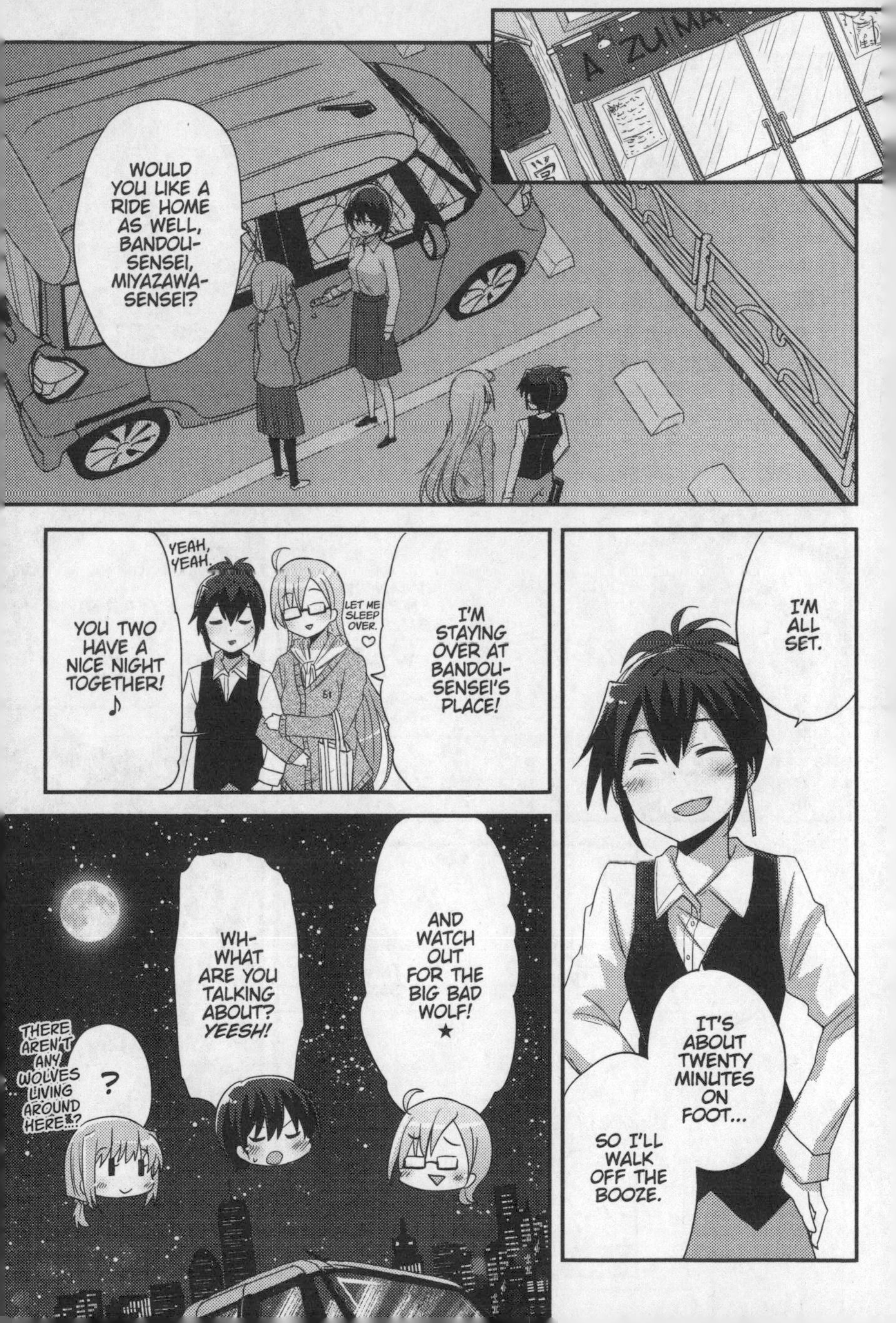
WOULD YOU LIKE A RIDE HOME AS WELL, BANDOU-SENSEI, MIYAZAWA-SENSEI?
I'M ALL SET.
IT'S ABOUT TWENTY MINUTES ON FOOT...
SO I'LL WALK OFF THE BOOZE.
I'M STAYING OVER AT BANDOU-SENSEI'S PLACE!
LET ME SLEEP OVER. ♡
YEAH, YEAH.
YOU TWO HAVE A NICE NIGHT TOGETHER! ♪
AND WATCH OUT FOR THE BIG BAD WOLF! ★
WH-WHAT ARE YOU TALKING ABOUT? YEESH!
?
THERE AREN'T ANY WOLVES LIVING AROUND HERE...?

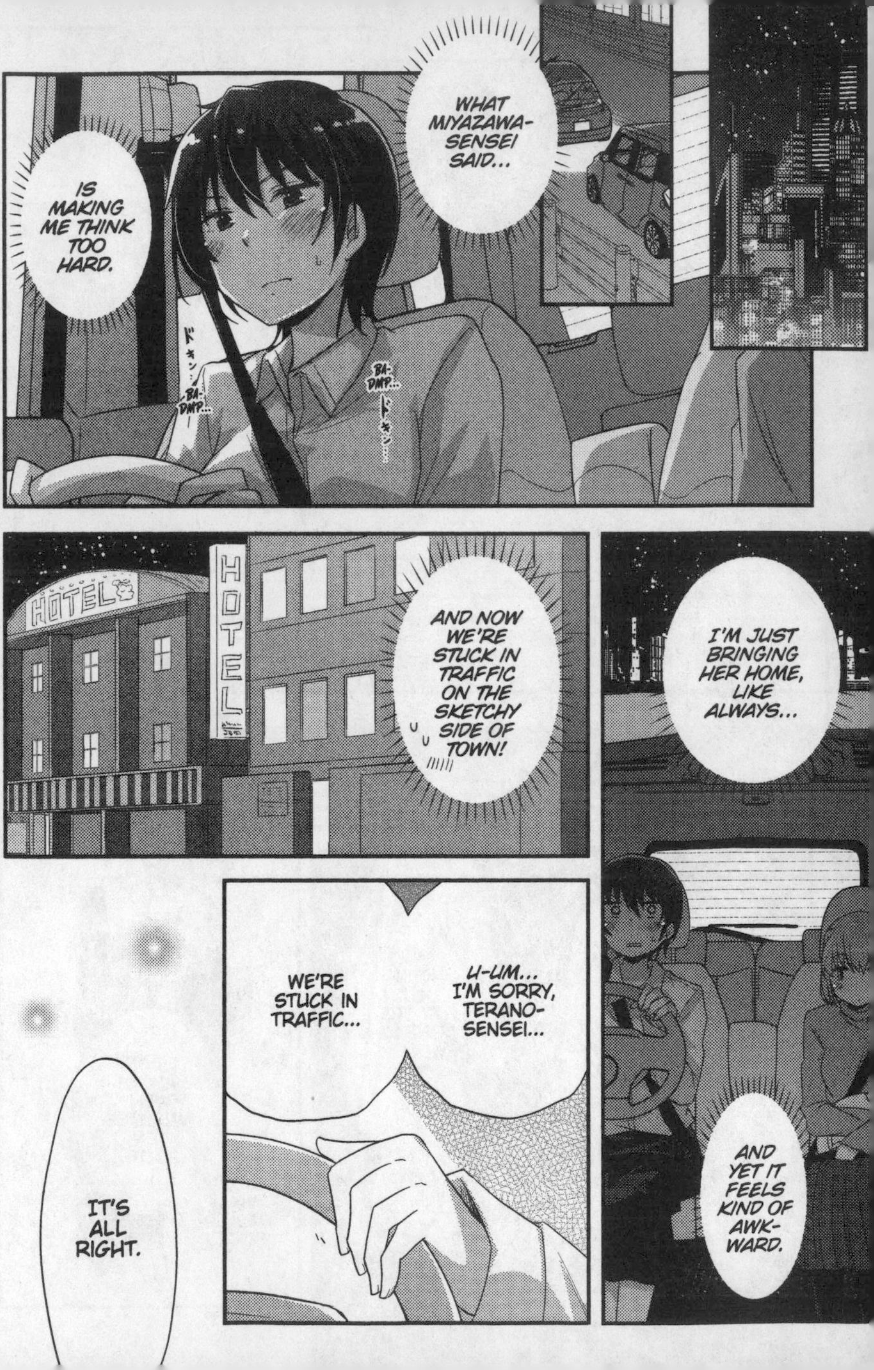
WHAT MIYAZAWA-SENSEI SAID...
IS MAKING ME THINK TOO HARD.
BA-DMP...
ドキン...
BA-DMP...
ドキン...
I'M JUST BRINGING HER HOME, LIKE ALWAYS...
AND YET IT FEELS KIND OF AWK-WARD.
HOTEL
HOTEL
AND NOW WE'RE STUCK IN TRAFFIC ON THE SKETCHY SIDE OF TOWN!
U-UM... I'M SORRY, TERANO-SENSEI...
WE'RE STUCK IN TRAFFIC...
IT'S ALL RIGHT.

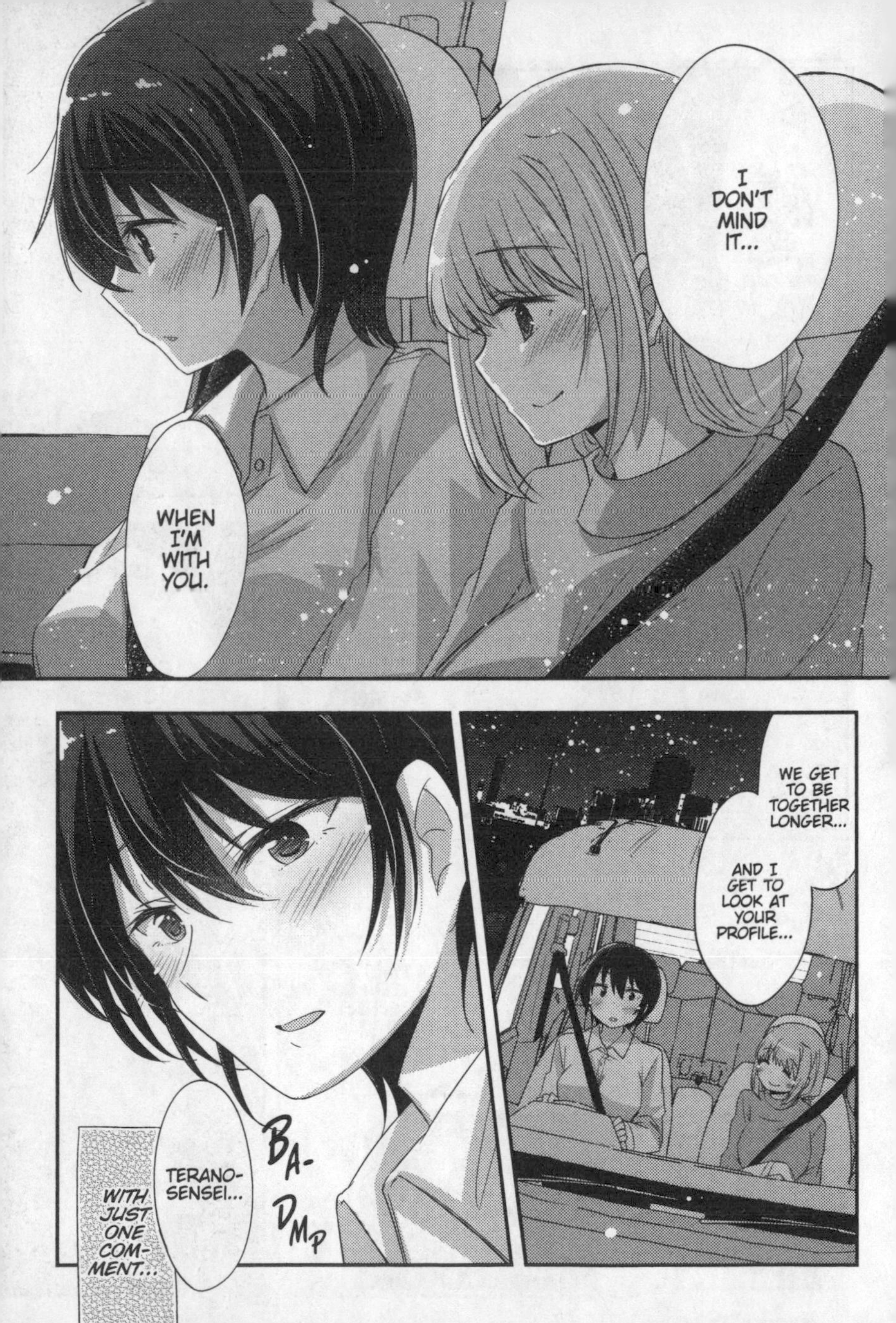
I DON'T MIND IT...
WHEN I'M WITH YOU.
WE GET TO BE TOGETHER LONGER...
AND I GET TO LOOK AT YOUR PROFILE...
BA-DMP
TERANO-SENSEI...
WITH JUST ONE COMMENT...

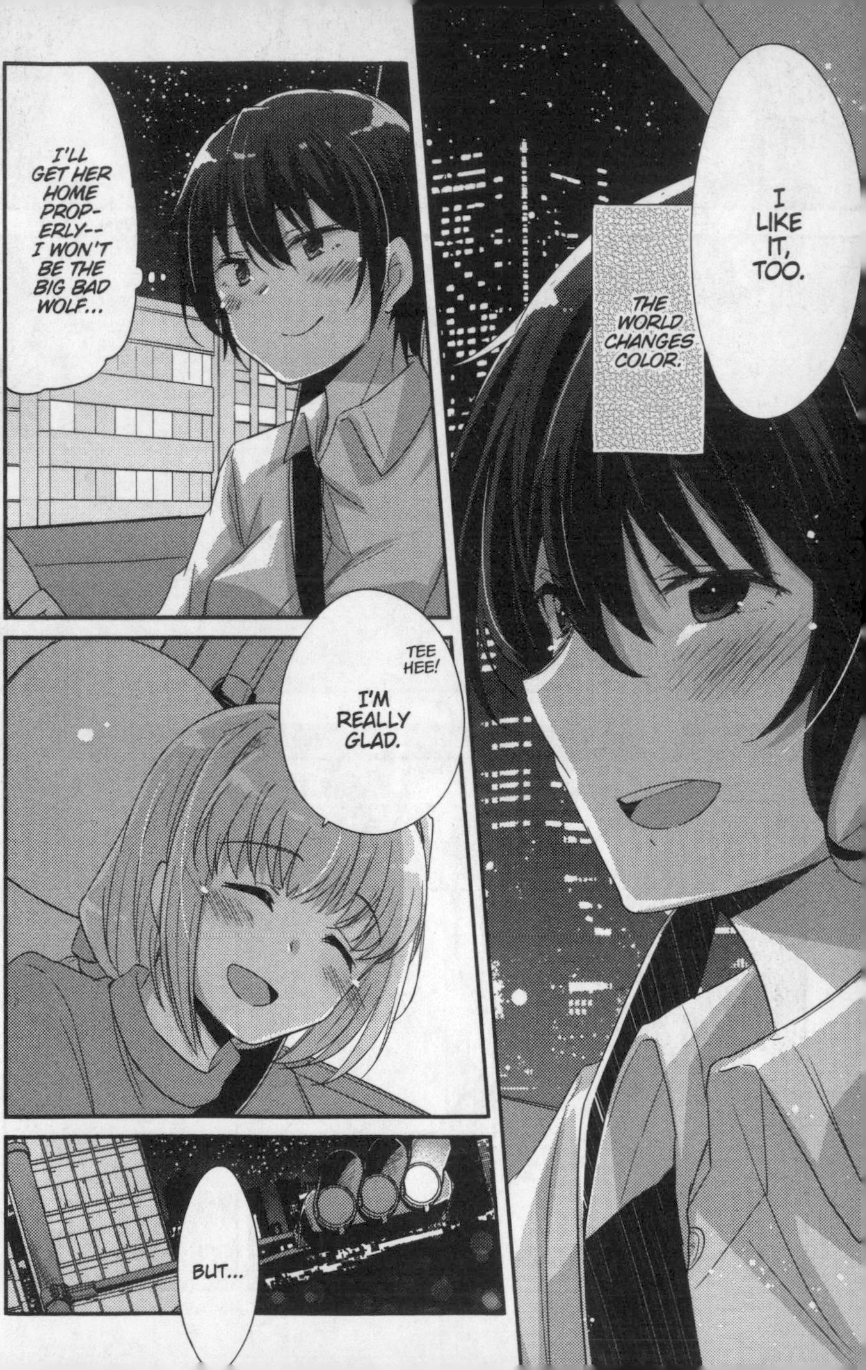
I LIKE IT, TOO.
THE WORLD CHANGES COLOR.
I'LL GET HER HOME PROPERLY-- I WON'T BE THE BIG BAD WOLF...
TEE HEE!
I'M REALLY GLAD.
BUT...

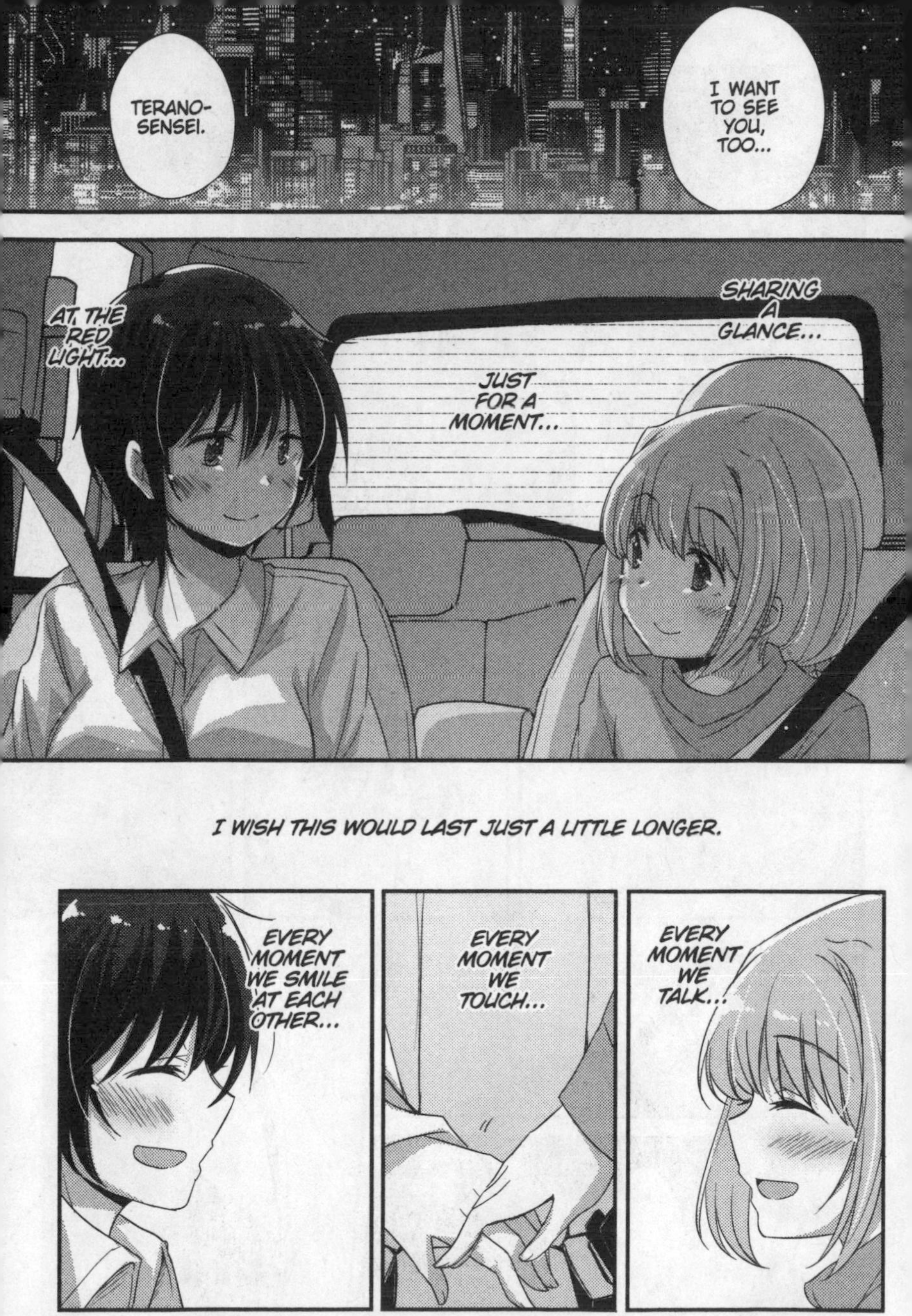
I WANT TO SEE YOU, TOO...
TERANO-SENSEI.
SHARING A GLANCE...
JUST FOR A MOMENT...
AT THE RED LIGHT...
I WISH THIS WOULD LAST JUST A LITTLE LONGER.
EVERY MOMENT WE TALK...
EVERY MOMENT WE TOUCH...
EVERY MOMENT WE SMILE AT EACH OTHER...

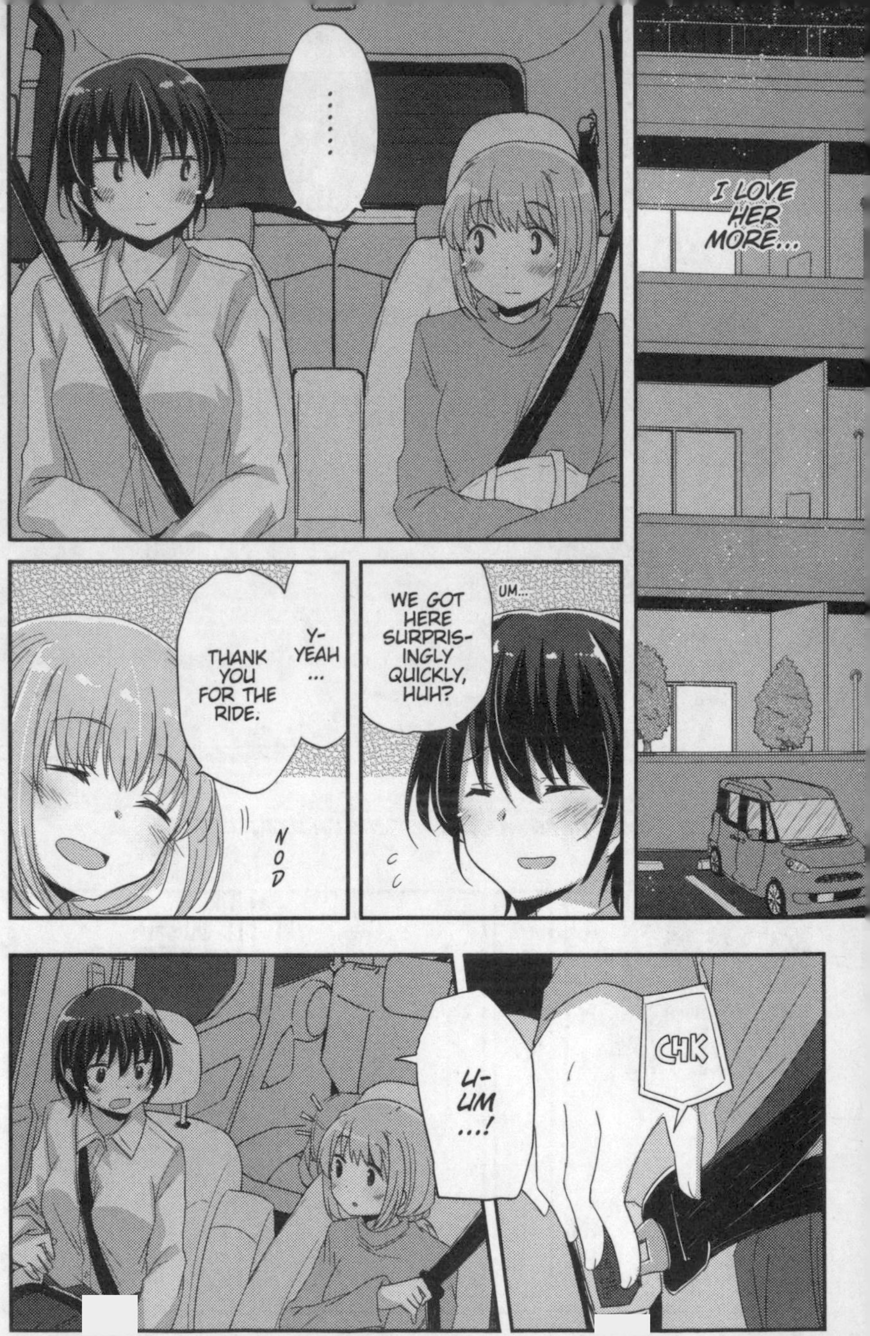
I LOVE HER MORE...
......
UM...
WE GOT HERE SURPRIS-INGLY QUICKLY, HUH?
Y-YEAH ...
THANK YOU FOR THE RIDE.
NOD
CHK
U-UM ...!

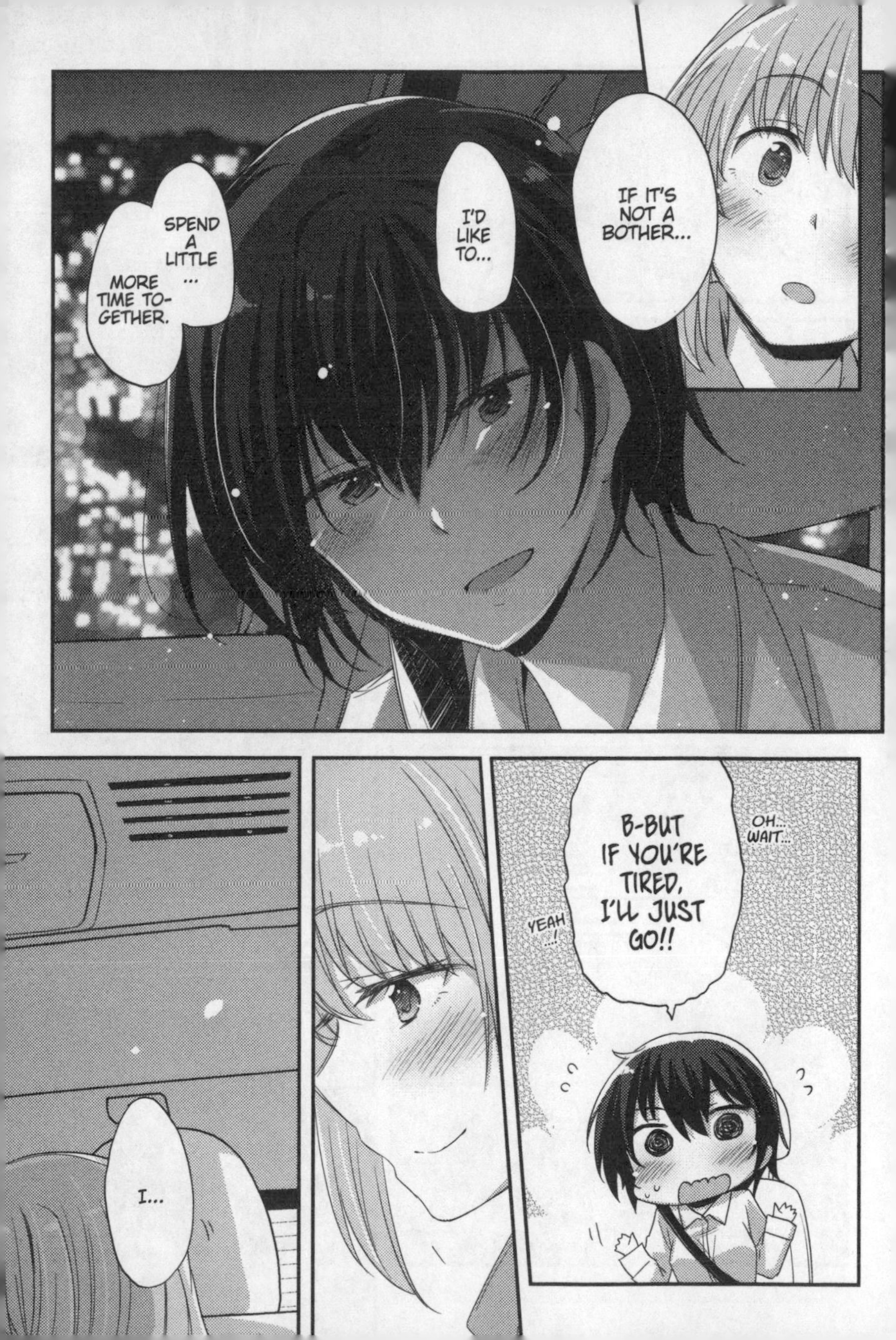
IF IT'S NOT A BOTHER...
I'D LIKE TO...
SPEND A LITTLE... MORE TIME TO-GETHER.
OH... WAIT...
B-BUT IF YOU'RE TIRED, I'LL JUST GO!!
YEAH...!
I...

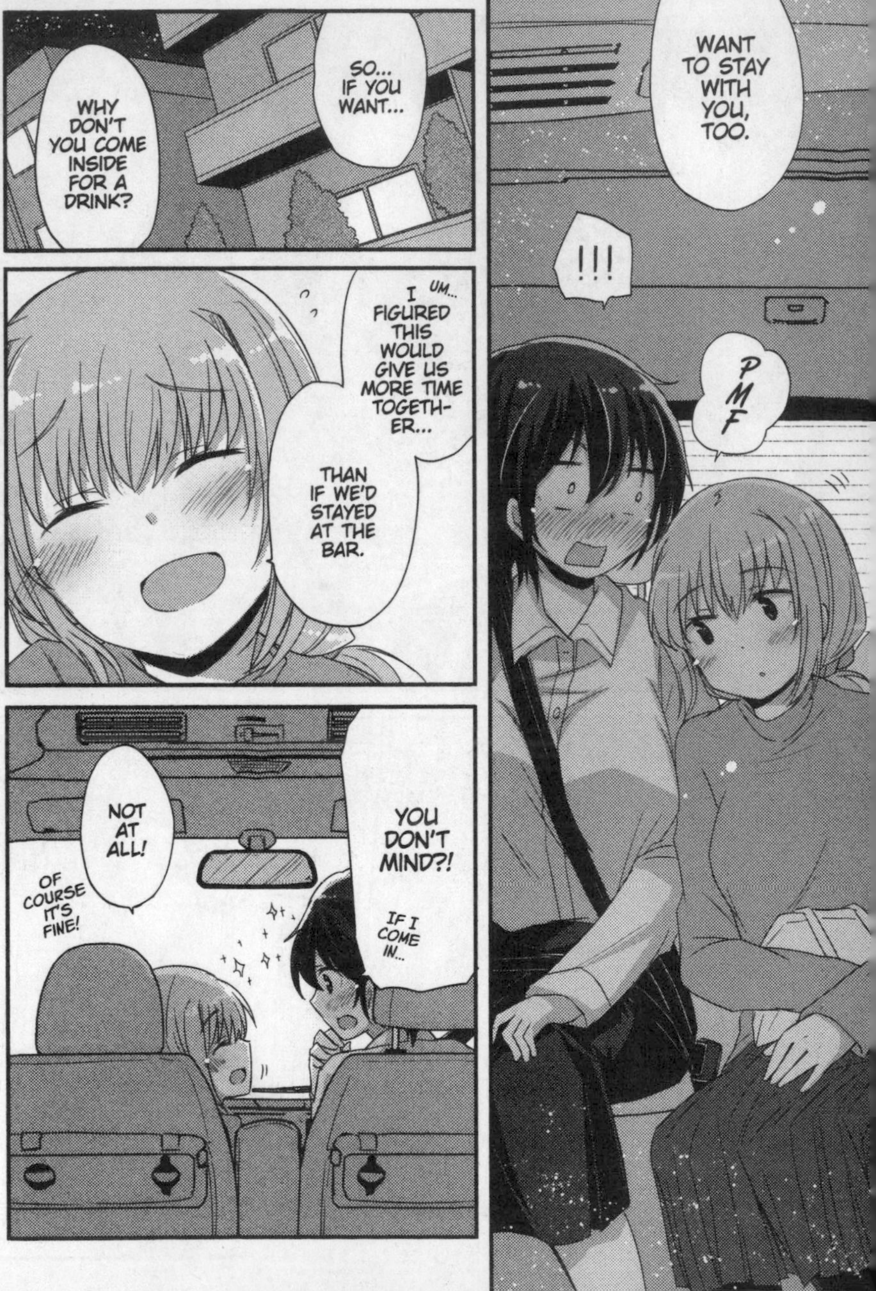
WANT TO STAY WITH YOU, TOO.
!!!
PMF
SO... IF YOU WANT...
WHY DON'T YOU COME INSIDE FOR A DRINK?
UM... I FIGURED THIS WOULD GIVE US MORE TIME TOGETH-ER...
THAN IF WE'D STAYED AT THE BAR.
YOU DON'T MIND?!
IF I COME IN...
NOT AT ALL!
OF COURSE IT'S FINE!

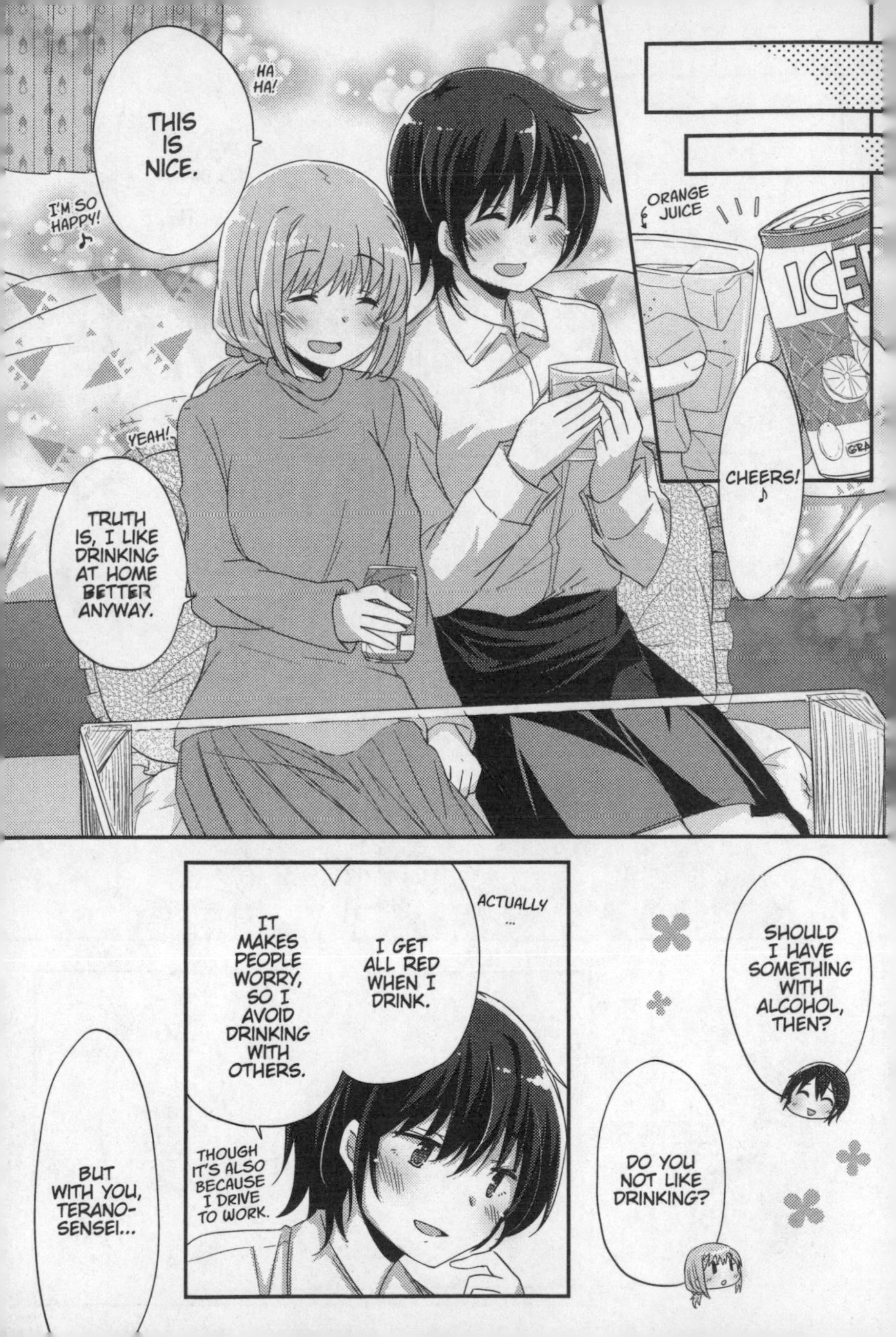
ORANGE JUICE
CHEERS! ♪
HA HA!
THIS IS NICE.
I'M SO HAPPY! ♪
YEAH!
TRUTH IS, I LIKE DRINKING AT HOME BETTER ANYWAY.
SHOULD I HAVE SOMETHING WITH ALCOHOL, THEN?
DO YOU NOT LIKE DRINKING?
ACTUALLY ...
I GET ALL RED WHEN I DRINK.
IT MAKES PEOPLE WORRY, SO I AVOID DRINKING WITH OTHERS.
THOUGH IT'S ALSO BECAUSE I DRIVE TO WORK.
BUT WITH YOU, TERANO-SENSEI...

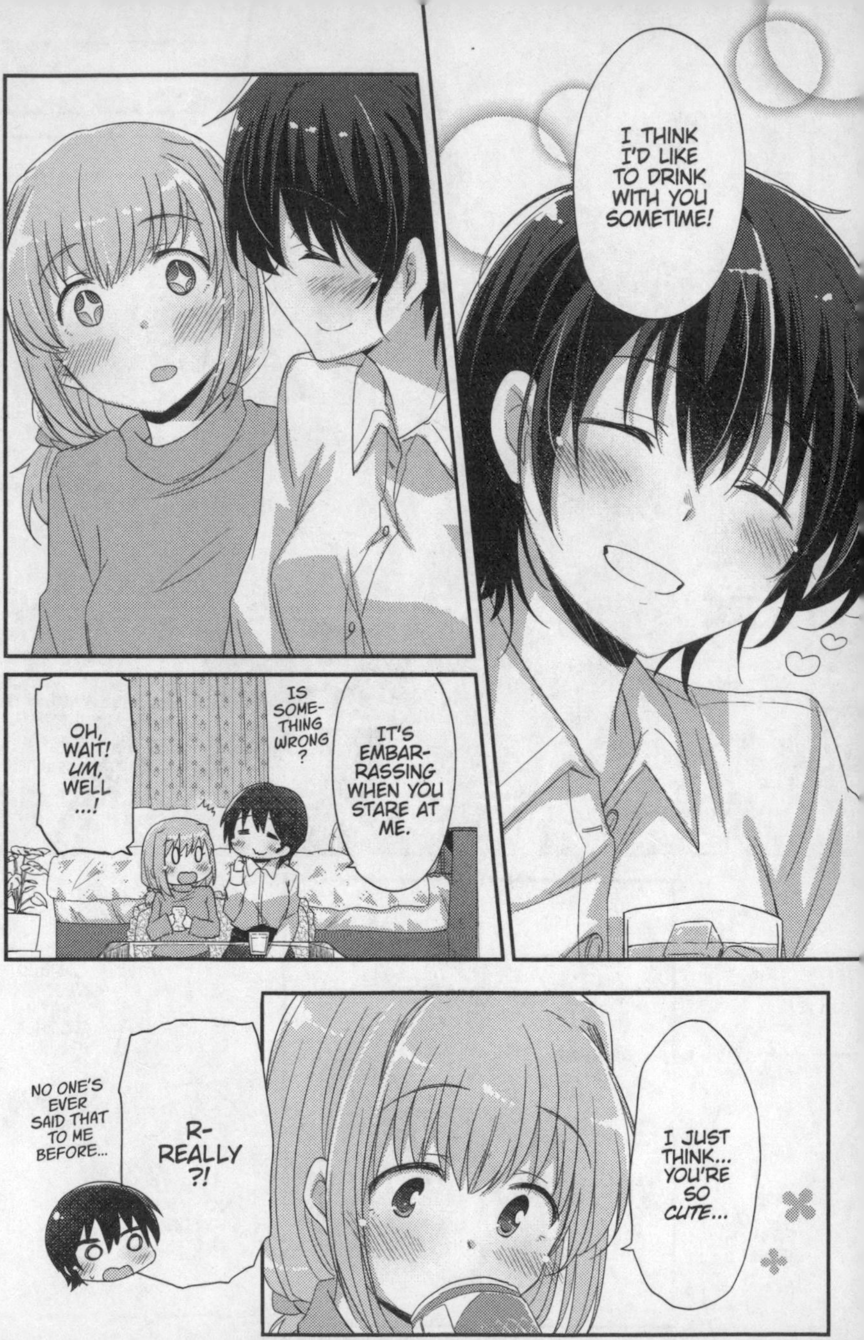
I THINK I'D LIKE TO DRINK WITH YOU SOMETIME!
IT'S EMBARRASSING WHEN YOU STARE AT ME.
IS SOMETHING WRONG?
OH, WAIT! UM, WELL...!
I JUST THINK... YOU'RE SO CUTE...
R-REALLY?!
NO ONE'S EVER SAID THAT TO ME BEFORE...

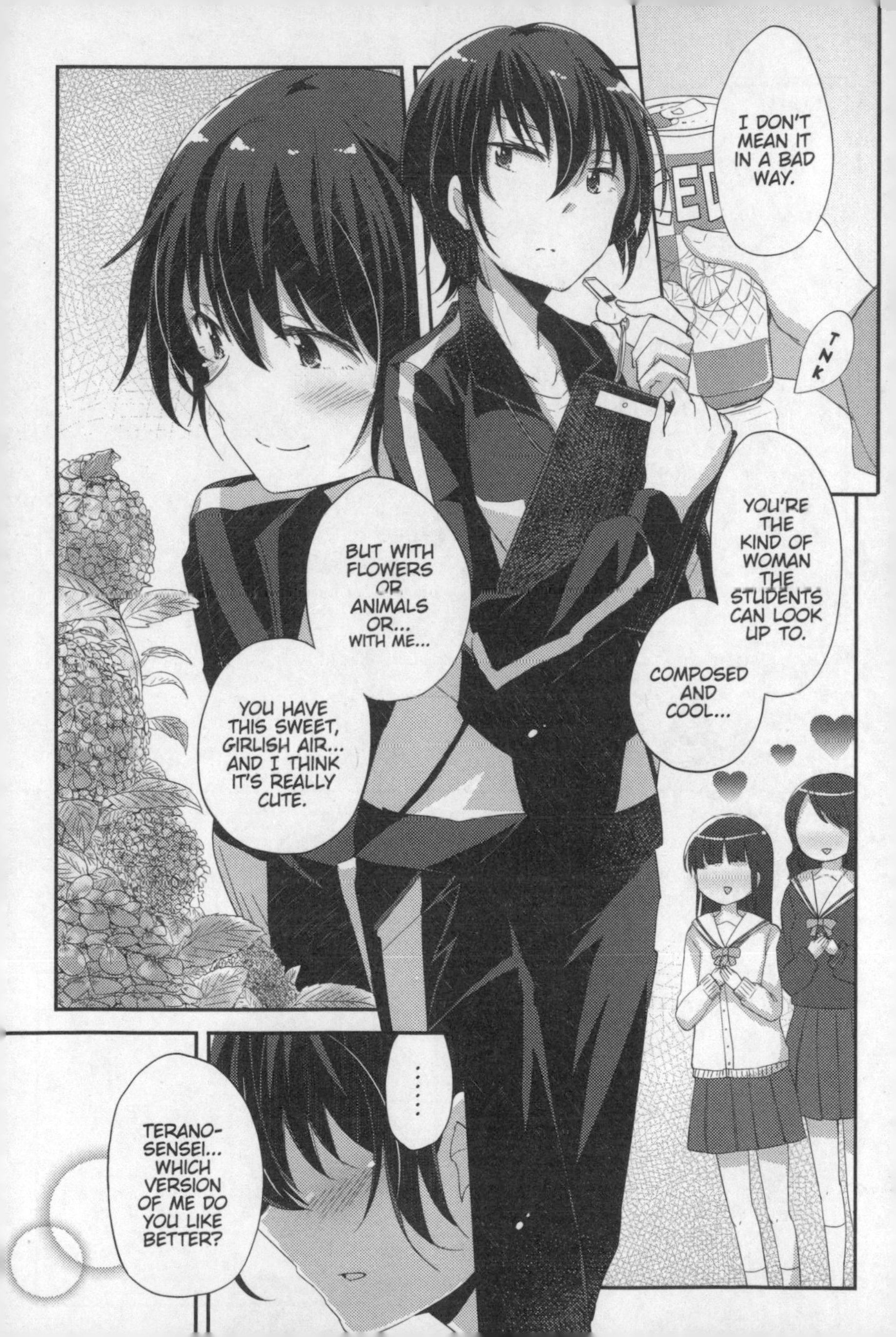
I DON'T MEAN IT IN A BAD WAY.
TNK
YOU'RE THE KIND OF WOMAN THE STUDENTS CAN LOOK UP TO.
COMPOSED AND COOL...
BUT WITH FLOWERS OR ANIMALS OR... WITH ME...
YOU HAVE THIS SWEET, GIRLISH AIR... AND I THINK IT'S REALLY CUTE.
......
TERANO-SENSEI... WHICH VERSION OF ME DO YOU LIKE BETTER?

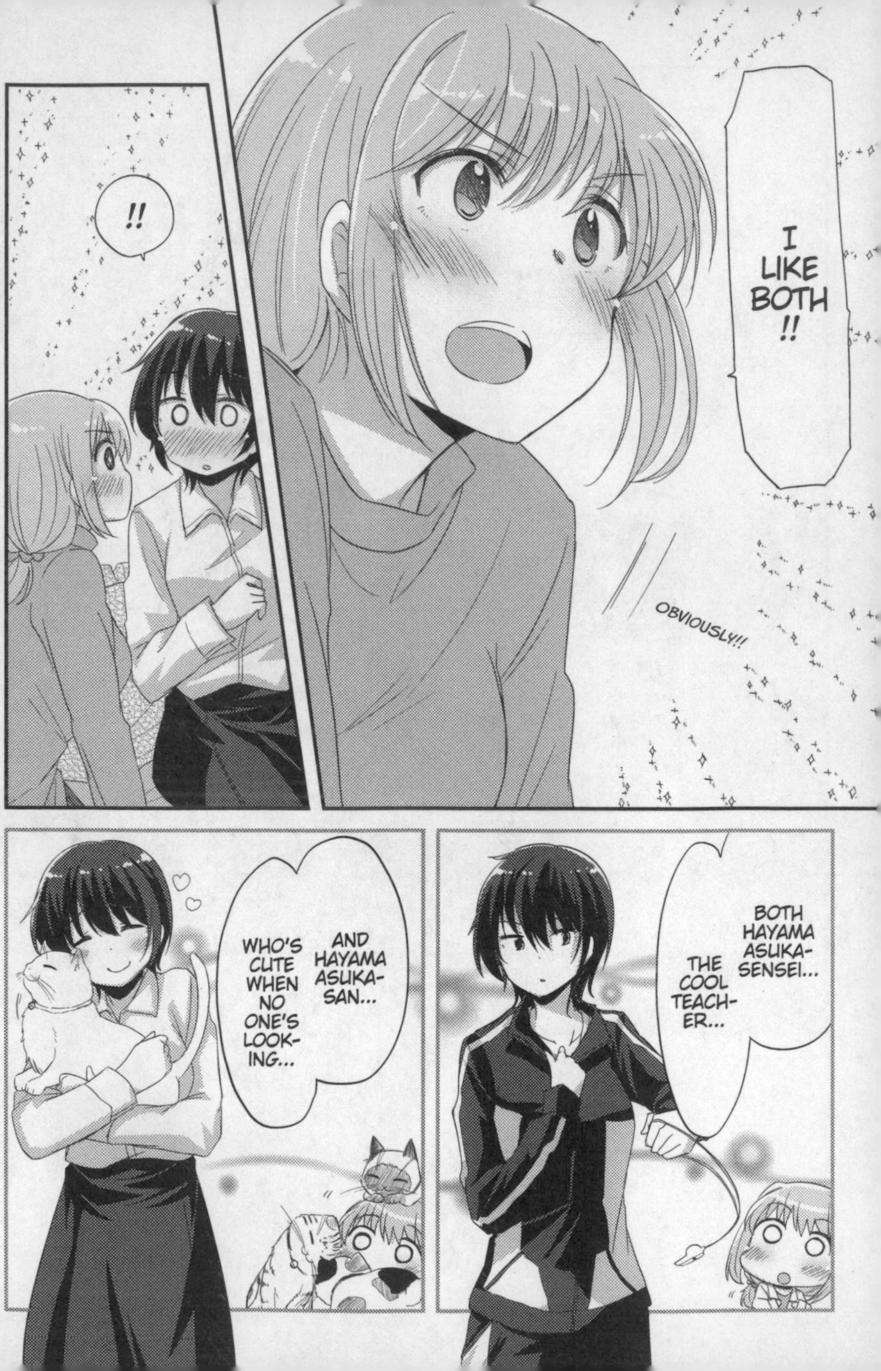
I LIKE BOTH!!
OBVIOUSLY!!!
!!
BOTH HAYAMA ASUKA-SENSEI...
THE COOL TEACHER...
AND HAYAMA ASUKA-SAN...
WHO'S CUTE WHEN NO ONE'S LOOKING...

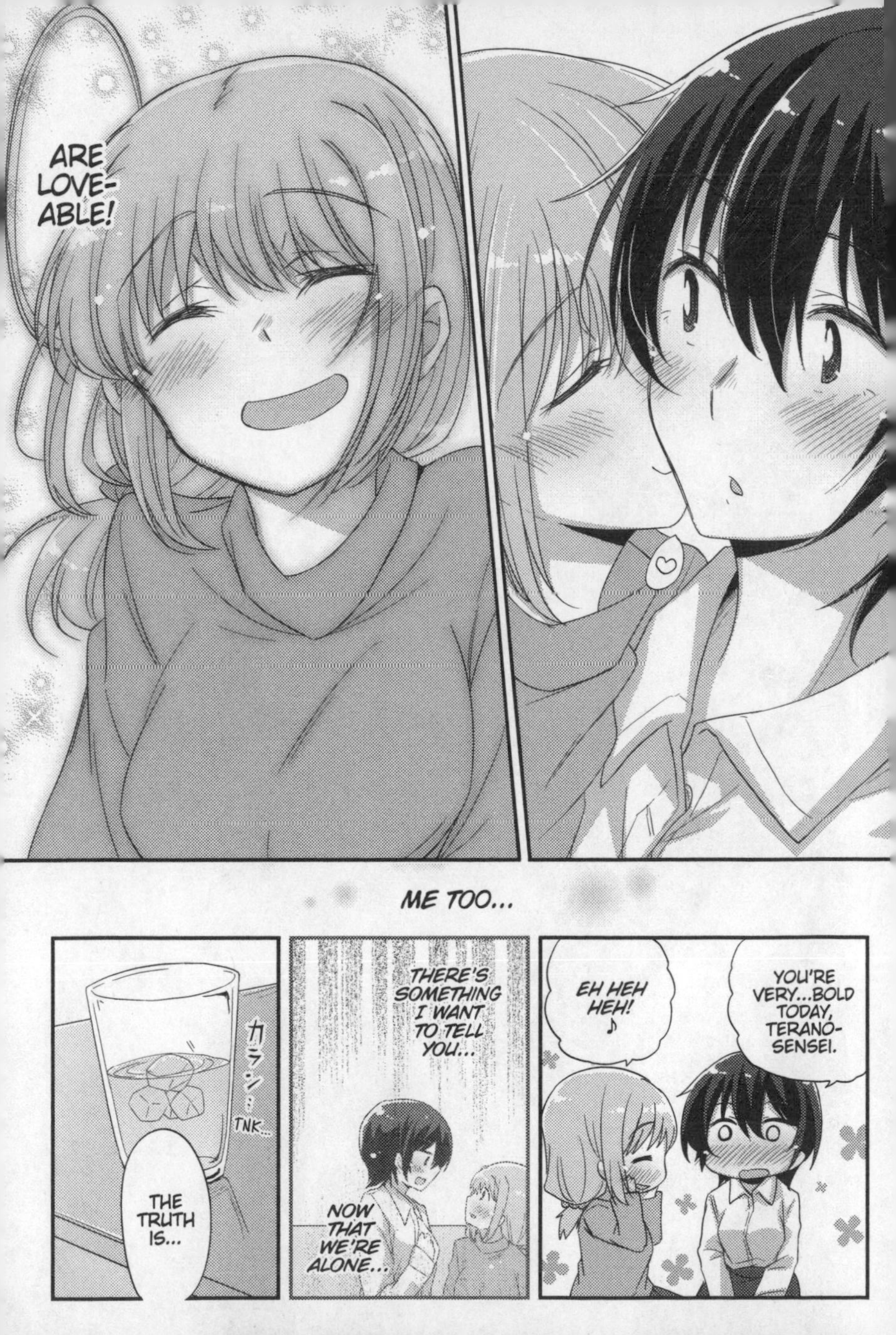
ARE LOVE-ABLE!
ME TOO...
YOU'RE VERY...BOLD TODAY, TERANO-SENSEI.
EH HEH HEH! ♪
THERE'S SOMETHING I WANT TO TELL YOU...
NOW THAT WE'RE ALONE...
カラン...
TNK...
THE TRUTH IS...

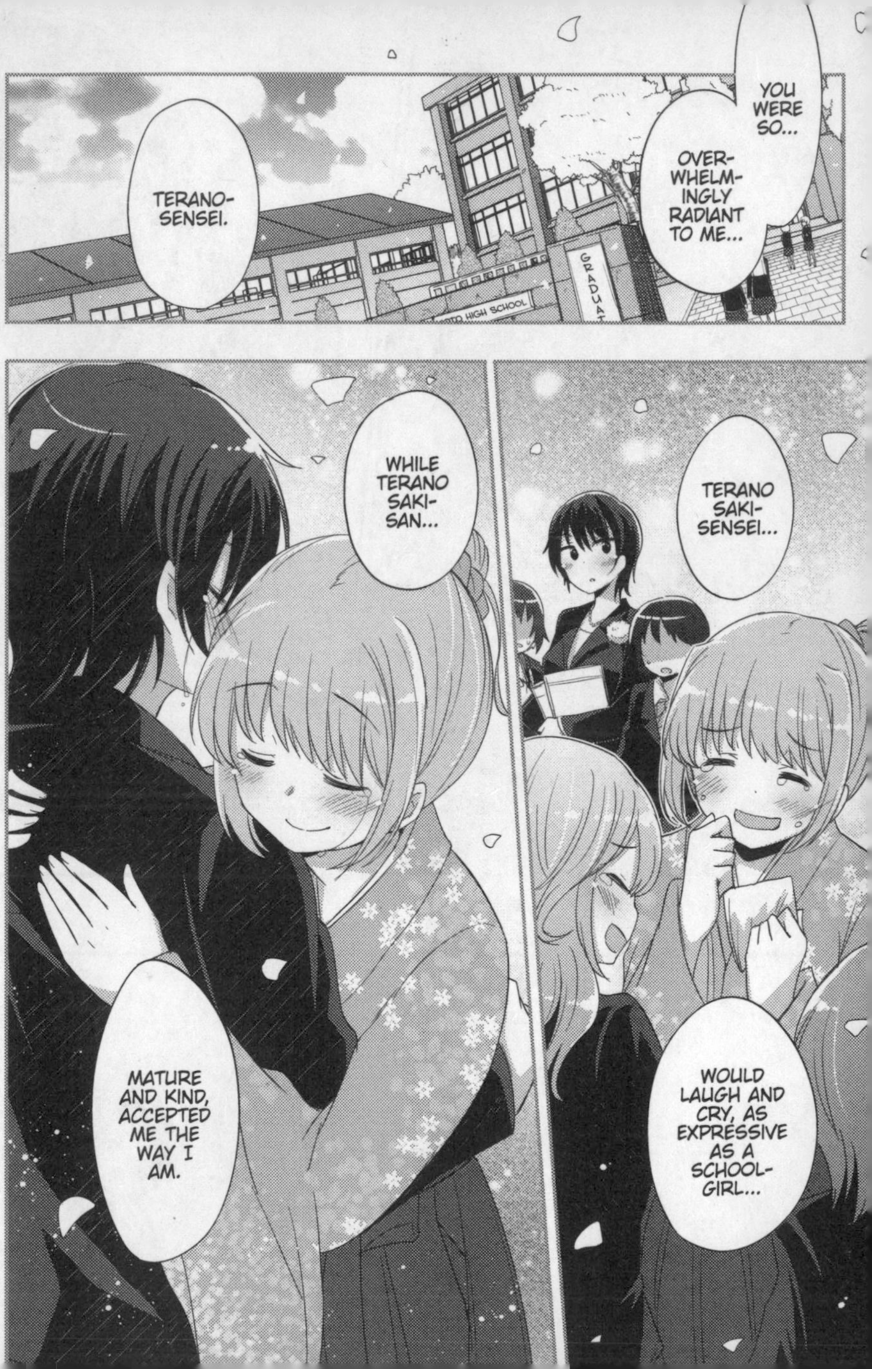
YOU WERE SO...
OVER-WHELM-INGLY RADIANT TO ME...
TERANO-SENSEI.
TERANO SAKI-SENSEI...
WOULD LAUGH AND CRY, AS EXPRESSIVE AS A SCHOOL-GIRL...
WHILE TERANO SAKI-SAN...
MATURE AND KIND, ACCEPTED ME THE WAY I AM.

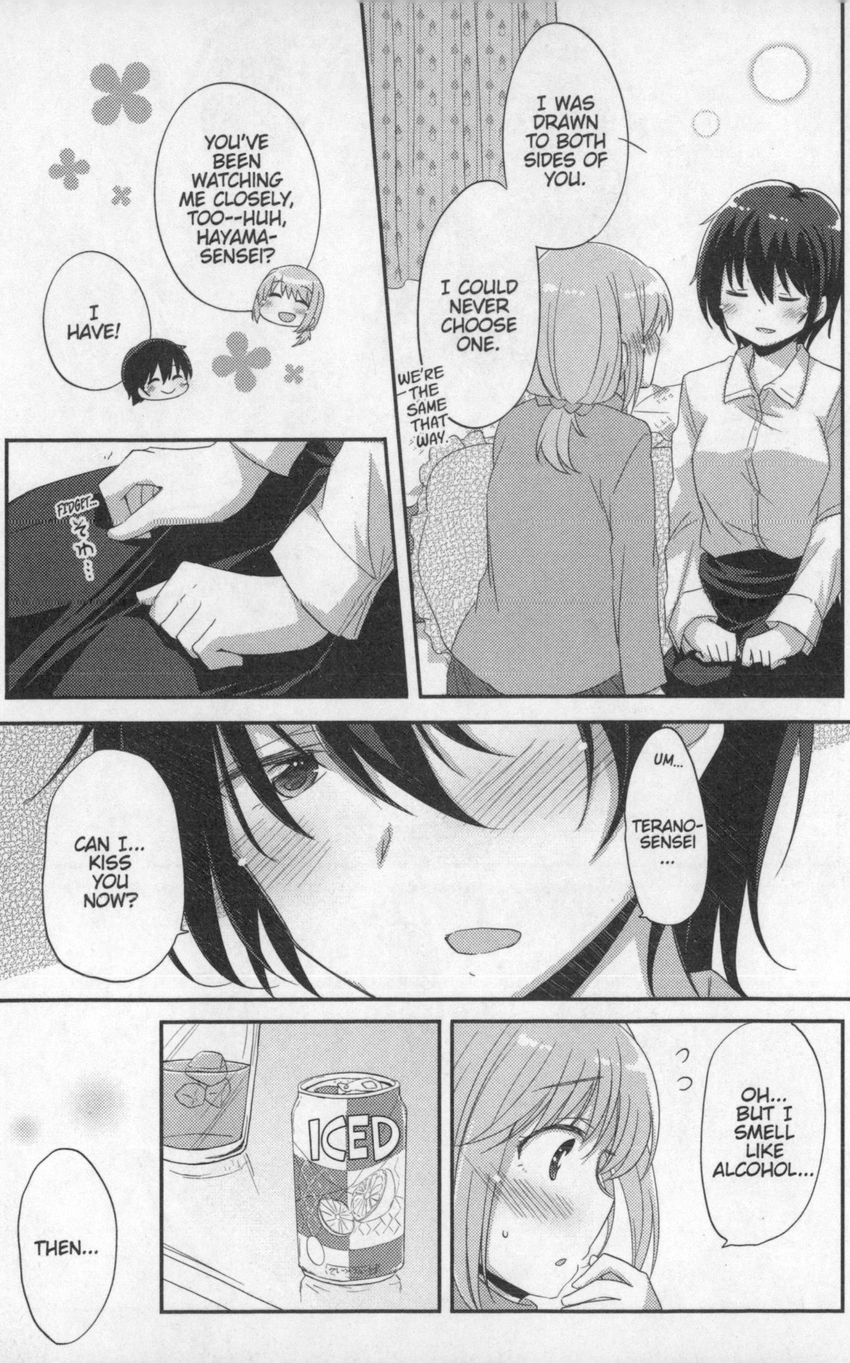
I WAS DRAWN TO BOTH SIDES OF YOU.
I COULD NEVER CHOOSE ONE.
WE'RE THE SAME THAT WAY.
YOU'VE BEEN WATCHING ME CLOSELY, TOO--HUH, HAYAMA-SENSEI?
I HAVE!
FIDGET...
そわ…
UM...
TERANO-SENSEI...
CAN I... KISS YOU NOW?
OH... BUT I SMELL LIKE ALCOHOL...
ICED
THEN...

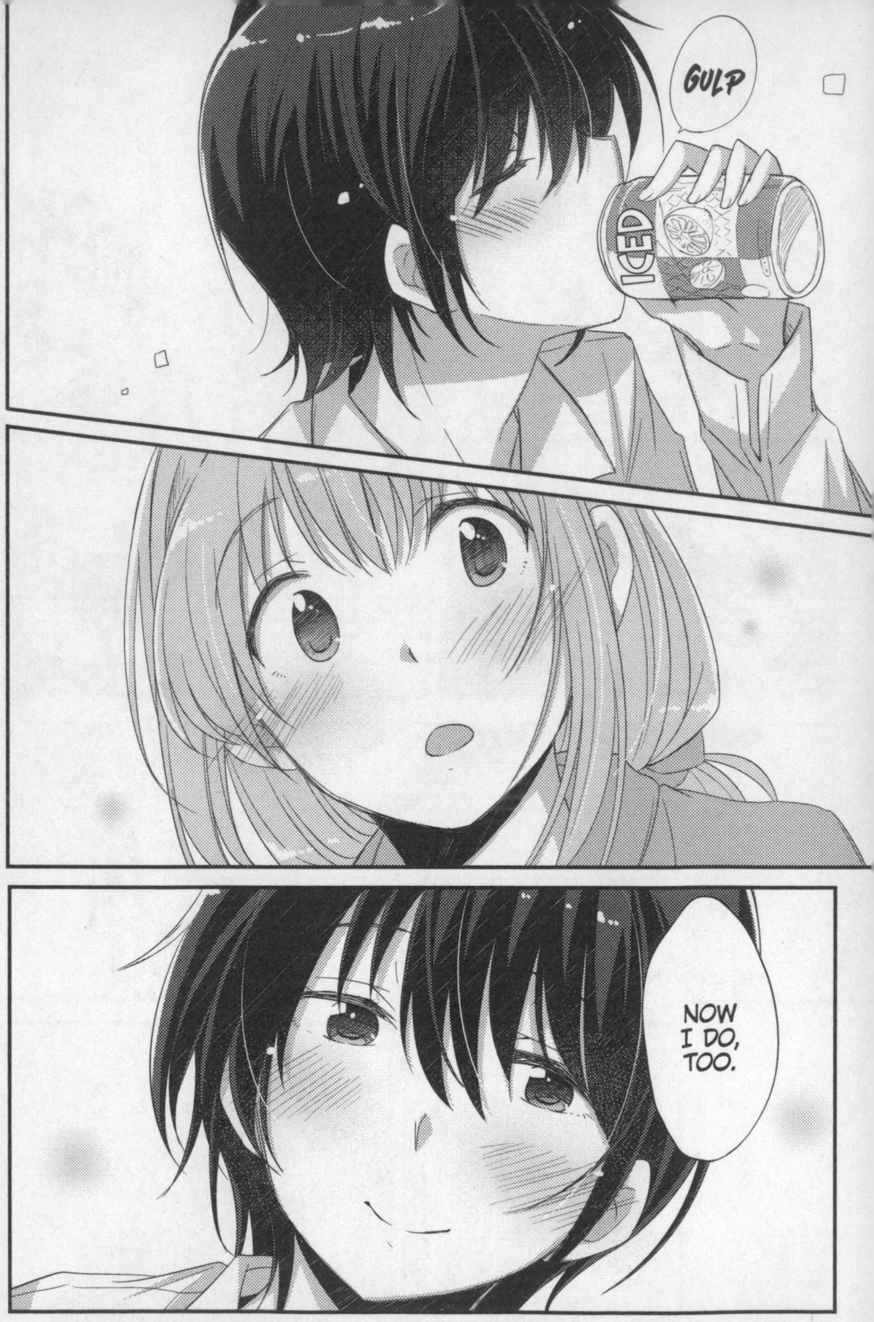
GULP
ICED
NOW I DO, TOO.

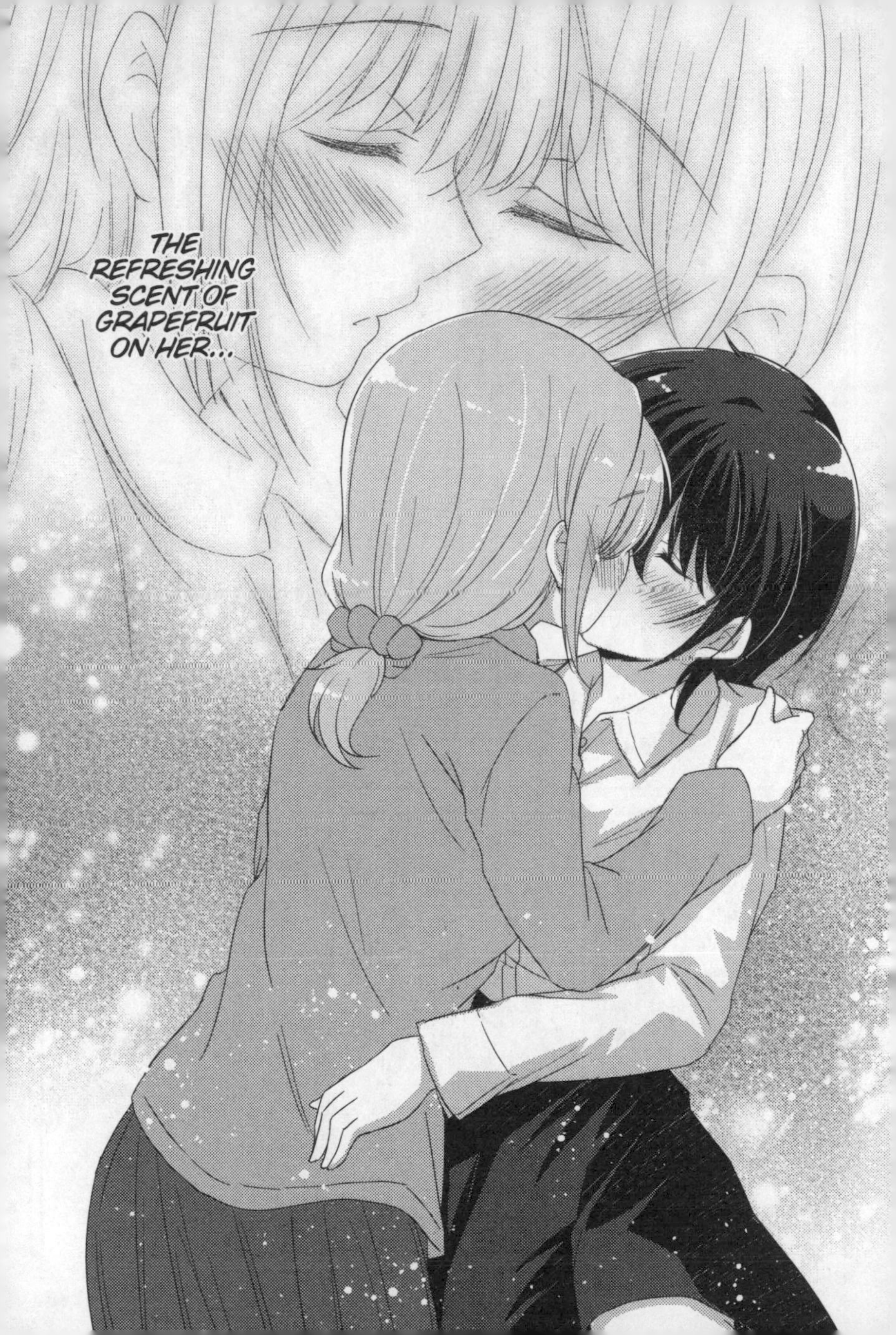
THE REFRESHING SCENT OF GRAPEFRUIT ON HER...

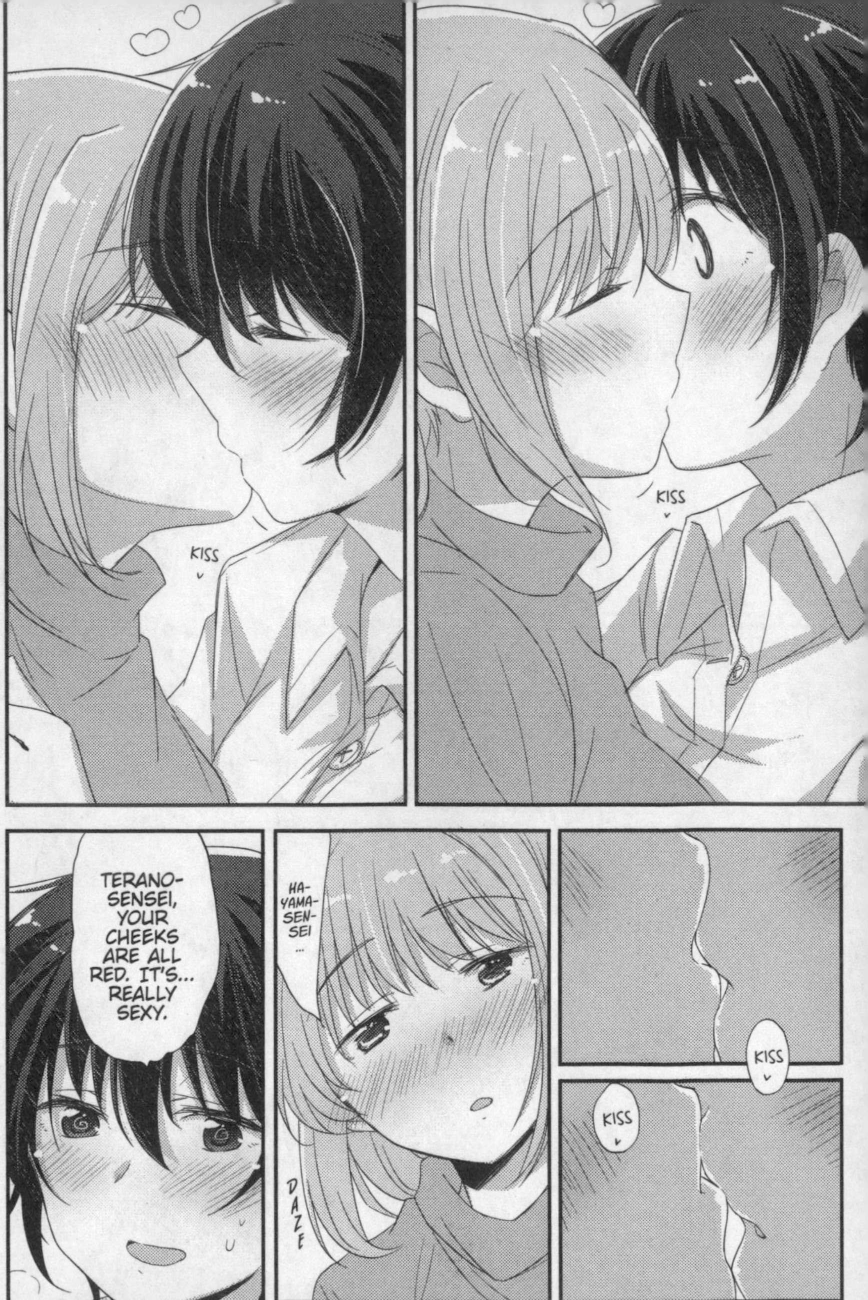

KISS
KISS
KISS
KISS
HA-YAMA-SEN-SEI...
DAZE
TERANO-SENSEI, YOUR CHEEKS ARE ALL RED. IT'S... REALLY SEXY.

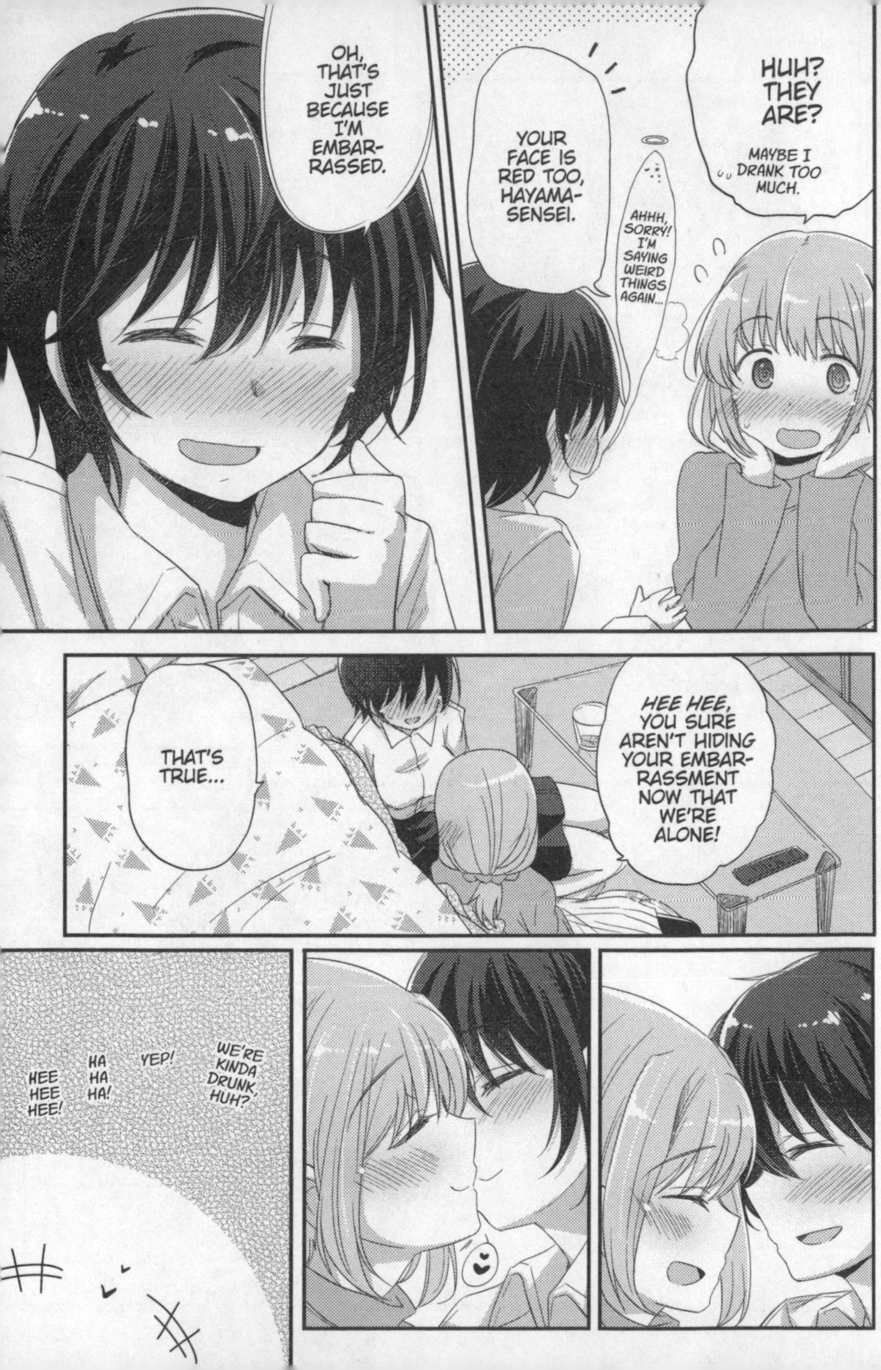
HUH? THEY ARE?
MAYBE I DRANK TOO MUCH.
YOUR FACE IS RED TOO, HAYAMA-SENSEI.
AHHH, SORRY! I'M SAYING WEIRD THINGS AGAIN...
OH, THAT'S JUST BECAUSE I'M EMBARRASSED.
HEE HEE, YOU SURE AREN'T HIDING YOUR EMBARRASSMENT NOW THAT WE'RE ALONE!
THAT'S TRUE...
WE'RE KINDA DRUNK, HUH?
YEP!
HA HA HA!
HEE HEE HEE!

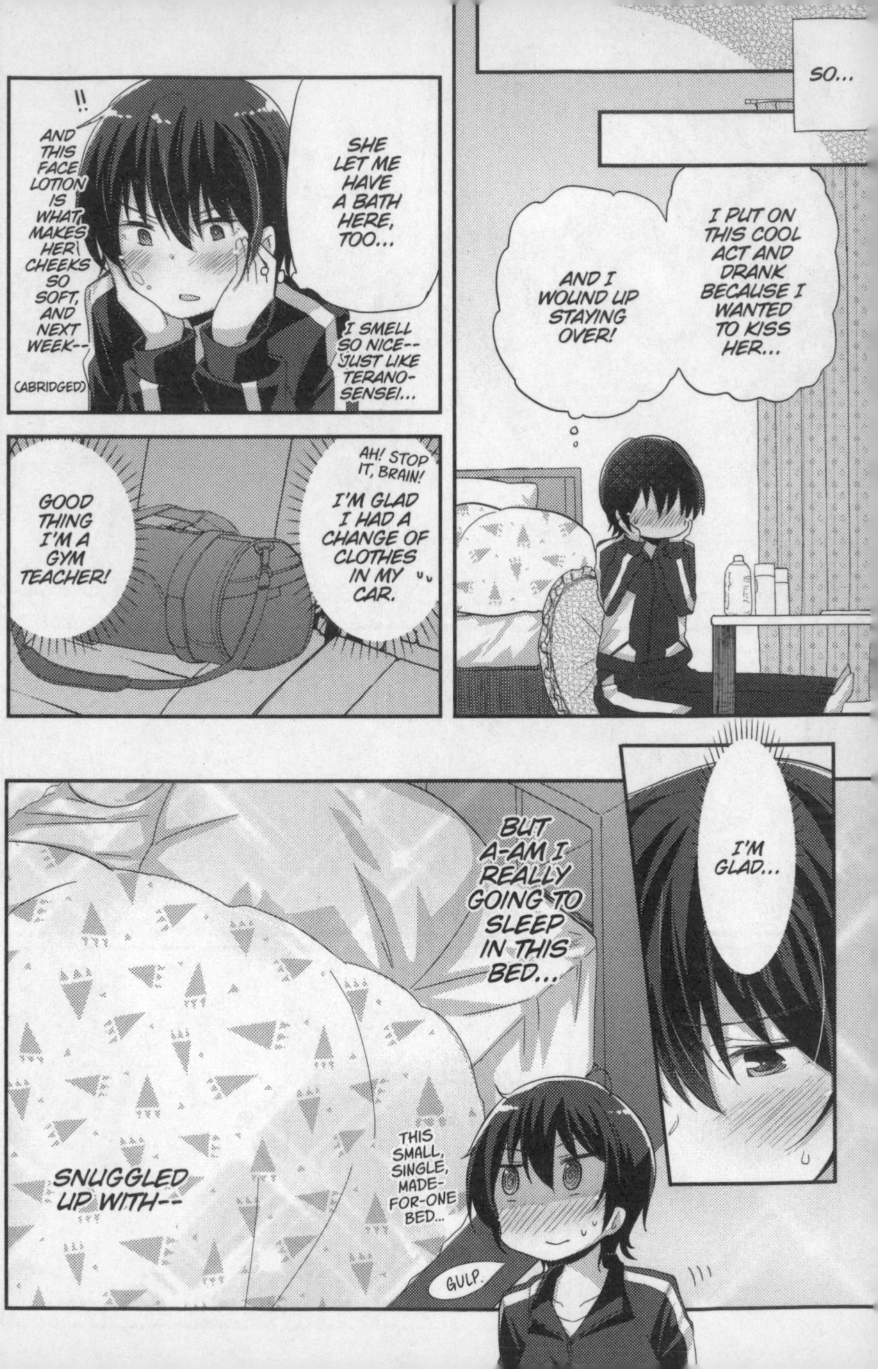
SO...
I PUT ON THIS COOL ACT AND DRANK BECAUSE I WANTED TO KISS HER...
AND I WOUND UP STAYING OVER!
SHE LET ME HAVE A BATH HERE, TOO...
I SMELL SO NICE--JUST LIKE TERANO-SENSEI...
!!
AND THIS FACE LOTION IS WHAT MAKES HER CHEEKS SO SOFT, AND NEXT WEEK--
(ABRIDGED)
AH! STOP IT, BRAIN!
I'M GLAD I HAD A CHANGE OF CLOTHES IN MY CAR.
GOOD THING I'M A GYM TEACHER!
I'M GLAD...
BUT A-AM I REALLY GOING TO SLEEP IN THIS BED...
THIS SMALL, SINGLE, MADE-FOR-ONE BED...
SNUGGLED UP WITH--
GULP.

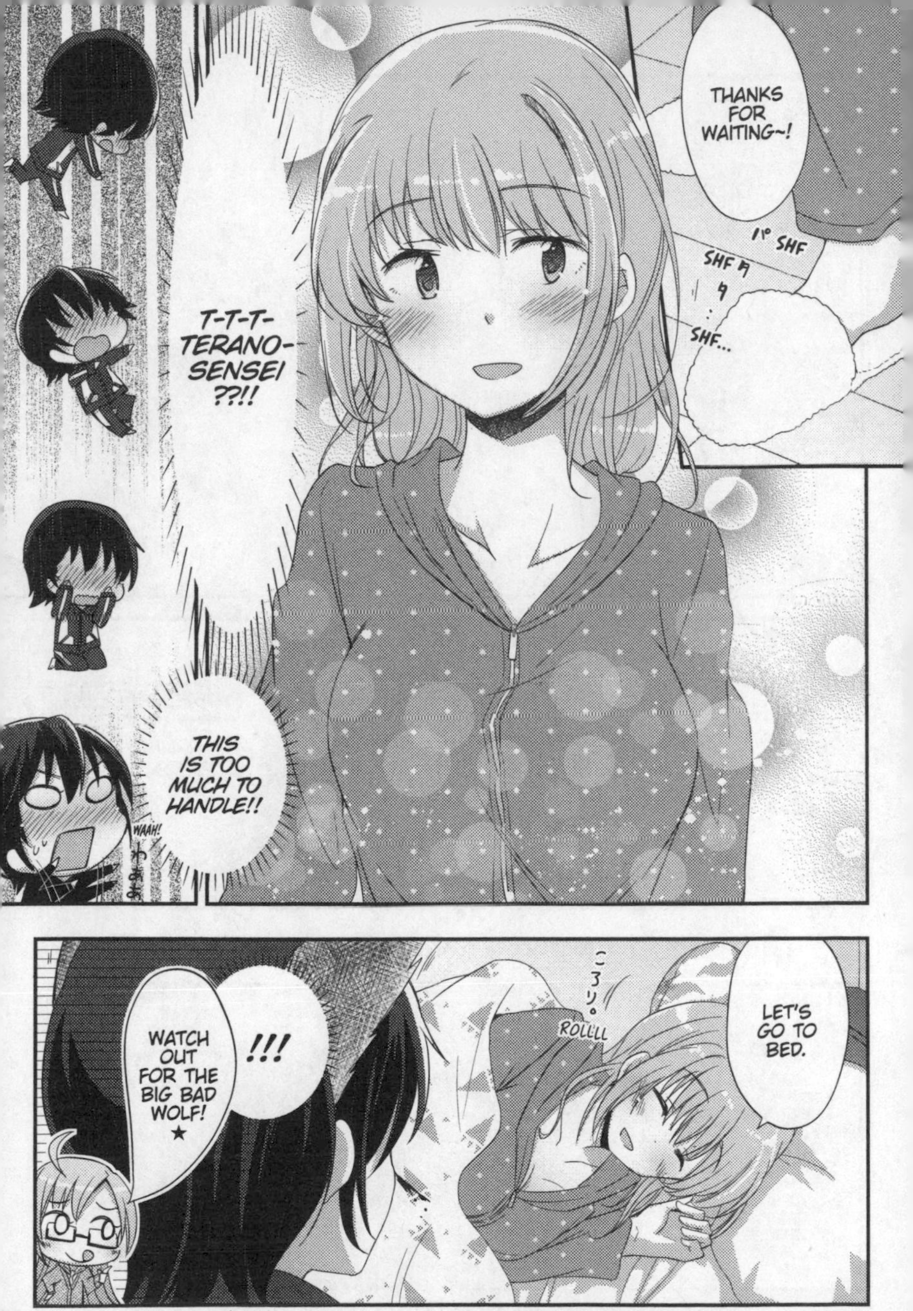

THANKS FOR WAITING~!
SHF SHF SHF...
T-T-T-TERANO-SENSEI??!!
THIS IS TOO MUCH TO HANDLE!!
WAAH!
LET'S GO TO BED.
ROLLLL
!!!
WATCH OUT FOR THE BIG BAD WOLF! ★

COMPLETELY DEFENSELESS.

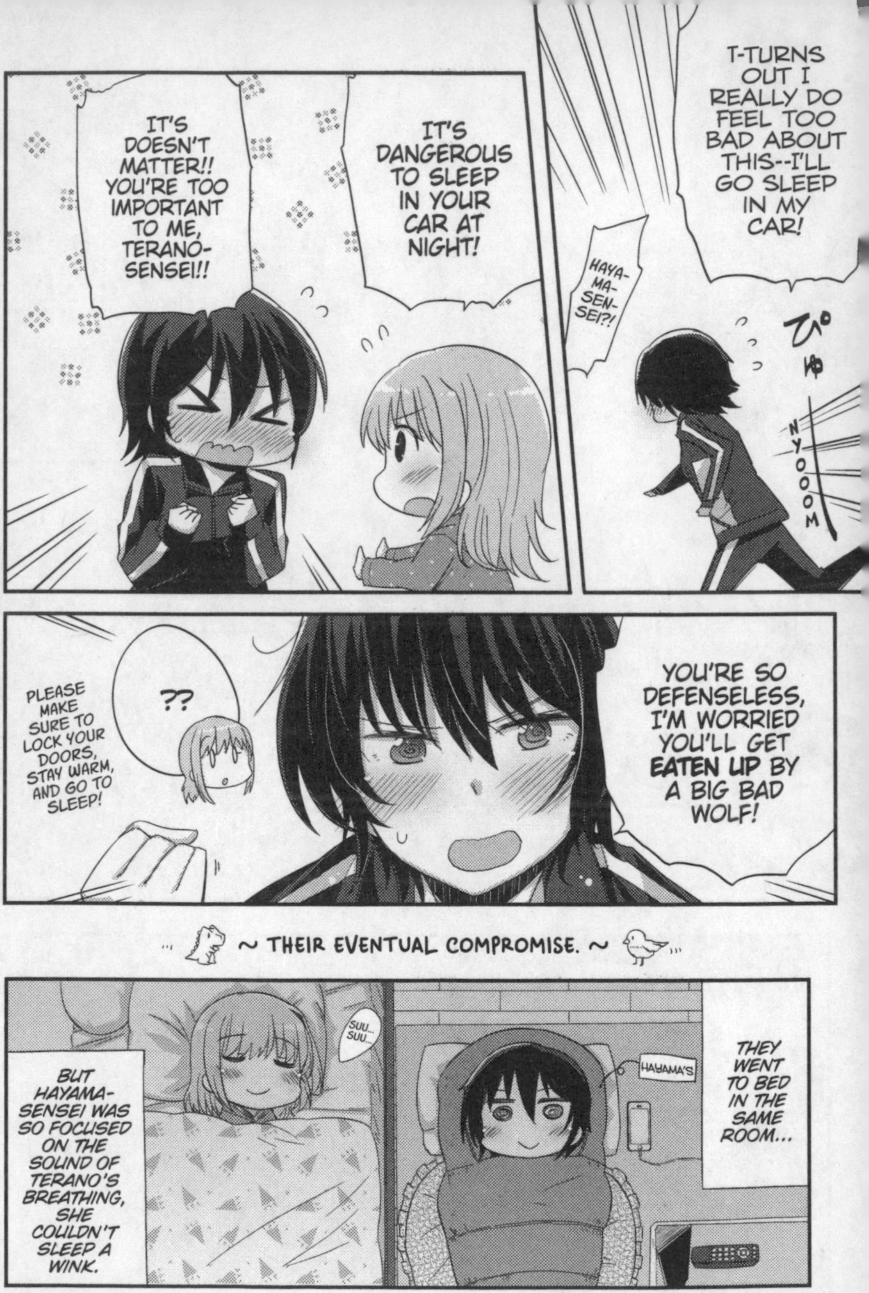
T-TURNS OUT I REALLY DO FEEL TOO BAD ABOUT THIS--I'LL GO SLEEP IN MY CAR!
HAYAMA-SENSEI?!
ぴゅ
NYOOOOM
IT'S DANGEROUS TO SLEEP IN YOUR CAR AT NIGHT!
IT'S DOESN'T MATTER!! YOU'RE TOO IMPORTANT TO ME, TERANO-SENSEI!!
YOU'RE SO DEFENSELESS, I'M WORRIED YOU'LL GET EATEN UP BY A BIG BAD WOLF!
??
PLEASE MAKE SURE TO LOCK YOUR DOORS, STAY WARM, AND GO TO SLEEP!
~ THEIR EVENTUAL COMPROMISE. ~
THEY WENT TO BED IN THE SAME ROOM...
HAYAMA'S
SUU... SUU...
BUT HAYAMA-SENSEI WAS SO FOCUSED ON THE SOUND OF TERANO'S BREATHING, SHE COULDN'T SLEEP A WINK.

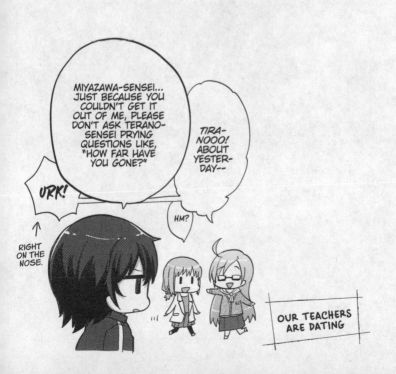

TIRA-NOOO! ABOUT YESTERDAY--
HM?
MIYAZAWA-SENSEI... JUST BECAUSE YOU COULDN'T GET IT OUT OF ME, PLEASE DON'T ASK TERANO-SENSEI PRYING QUESTIONS LIKE, "HOW FAR HAVE YOU GONE?"
URK!
RIGHT ON THE NOSE.

OUR TEACHERS ARE DATING

Our Teachers are Dating!

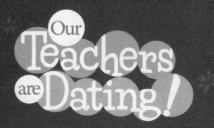

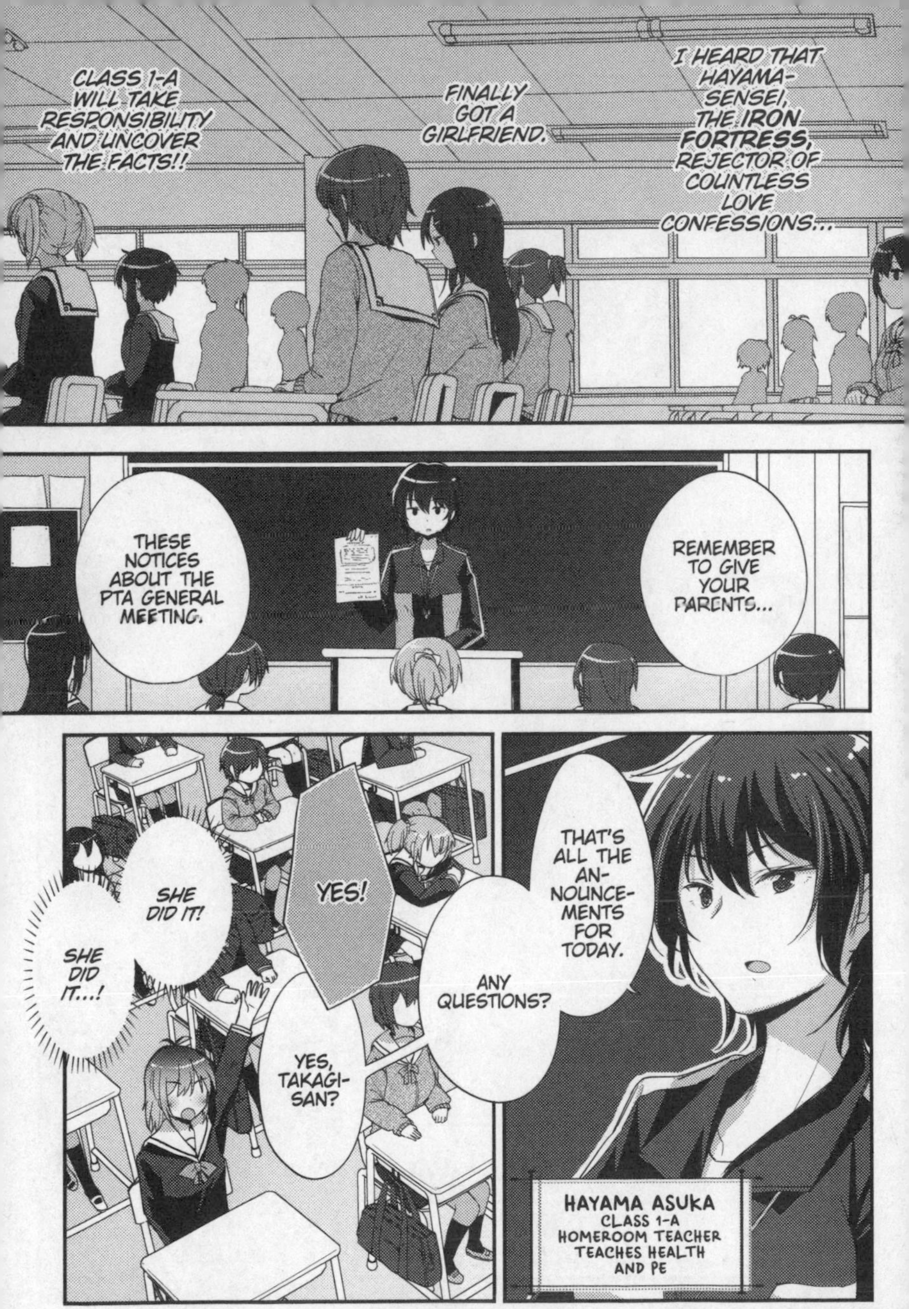

I HEARD THAT HAYAMA-SENSEI, THE IRON FORTRESS, REJECTOR OF COUNTLESS LOVE CONFESSIONS...
FINALLY GOT A GIRLFRIEND.
CLASS 1-A WILL TAKE RESPONSIBILITY AND UNCOVER THE FACTS!!
REMEMBER TO GIVE YOUR PARENTS...
THESE NOTICES ABOUT THE PTA GENERAL MEETING.
THAT'S ALL THE AN-NOUNCE-MENTS FOR TODAY.
ANY QUESTIONS?
HAYAMA ASUKA
CLASS 1-A HOMEROOM TEACHER
TEACHES HEALTH AND PE
YES!
SHE DID IT!
SHE DID IT...!
YES, TAKAGI-SAN?

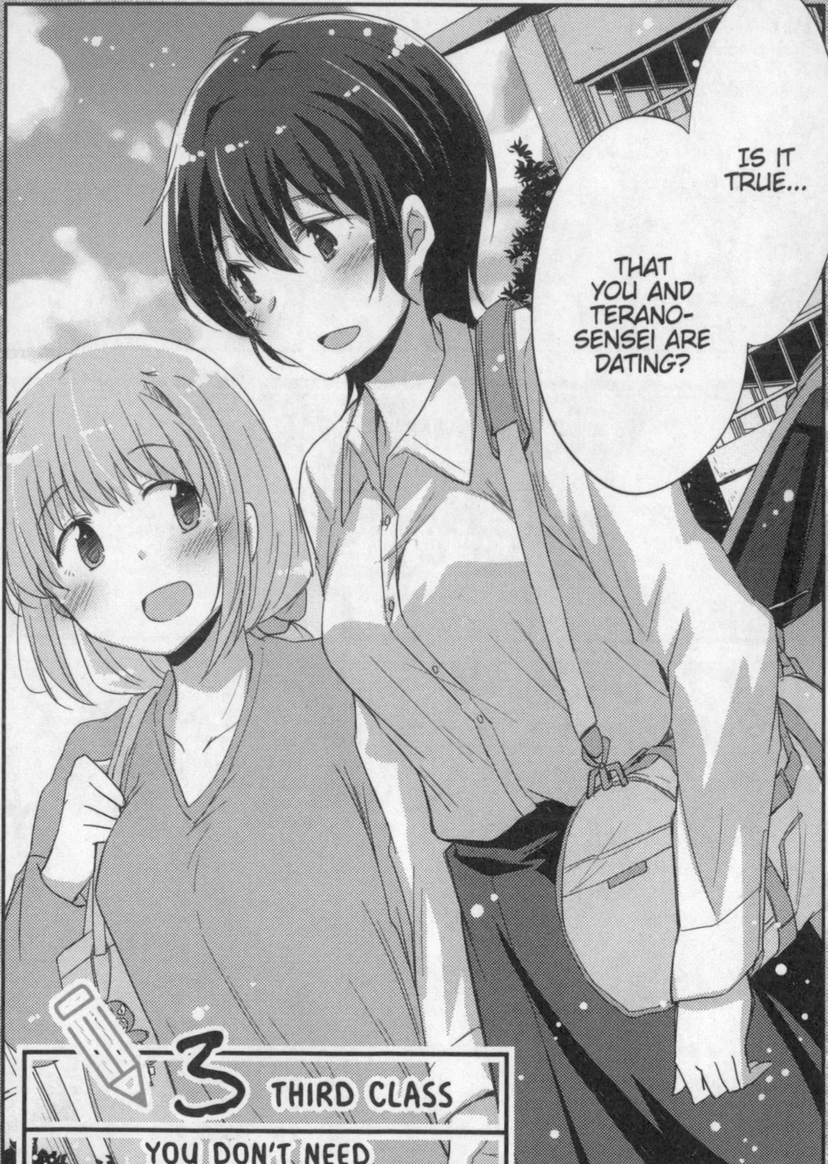

IS IT TRUE...
THAT YOU AND TERANO-SENSEI ARE DATING?
3 THIRD CLASS
YOU DON'T NEED TO WORRY ANYMORE

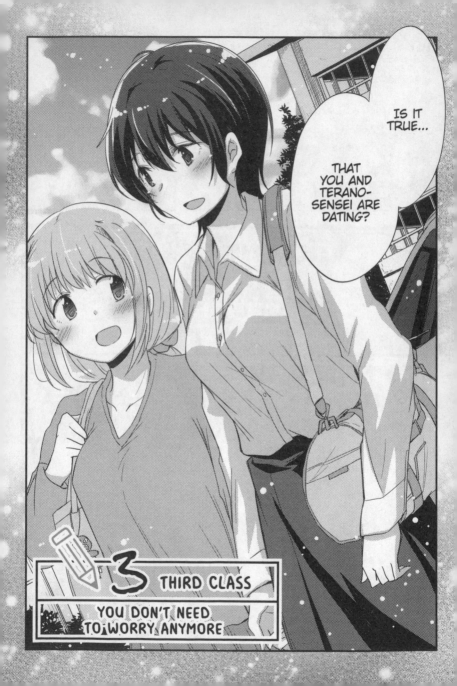

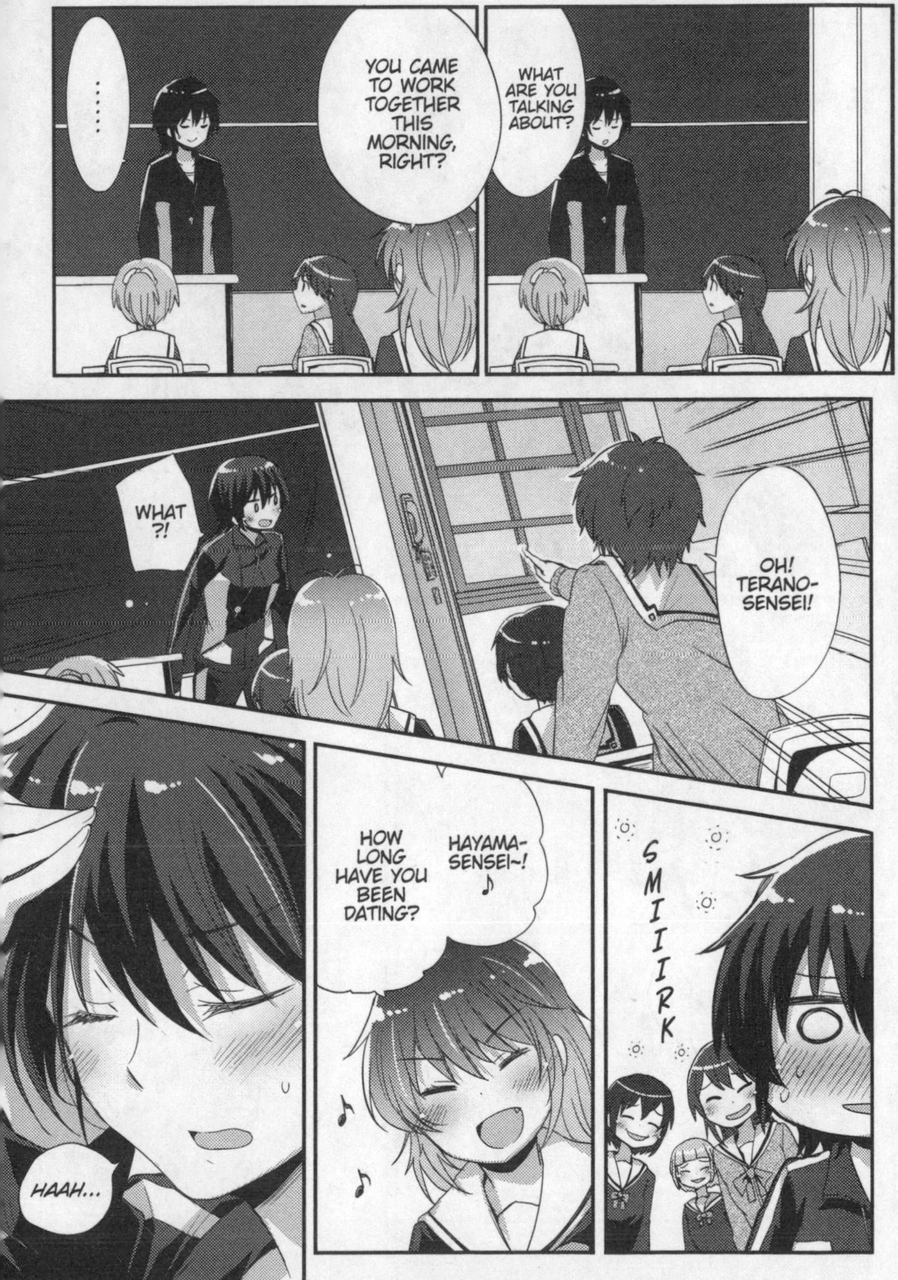
WHAT ARE YOU TALKING ABOUT?
YOU CAME TO WORK TOGETHER THIS MORNING, RIGHT?
......
OH! TERANO-SENSEI!
WHAT ?!
SMIIIRK
HAYAMA-SENSEI~! ♪
HOW LONG HAVE YOU BEEN DATING?
HAAH...

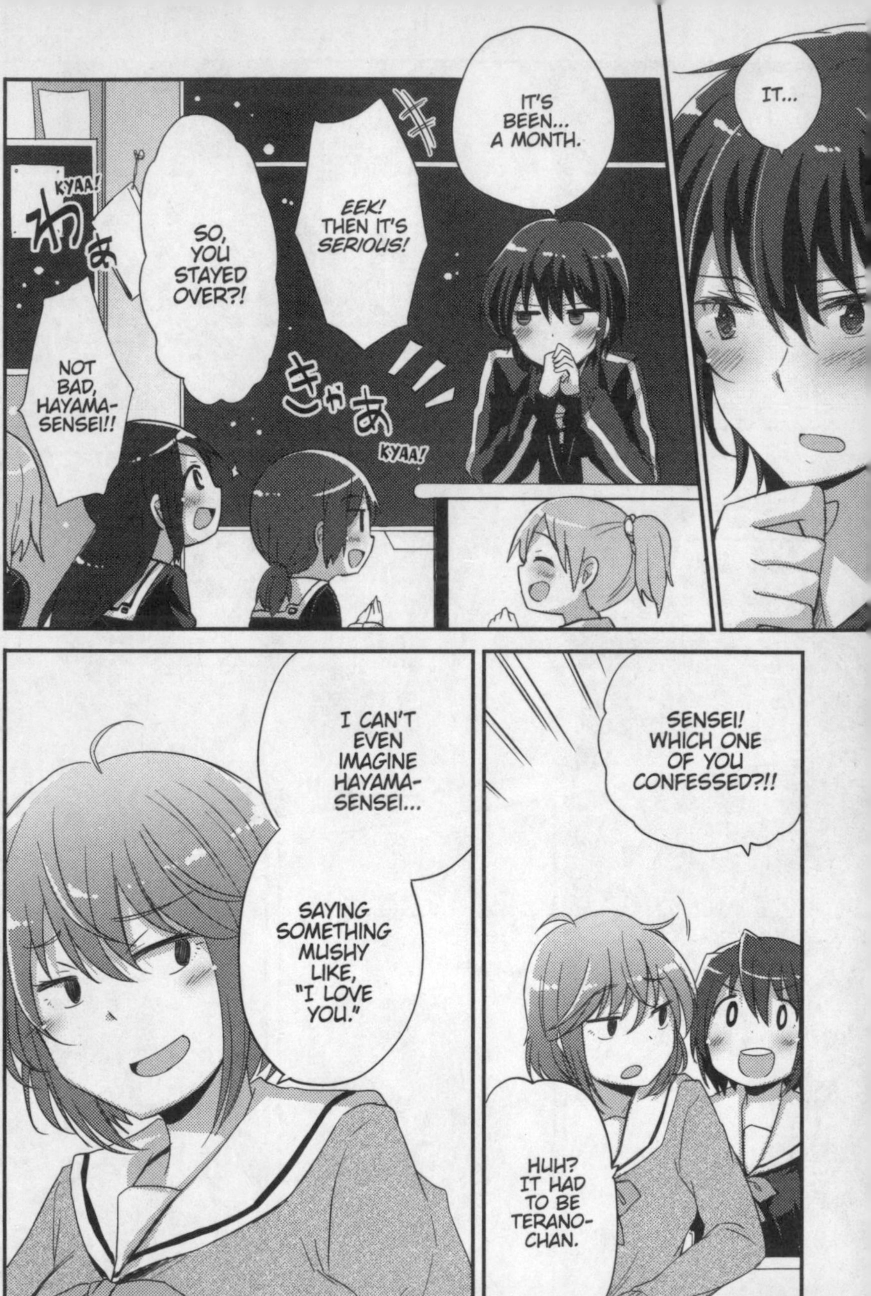
IT...
IT'S BEEN... A MONTH.
EEK! THEN IT'S SERIOUS!
きゃあ
KYAA!
SO, YOU STAYED OVER?!
わぁ
KYAA!
NOT BAD, HAYAMA-SENSEI!!
SENSEI! WHICH ONE OF YOU CONFESSED?!!
HUH? IT HAD TO BE TERANO-CHAN.
I CAN'T EVEN IMAGINE HAYAMA-SENSEI...
SAYING SOMETHING MUSHY LIKE, "I LOVE YOU."

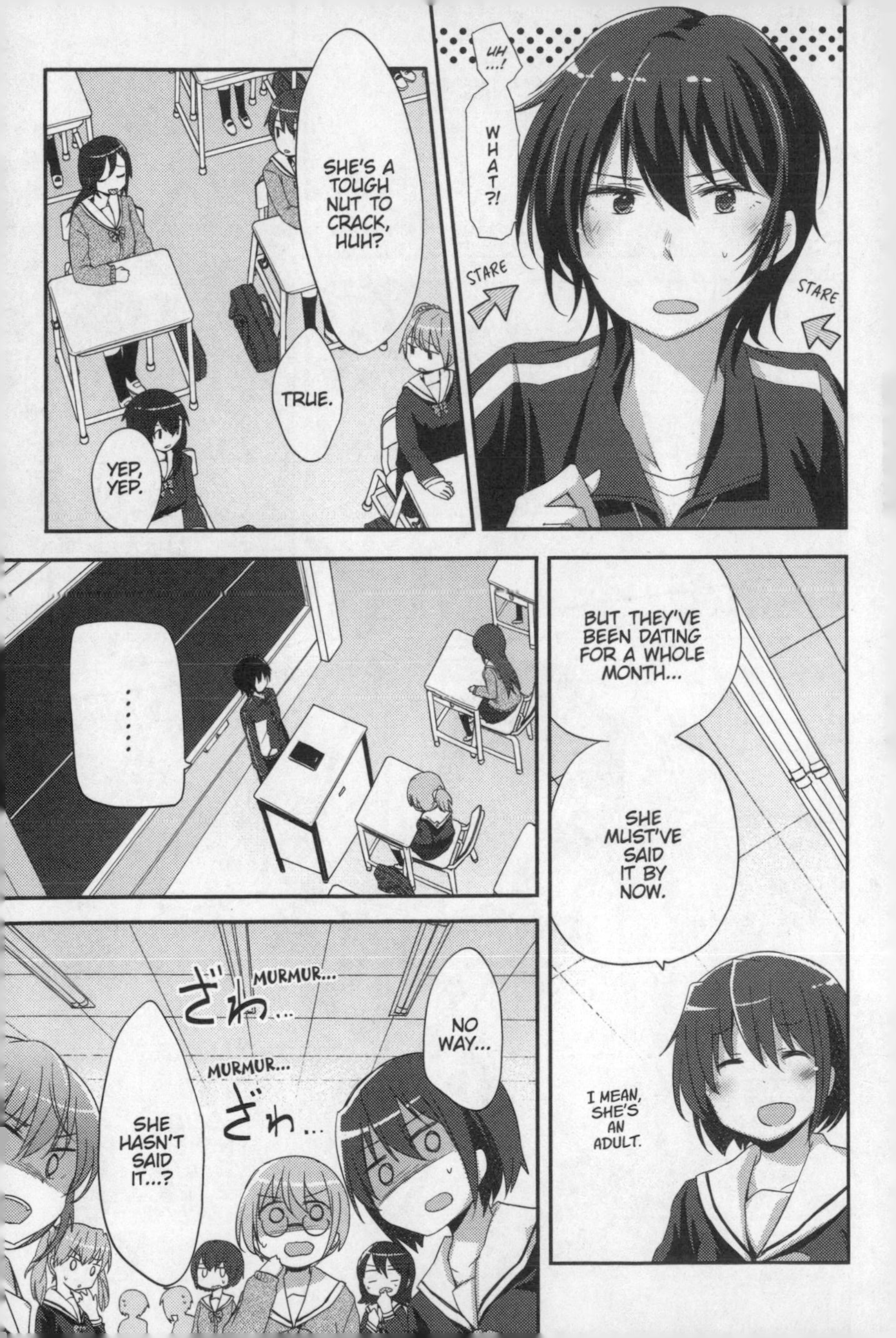
UH ...! WHAT?!
STARE
STARE
SHE'S A TOUGH NUT TO CRACK, HUH?
TRUE.
YEP, YEP.
BUT THEY'VE BEEN DATING FOR A WHOLE MONTH...
SHE MUST'VE SAID IT BY NOW.
I MEAN, SHE'S AN ADULT.
......
ざわ... MURMUR...
NO WAY...
ざわ... MURMUR...
SHE HASN'T SAID IT...?

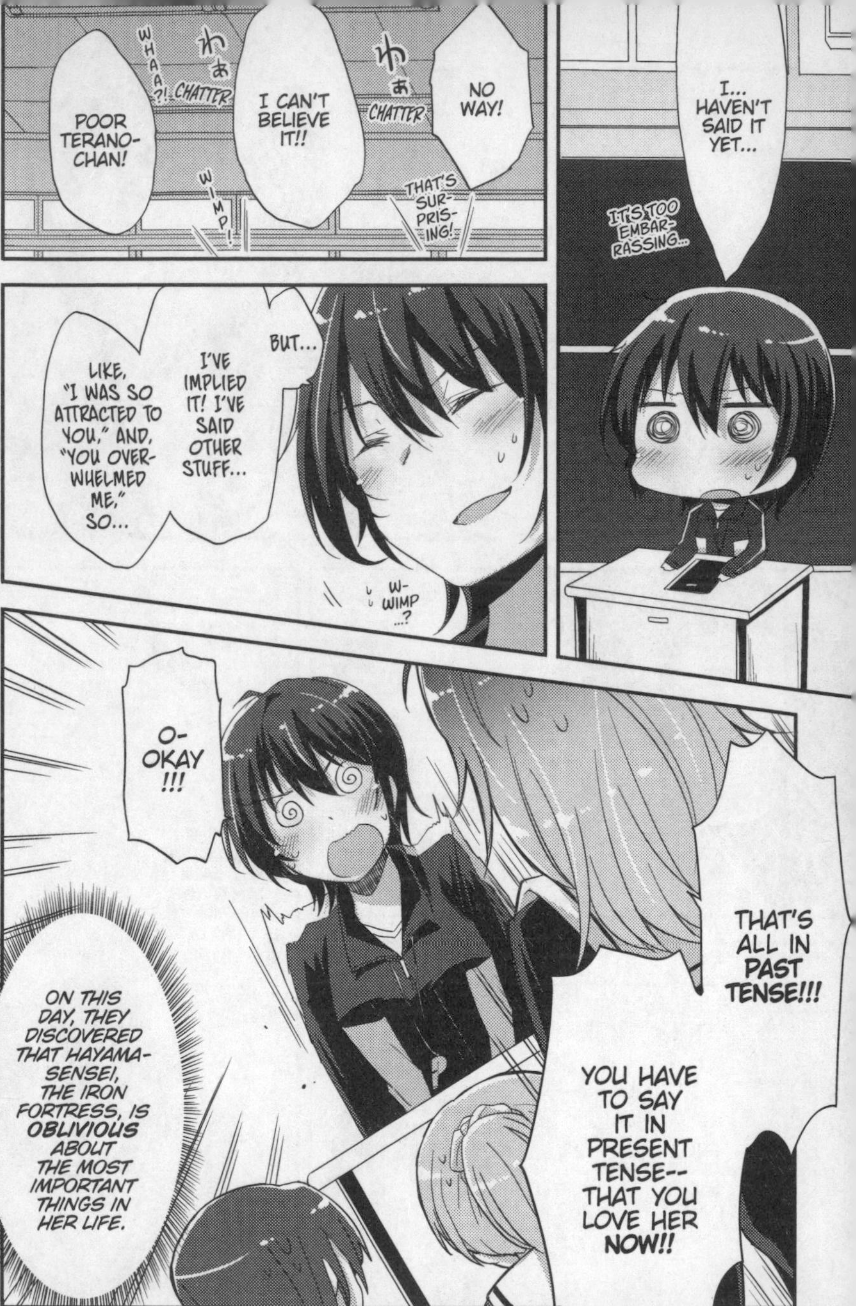

I... HAVEN'T SAID IT YET...
IT'S TOO EMBARRASSING...
NO WAY!
わあ
CHATTER
THAT'S SURPRISING!
I CAN'T BELIEVE IT!!
わあ
CHATTER
WHAA?!
WIMP!
POOR TERANO-CHAN!
BUT...
I'VE IMPLIED IT! I'VE SAID OTHER STUFF...
LIKE, "I WAS SO ATTRACTED TO YOU," AND, "YOU OVERWHELMED ME," SO...
W-WIMP...?
THAT'S ALL IN PAST TENSE!!!
YOU HAVE TO SAY IT IN PRESENT TENSE--THAT YOU LOVE HER NOW!!
O-OKAY!!!
ON THIS DAY, THEY DISCOVERED THAT HAYAMA-SENSEI, THE IRON FORTRESS, IS OBLIVIOUS ABOUT THE MOST IMPORTANT THINGS IN HER LIFE.

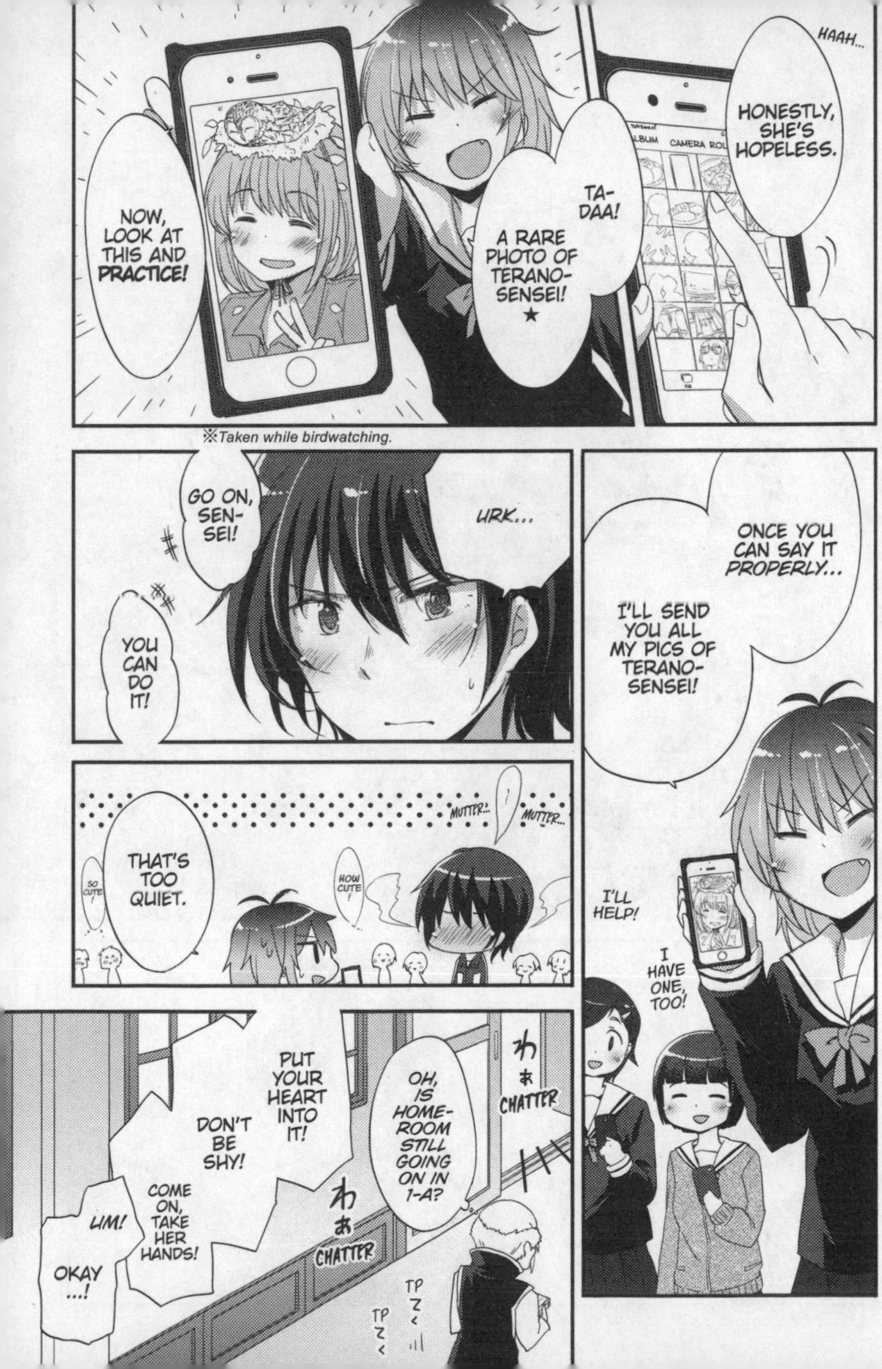
HAAH...
HONESTLY, SHE'S HOPELESS.
TA-DAA!
A RARE PHOTO OF TERANO-SENSEI! ★
NOW, LOOK AT THIS AND PRACTICE!
ONCE YOU CAN SAY IT PROPERLY...
I'LL SEND YOU ALL MY PICS OF TERANO-SENSEI!
I'LL HELP!
I HAVE ONE, TOO!
URK...
GO ON, SEN-SEI!
YOU CAN DO IT!
MUTTER...
MUTTER...
HOW CUTE!
THAT'S TOO QUIET.
SO CUTE!
わぁ CHATTER
OH, IS HOME-ROOM STILL GOING ON IN 1-A?
PUT YOUR HEART INTO IT!
DON'T BE SHY!
わぁ CHATTER
COME ON, TAKE HER HANDS!
UM!
OKAY ...!
TP てく
TP てく

※Taken while birdwatching.

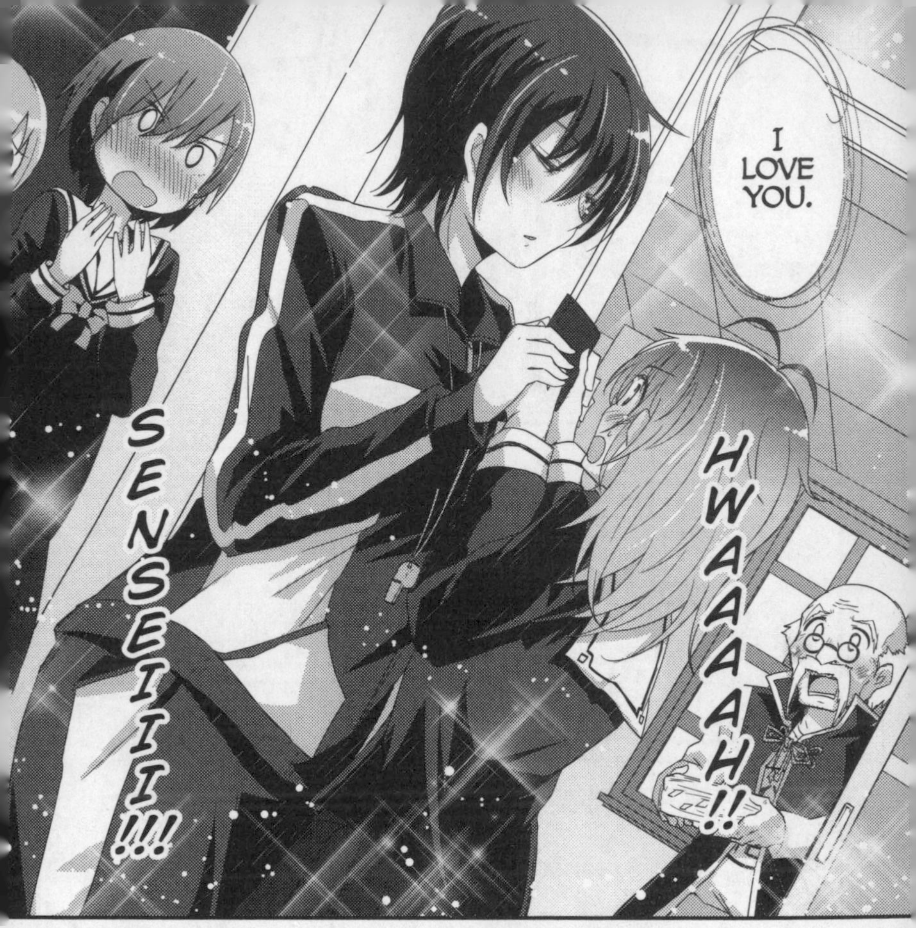
I LOVE YOU.
HWAAAAAH!!
SENSEIIII!!!

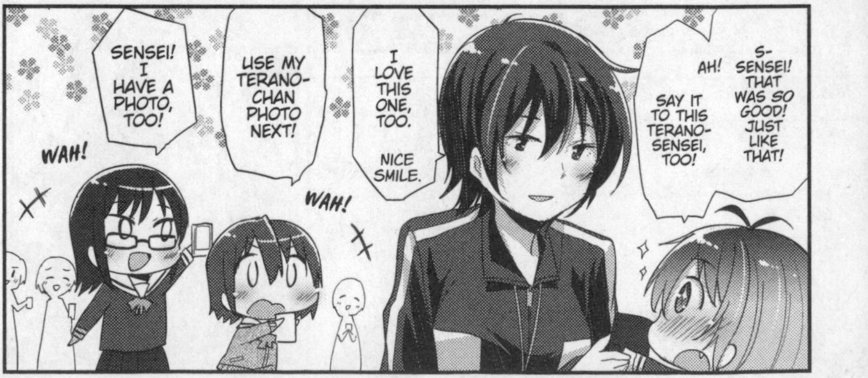
S-SENSEI! THAT WAS SO GOOD! JUST LIKE THAT!
AH!
SAY IT TO THIS TERANO-SENSEI, TOO!
I LOVE THIS ONE, TOO.
NICE SMILE.
USE MY TERANO-CHAN PHOTO NEXT!
SENSEI! I HAVE A PHOTO, TOO!
WAH!
WAH!

TERANO SOMMELIER

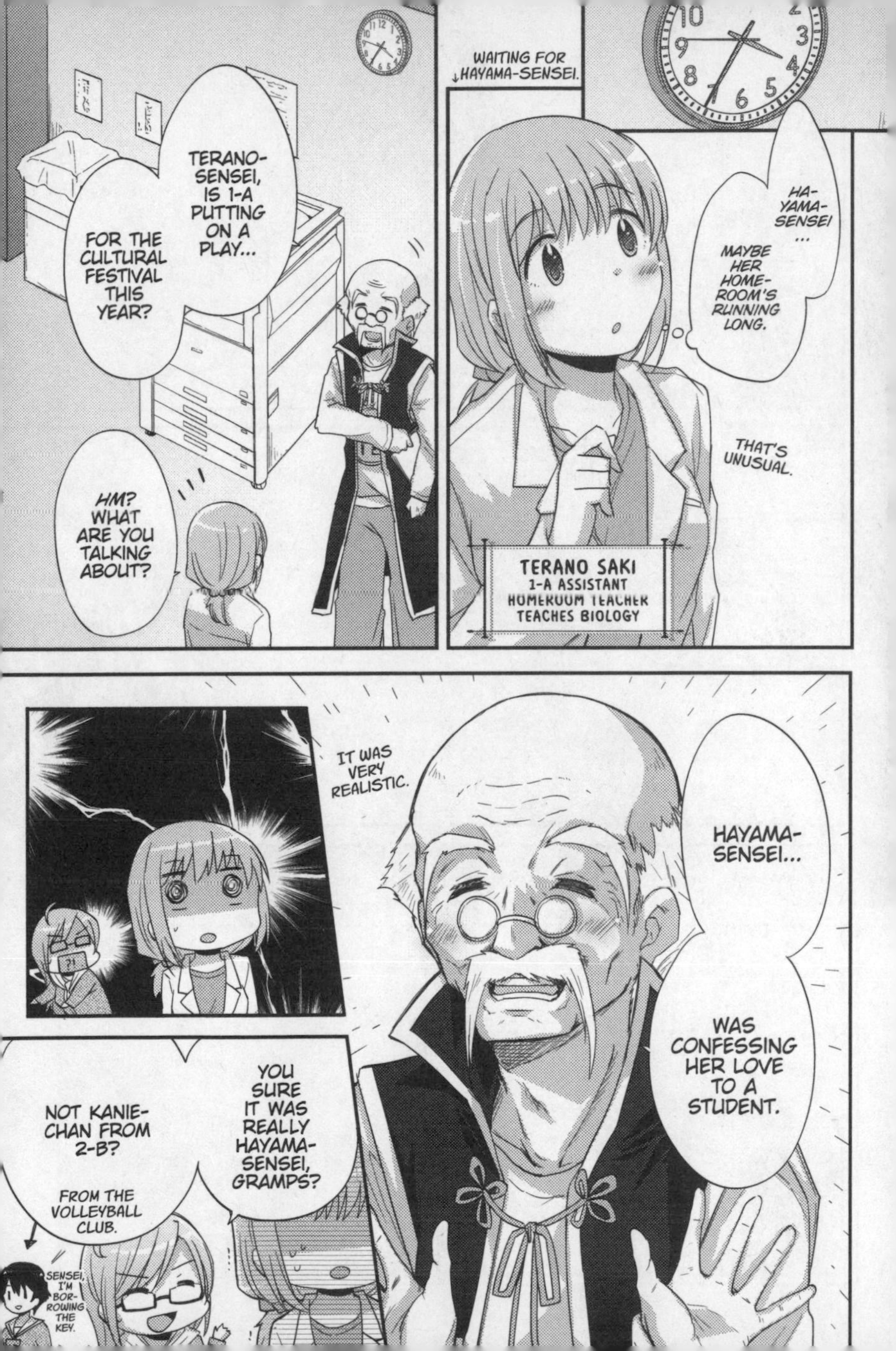
WAITING FOR ↓HAYAMA-SENSEI.
HAYAMA-SENSEI...
MAYBE HER HOMEROOM'S RUNNING LONG.
THAT'S UNUSUAL.
TERANO SAKI
1-A ASSISTANT HOMEROOM TEACHER
TEACHES BIOLOGY
TERANO-SENSEI, IS 1-A PUTTING ON A PLAY...
FOR THE CULTURAL FESTIVAL THIS YEAR?
HM? WHAT ARE YOU TALKING ABOUT?
HAYAMA-SENSEI...
WAS CONFESSING HER LOVE TO A STUDENT.
IT WAS VERY REALISTIC.
YOU SURE IT WAS REALLY HAYAMA-SENSEI, GRAMPS?
NOT KANIE-CHAN FROM 2-B?
FROM THE VOLLEYBALL CLUB.
SENSEI, I'M BORROWING THE KEY.

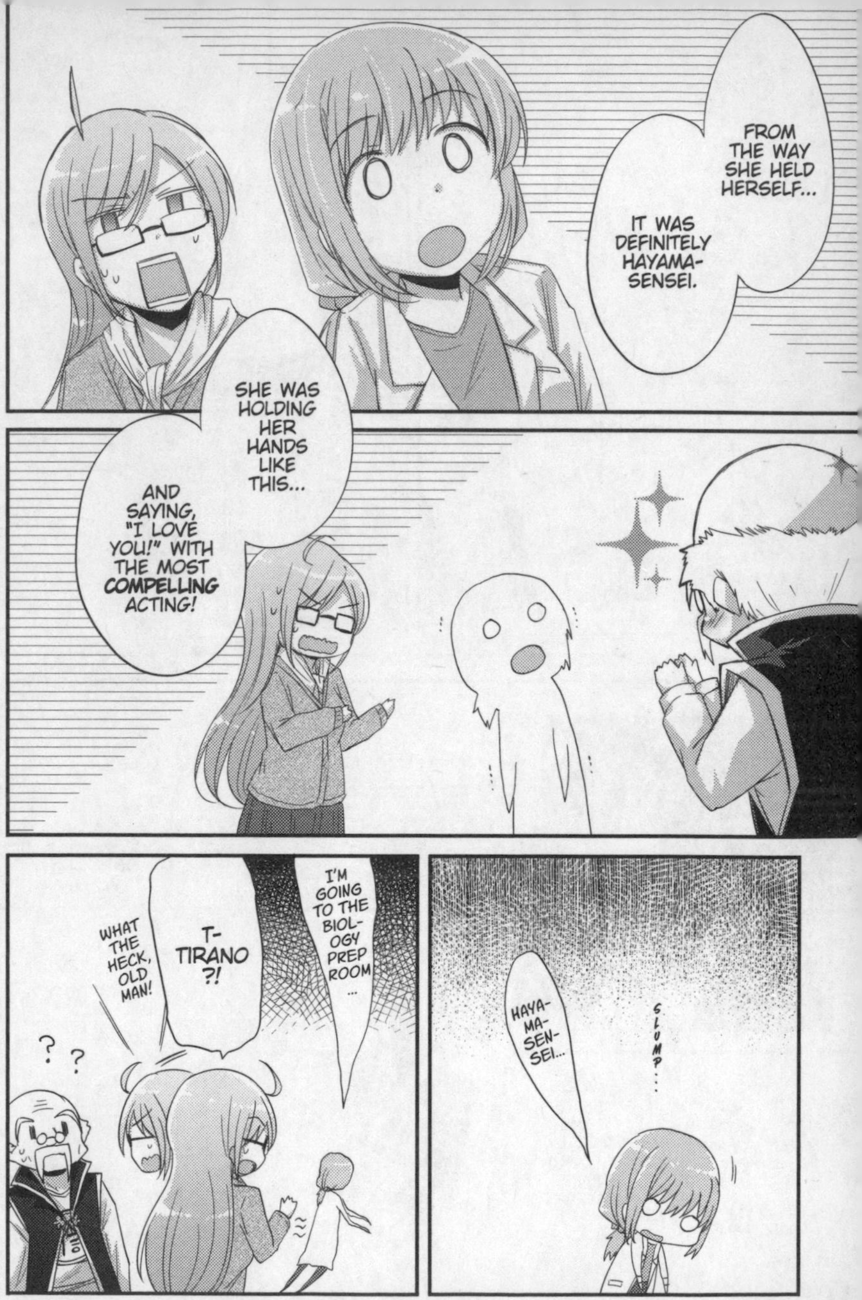
FROM THE WAY SHE HELD HERSELF...
IT WAS DEFINITELY HAYAMA-SENSEI.
SHE WAS HOLDING HER HANDS LIKE THIS...
AND SAYING, "I LOVE YOU!" WITH THE MOST **COMPELLING** ACTING!
HAYAMA-SENSEI...
SLUMP...
I'M GOING TO THE BIOLOGY PREP ROOM...
T-TIRANO?!
WHAT THE HECK, OLD MAN!
? ?

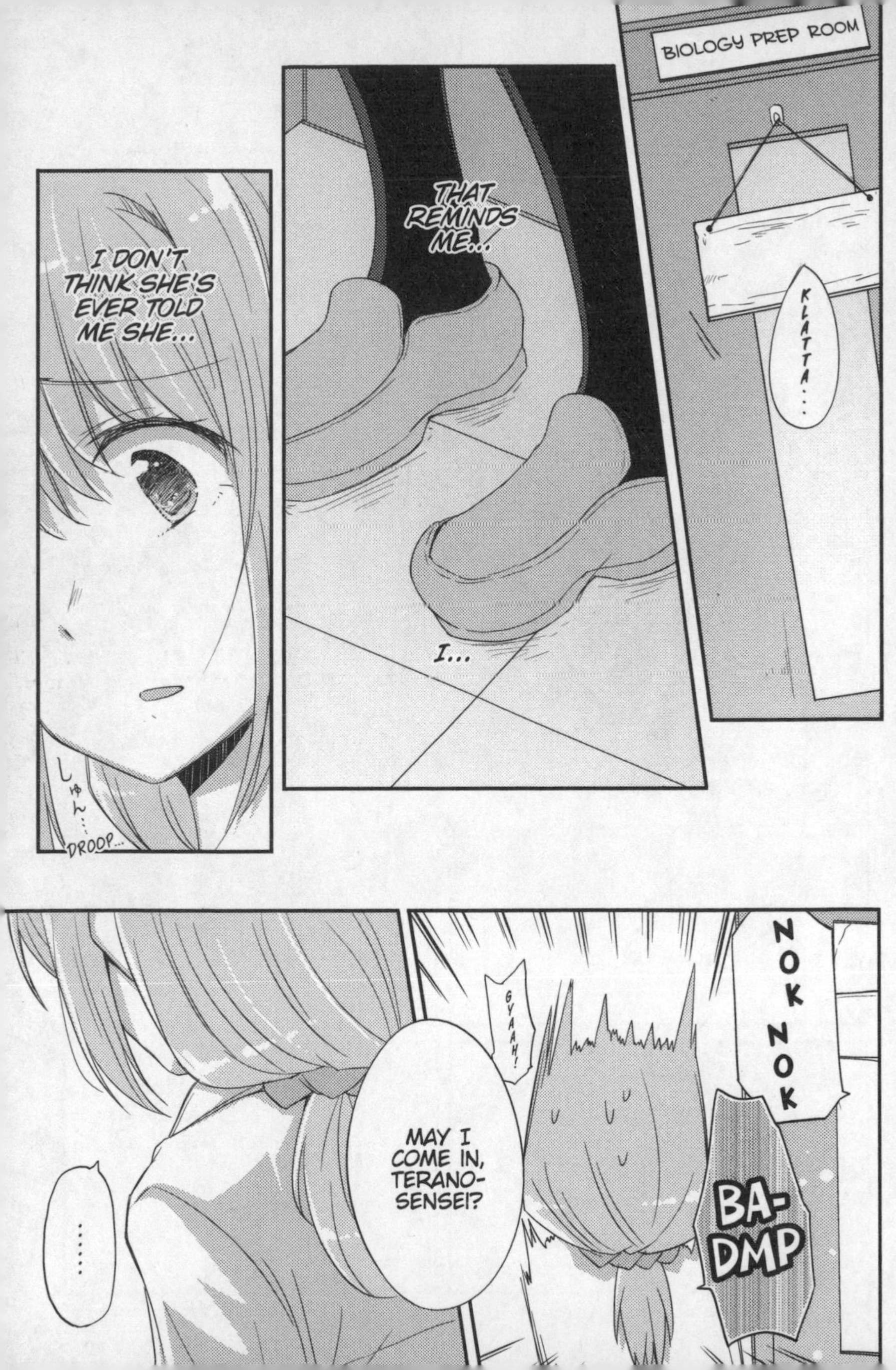
BIOLOGY PREP ROOM
KLATTA...
THAT REMINDS ME...
I...
I DON'T THINK SHE'S EVER TOLD ME SHE...
しゅん...
DROOP...
NOK NOK NOK
BA-DMP
GYAAH!
MAY I COME IN, TERANO-SENSEI?
......

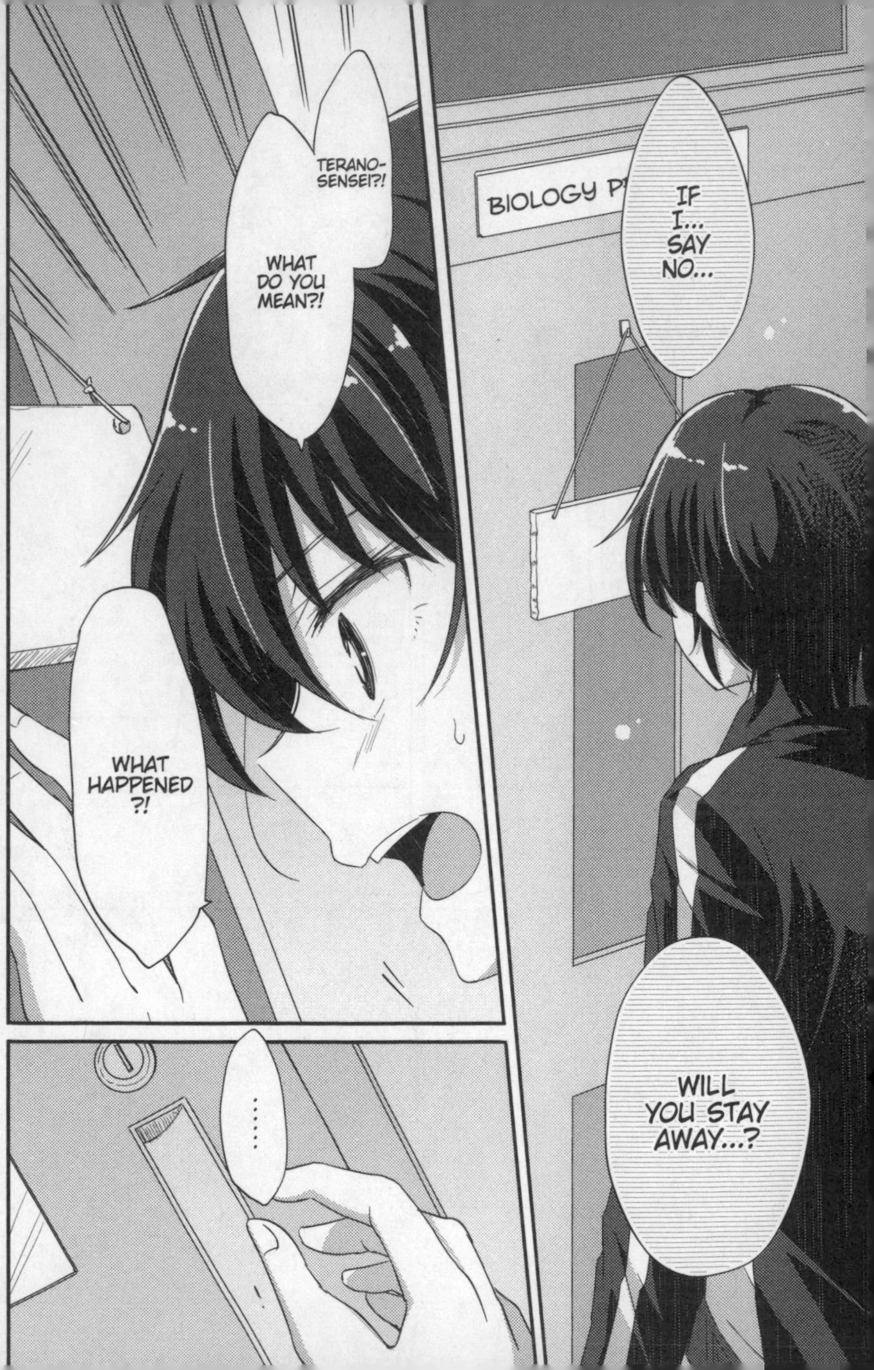
BIOLOGY
IF I... SAY NO...
WILL YOU STAY AWAY...?
TERANO-SENSEI?!
WHAT DO YOU MEAN?!
WHAT HAPPENED?!
......

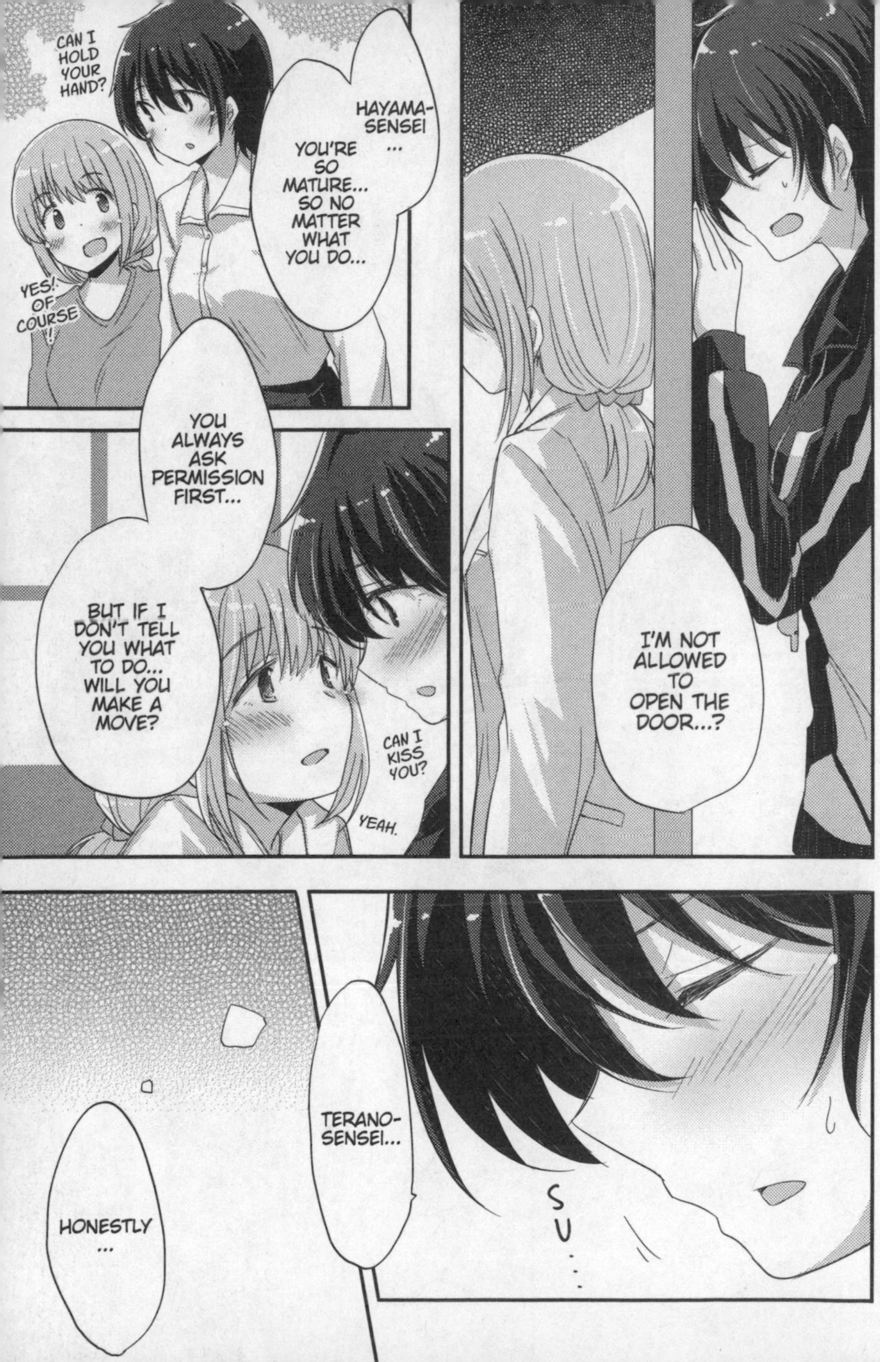
I'M NOT ALLOWED TO OPEN THE DOOR...?
HAYAMA-SENSEI ... YOU'RE SO MATURE... SO NO MATTER WHAT YOU DO...
CAN I HOLD YOUR HAND?
YES! OF COURSE!
YOU ALWAYS ASK PERMISSION FIRST...
BUT IF I DON'T TELL YOU WHAT TO DO... WILL YOU MAKE A MOVE?
CAN I KISS YOU?
YEAH.
TERANO-SENSEI...
SU...
HONESTLY ...

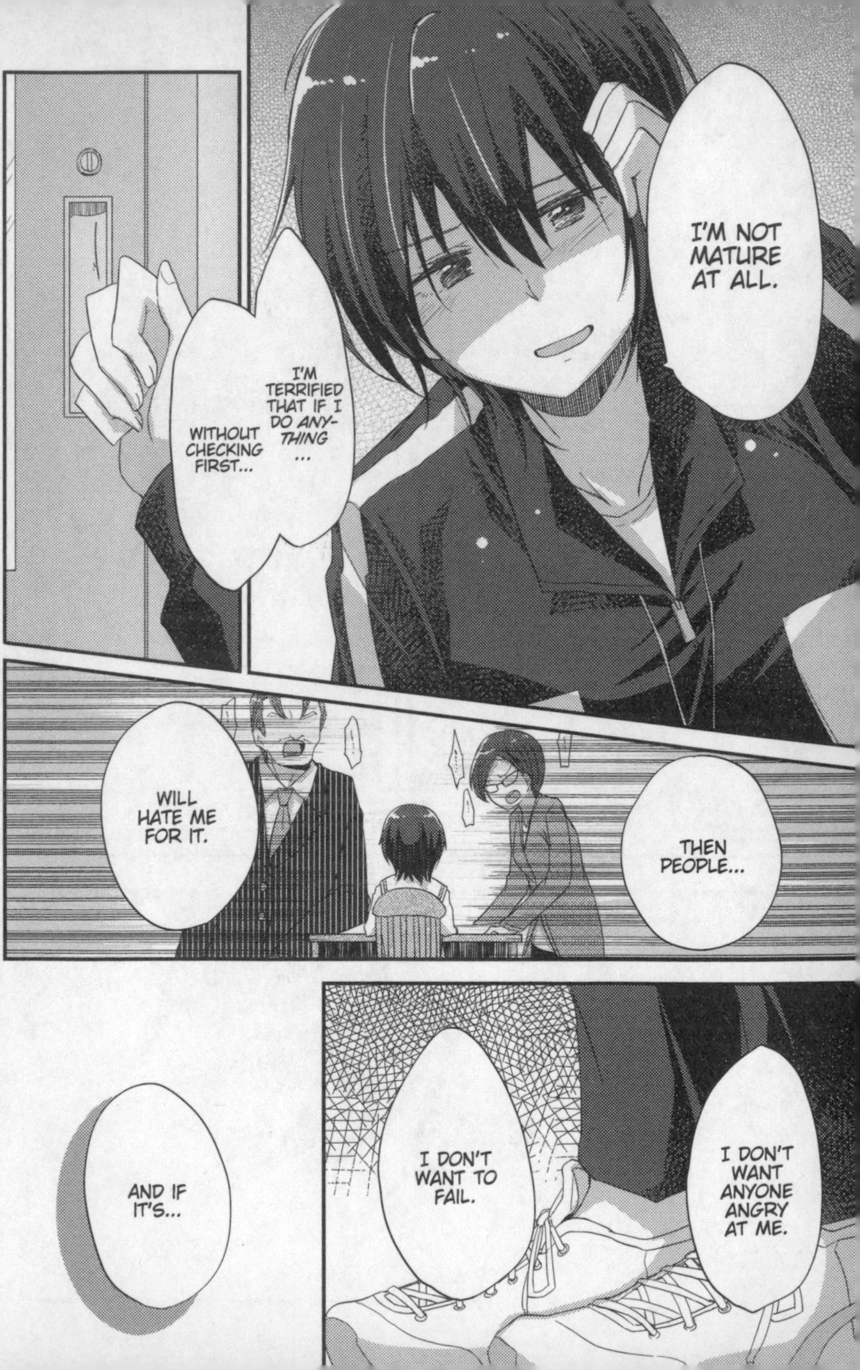
I'M NOT MATURE AT ALL.
I'M TERRIFIED THAT IF I DO *ANYTHING* ... WITHOUT CHECKING FIRST...
THEN PEOPLE...
WILL HATE ME FOR IT.
I DON'T WANT ANYONE ANGRY AT ME.
I DON'T WANT TO FAIL.
AND IF IT'S...

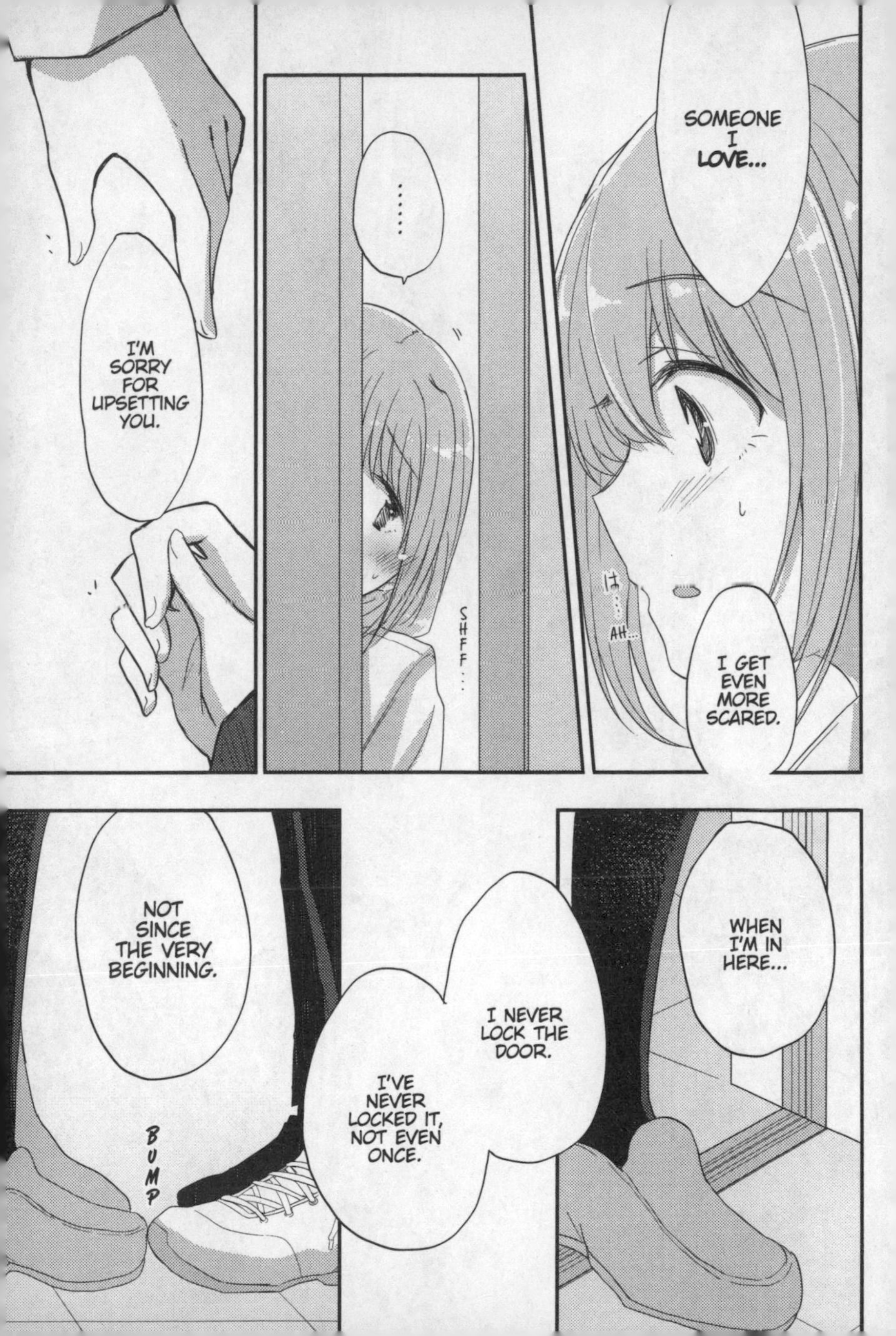
SOMEONE I LOVE...
は…
AH...
I GET EVEN MORE SCARED.
......
SHFF...
I'M SORRY FOR UPSETTING YOU.
WHEN I'M IN HERE...
I NEVER LOCK THE DOOR.
I'VE NEVER LOCKED IT, NOT EVEN ONCE.
NOT SINCE THE VERY BEGINNING.
BUMP

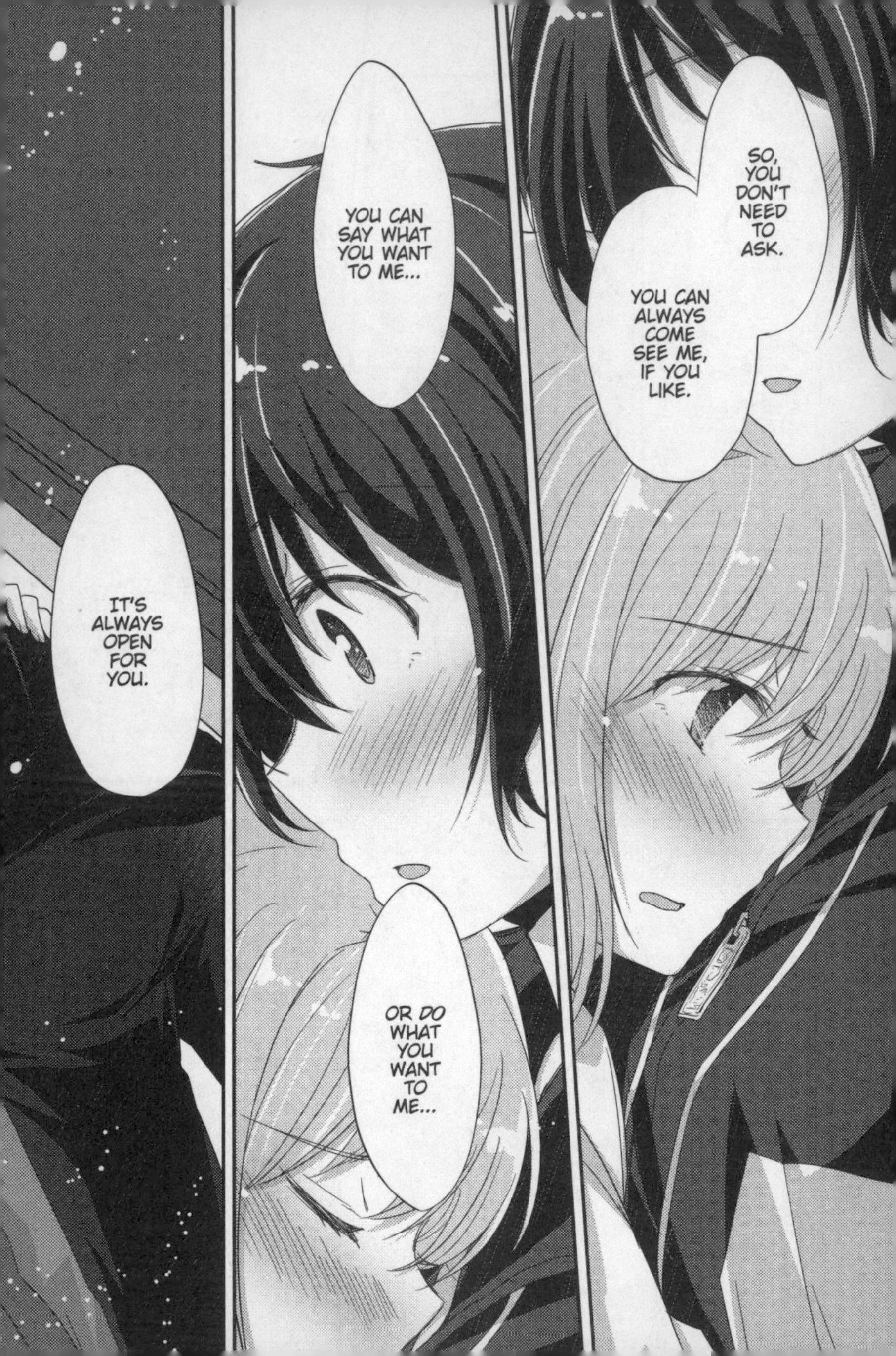
SO, YOU DON'T NEED TO ASK.
YOU CAN ALWAYS COME SEE ME, IF YOU LIKE.
YOU CAN SAY WHAT YOU WANT TO ME...
OR *DO* WHAT YOU WANT TO ME...
IT'S ALWAYS OPEN FOR YOU.

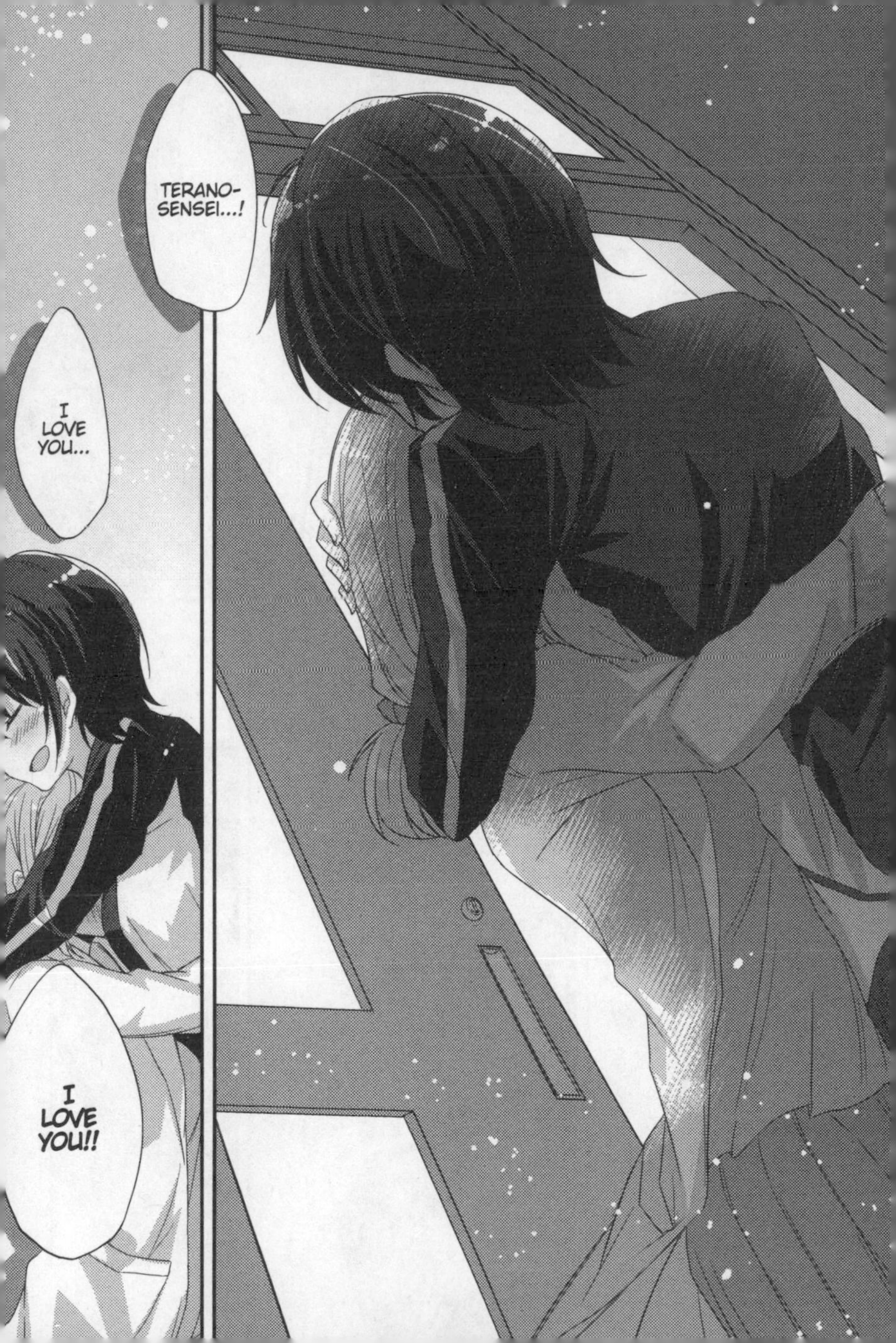
TERANO-SENSEI...!
I LOVE YOU...
I LOVE YOU!!

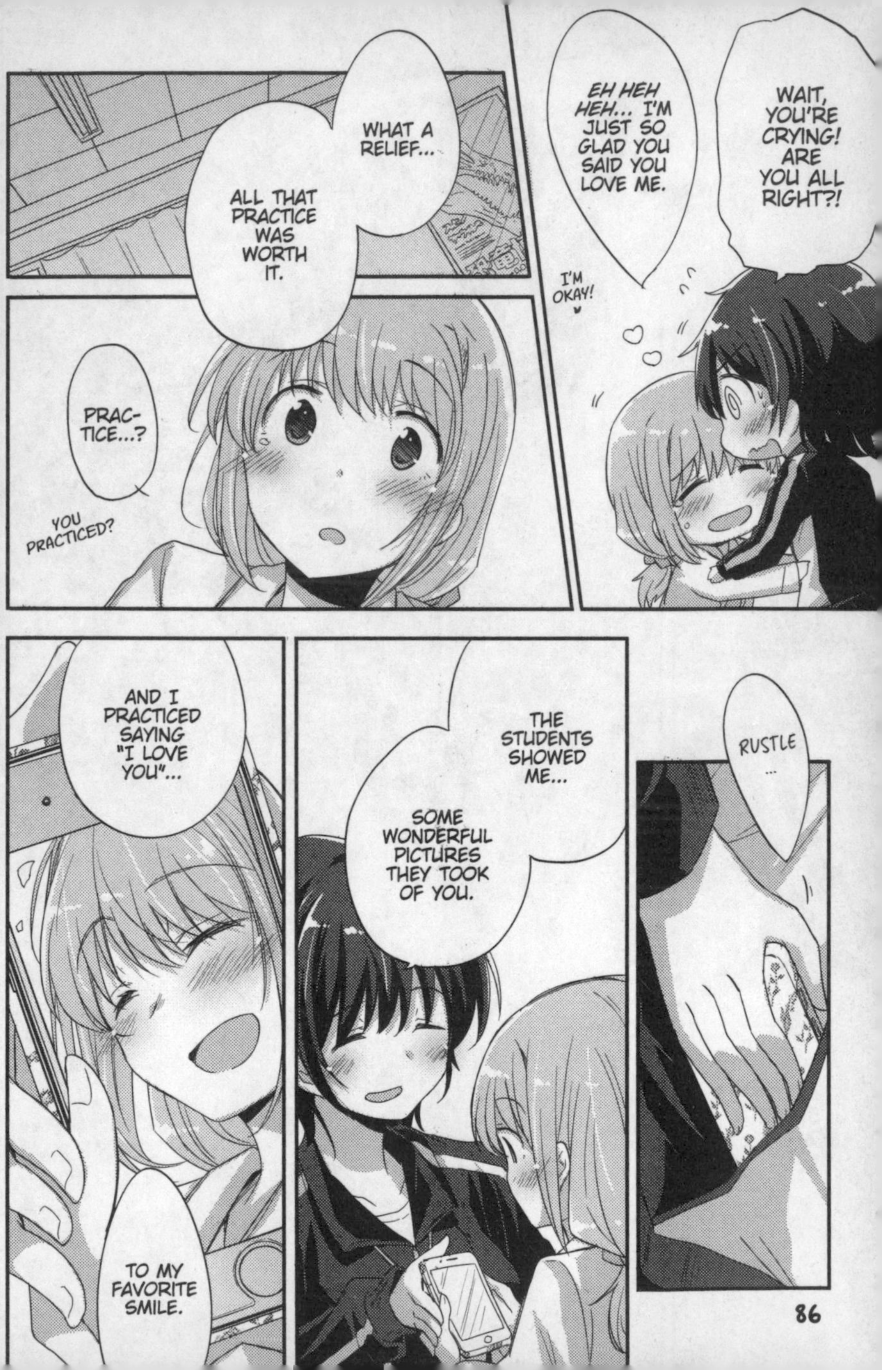
WAIT, YOU'RE CRYING! ARE YOU ALL RIGHT?!
EH HEH HEH... I'M JUST SO GLAD YOU SAID YOU LOVE ME.
I'M OKAY!
WHAT A RELIEF...
ALL THAT PRACTICE WAS WORTH IT.
PRAC-TICE...?
YOU PRACTICED?
RUSTLE...
THE STUDENTS SHOWED ME...
SOME WONDERFUL PICTURES THEY TOOK OF YOU.
AND I PRACTICED SAYING "I LOVE YOU"...
TO MY FAVORITE SMILE.

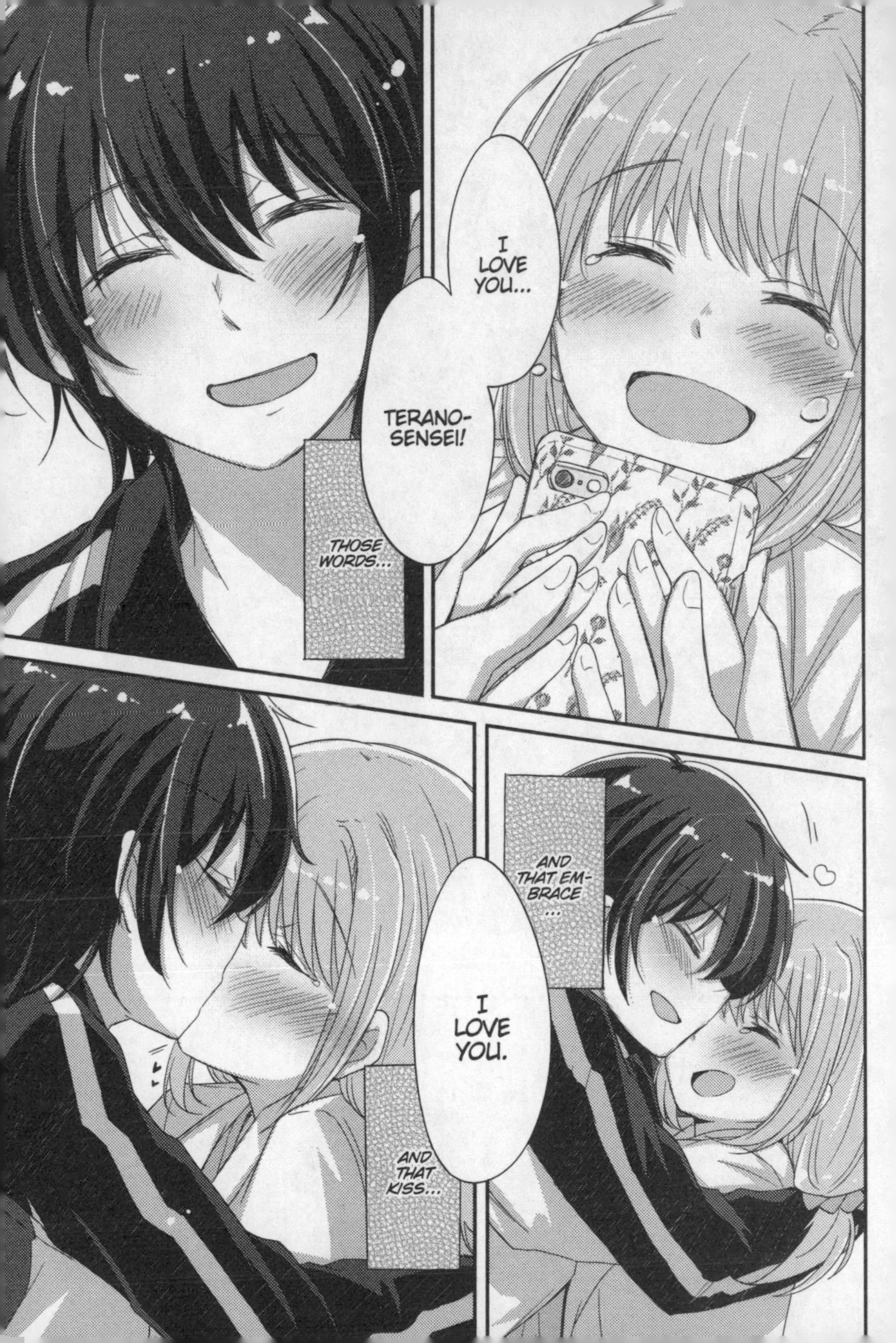
I LOVE YOU...
TERANO-SENSEI!
THOSE WORDS...
AND THAT EMBRACE...
I LOVE YOU.
AND THAT KISS...

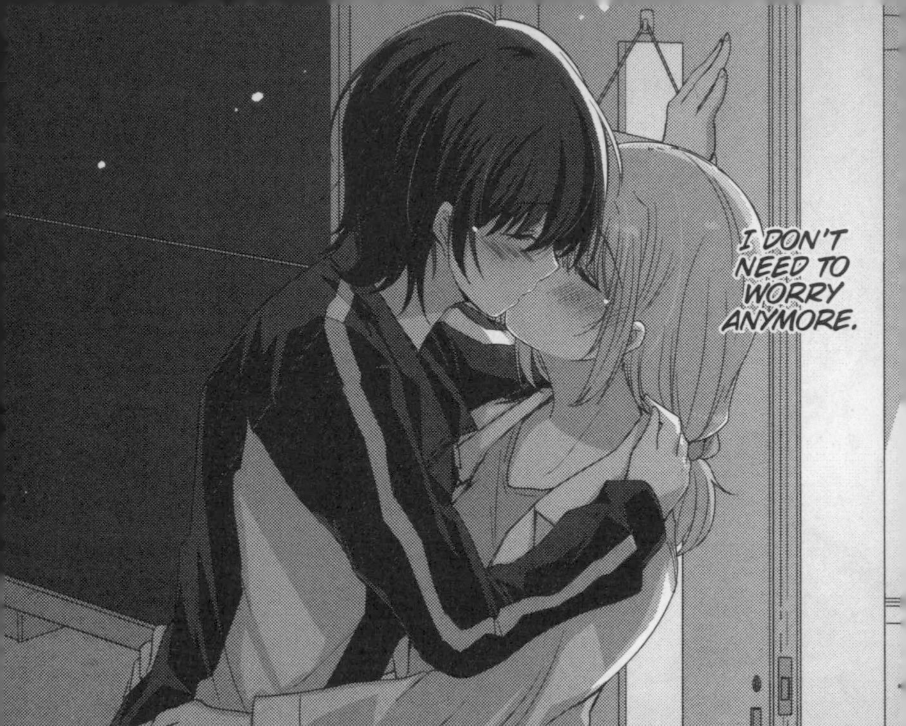
I DON'T NEED TO WORRY ANYMORE.

THE NEXT DAY...

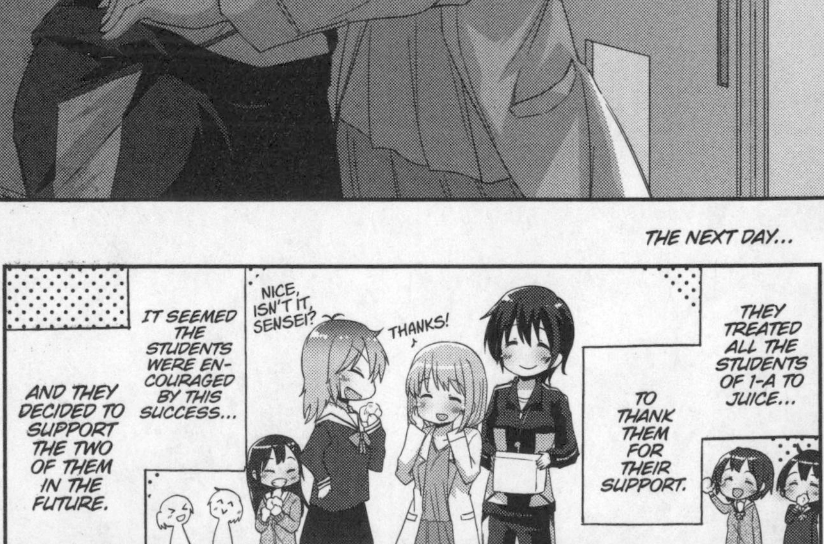
THEY TREATED ALL THE STUDENTS OF 1-A TO JUICE...
TO THANK THEM FOR THEIR SUPPORT.
THANKS!
NICE, ISN'T IT, SENSEI?
IT SEEMED THE STUDENTS WERE ENCOURAGED BY THIS SUCCESS...
AND THEY DECIDED TO SUPPORT THE TWO OF THEM IN THE FUTURE.

DIDN'T TAKE MUCH!

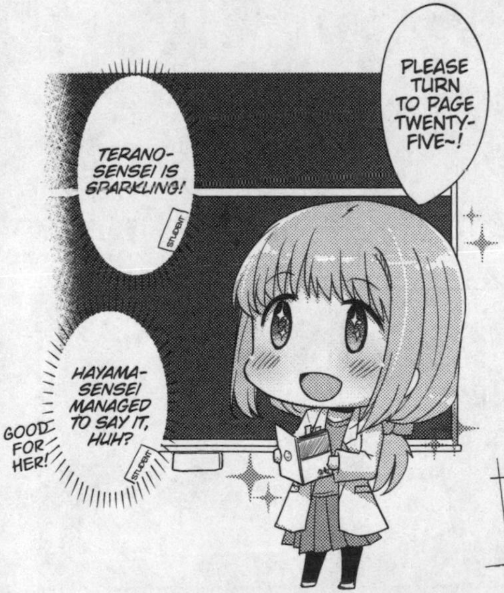
PLEASE TURN TO PAGE TWENTY-FIVE~!
TERANO-SENSEI IS SPARKLING!
STUDENT
HAYAMA-SENSEI MANAGED TO SAY IT, HUH?
STUDENT
GOOD FOR HER!

OUR TEACHERS ARE DATING

Our Teachers are Dating!

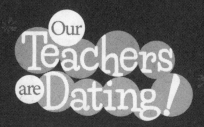

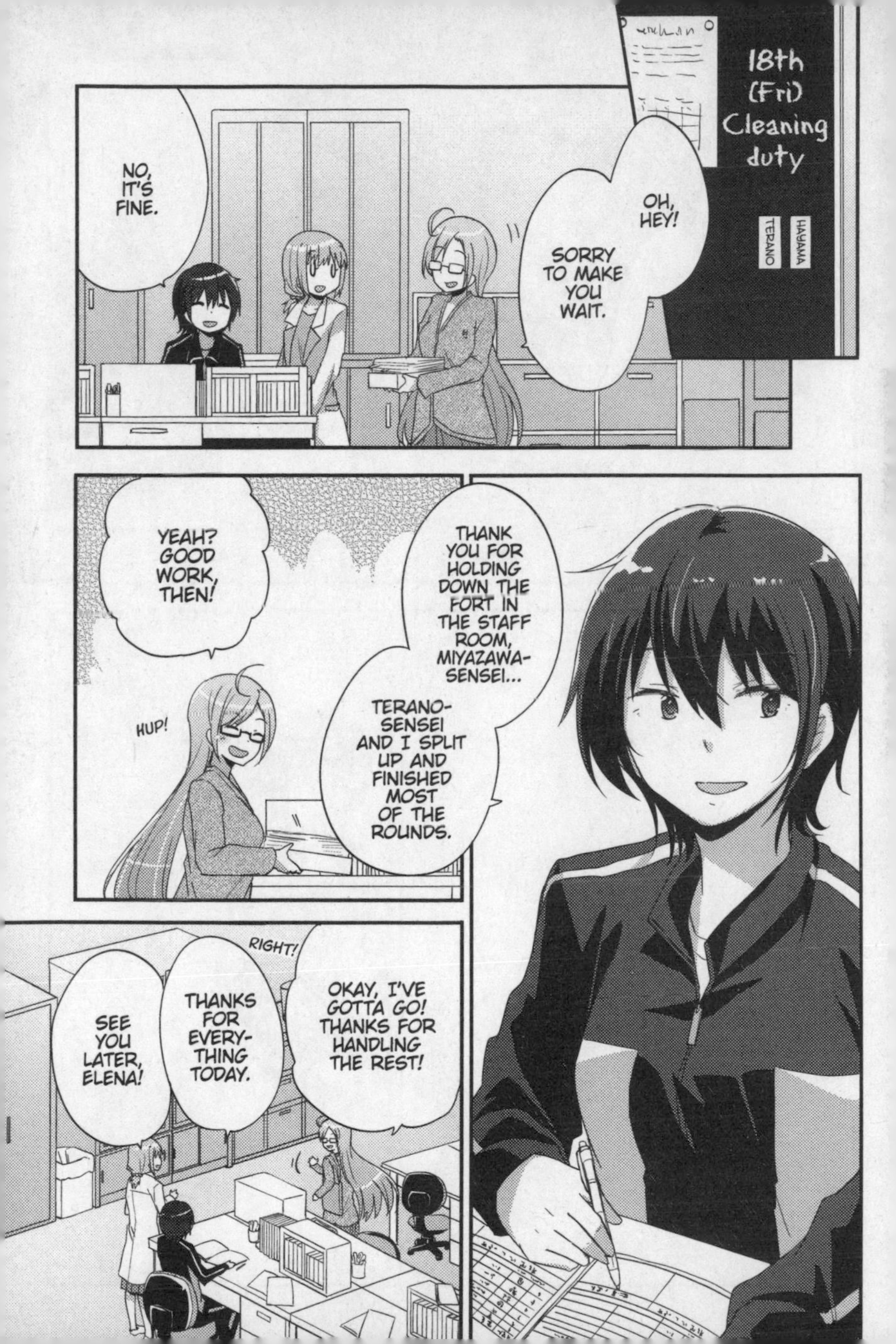
18th (Fri) Cleaning duty
HAYAMA
TERANO
OH, HEY!
SORRY TO MAKE YOU WAIT.
NO, IT'S FINE.
THANK YOU FOR HOLDING DOWN THE FORT IN THE STAFF ROOM, MIYAZAWA-SENSEI...
TERANO-SENSEI AND I SPLIT UP AND FINISHED MOST OF THE ROUNDS.
YEAH? GOOD WORK, THEN!
HUP!
OKAY, I'VE GOTTA GO! THANKS FOR HANDLING THE REST!
RIGHT!
THANKS FOR EVERYTHING TODAY.
SEE YOU LATER, ELENA!

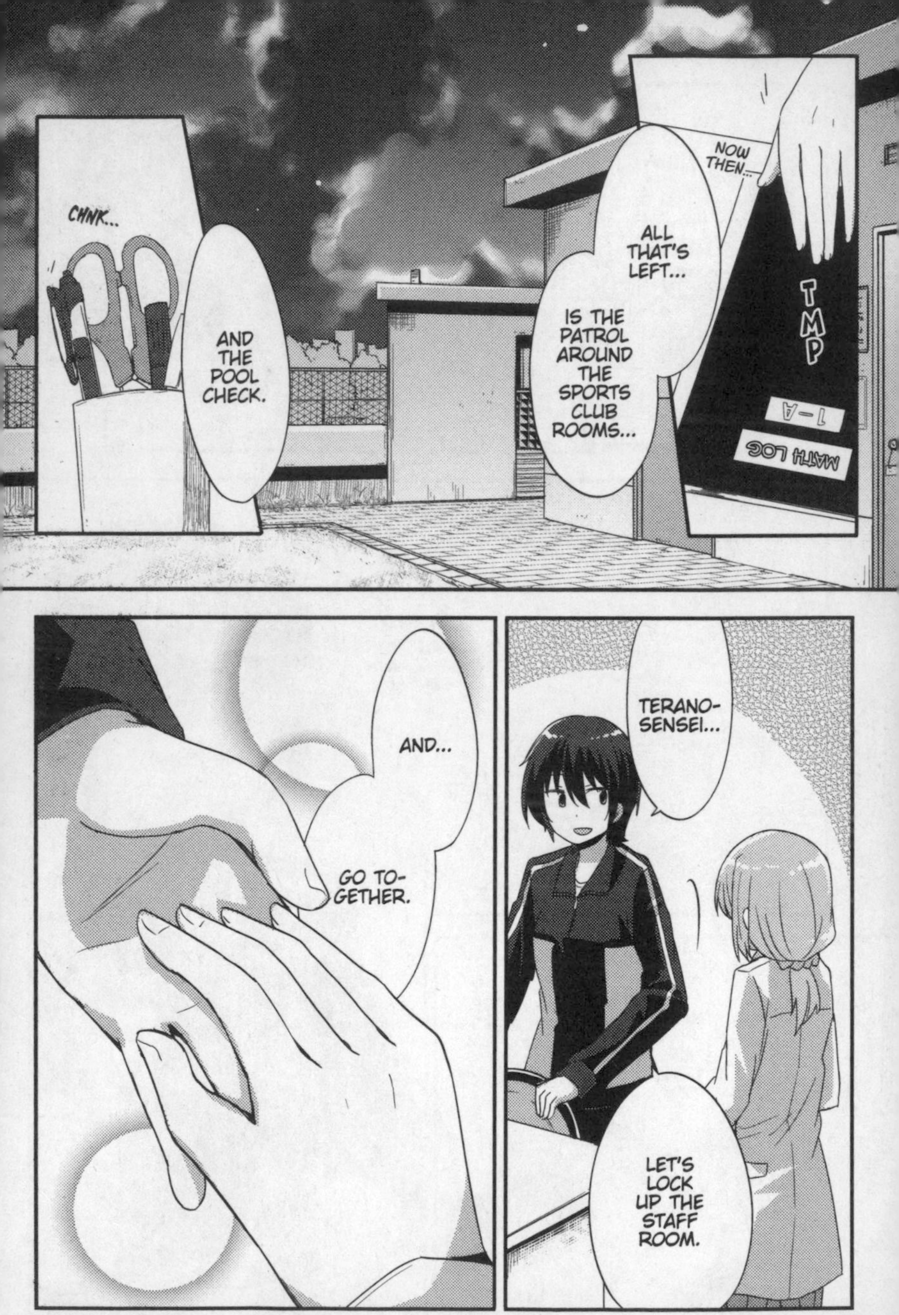
NOW THEN...
ALL THAT'S LEFT...
IS THE PATROL AROUND THE SPORTS CLUB ROOMS...
TMP
1-A
MATH LOG
CHNK...
AND THE POOL CHECK.
TERANO-SENSEI...
LET'S LOCK UP THE STAFF ROOM.
AND...
GO TO-GETHER.

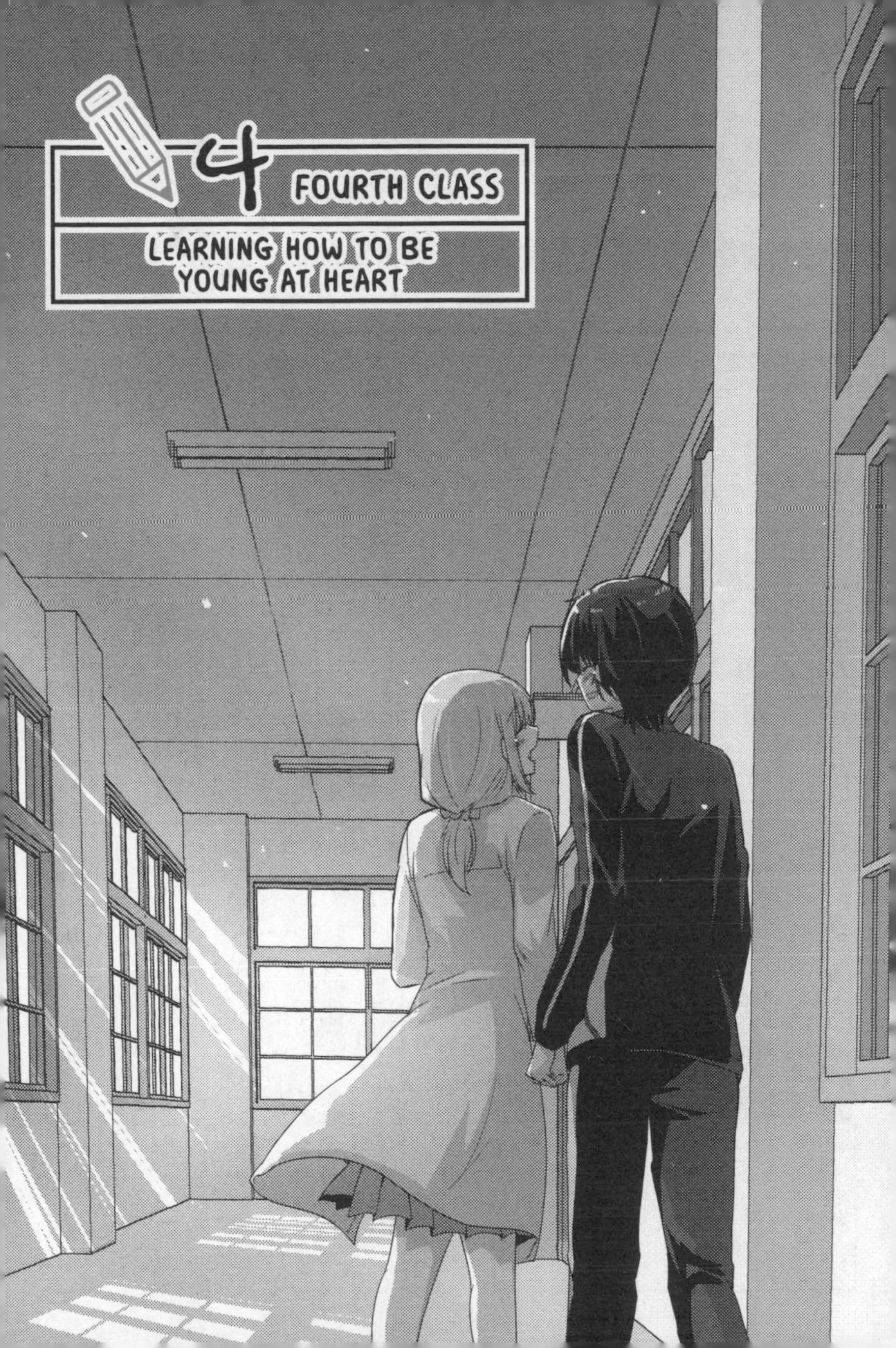
4 FOURTH CLASS
LEARNING HOW TO BE YOUNG AT HEART

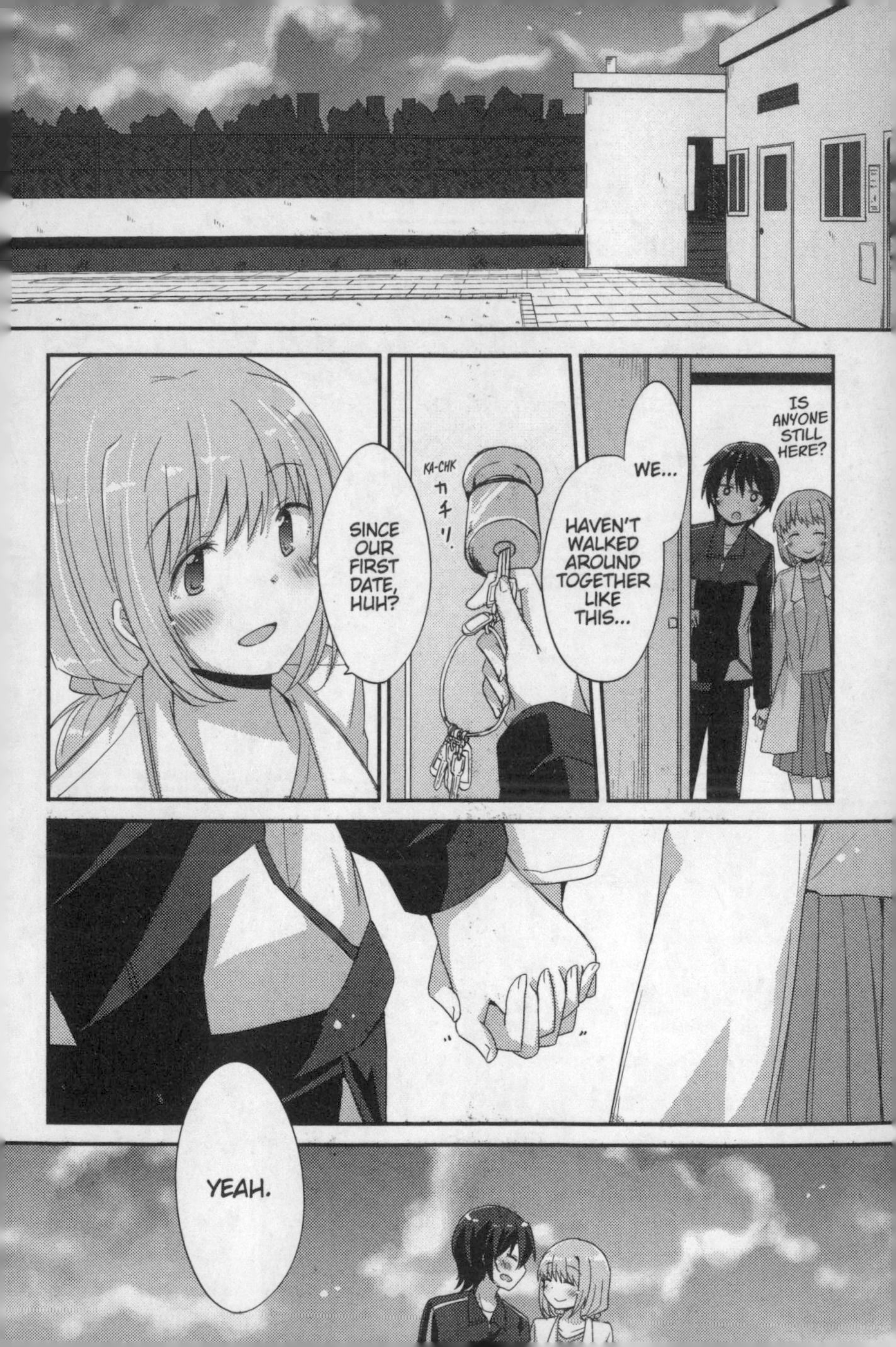
IS ANYONE STILL HERE?
WE...
HAVEN'T WALKED AROUND TOGETHER LIKE THIS...
KA-CHK
カチッ
SINCE OUR FIRST DATE, HUH?
YEAH.

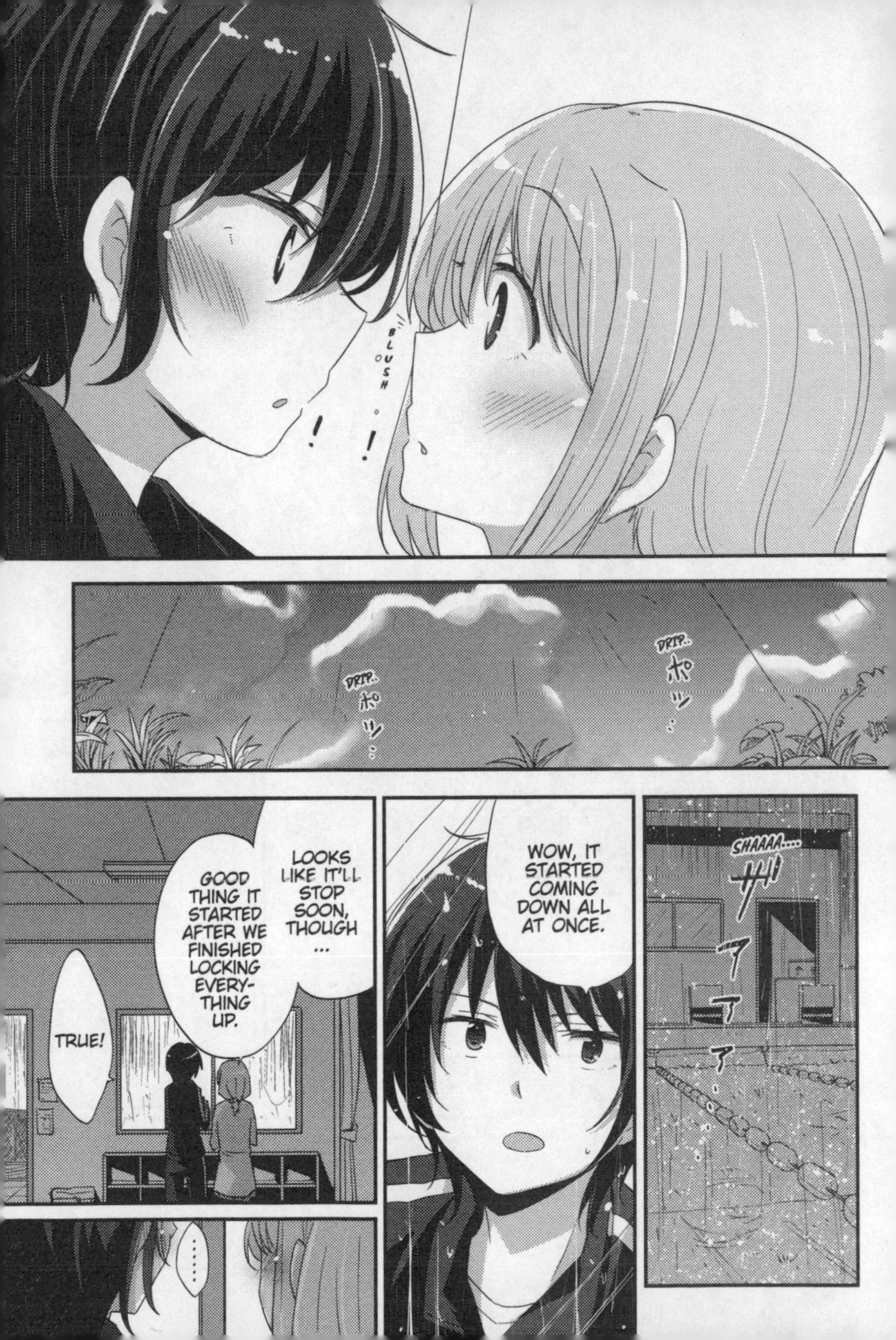

BLUSH
!
!
DRIP..
ポツ…
DRIP..
ポツ…
SHAAAA....
ザァァァ…
WOW, IT STARTED COMING DOWN ALL AT ONCE.
LOOKS LIKE IT'LL STOP SOON, THOUGH ...
GOOD THING IT STARTED AFTER WE FINISHED LOCKING EVERY-THING UP.
TRUE!
......

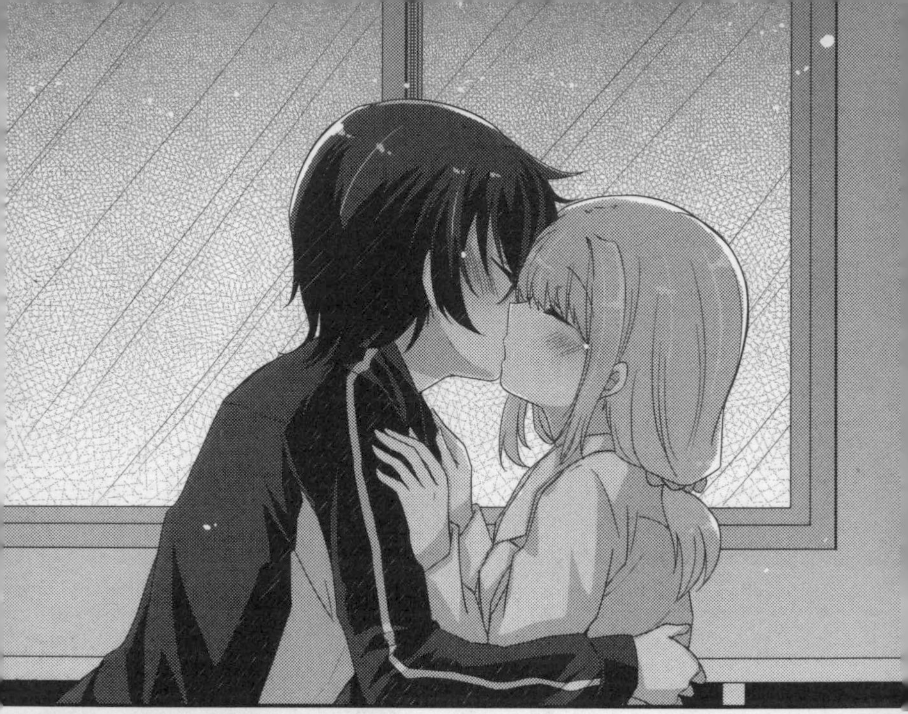

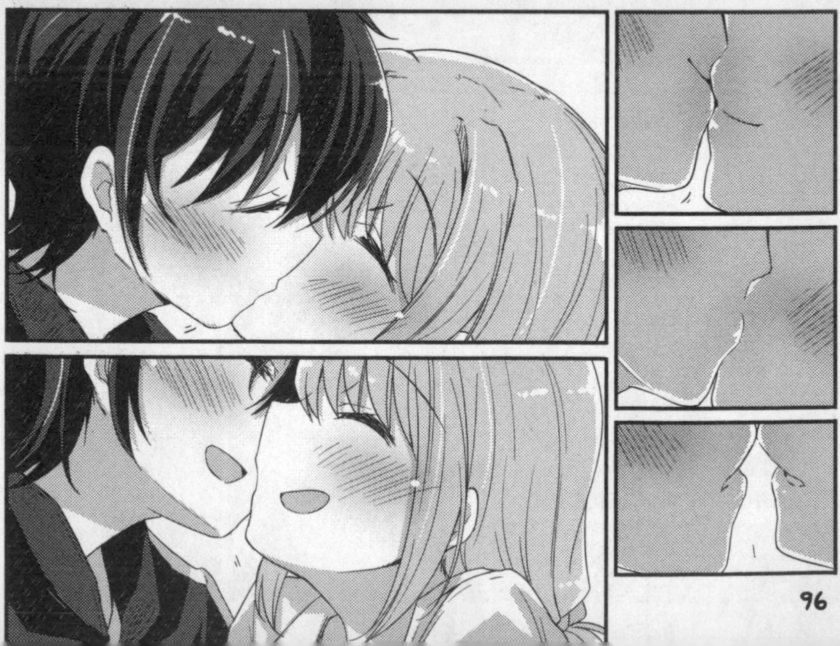

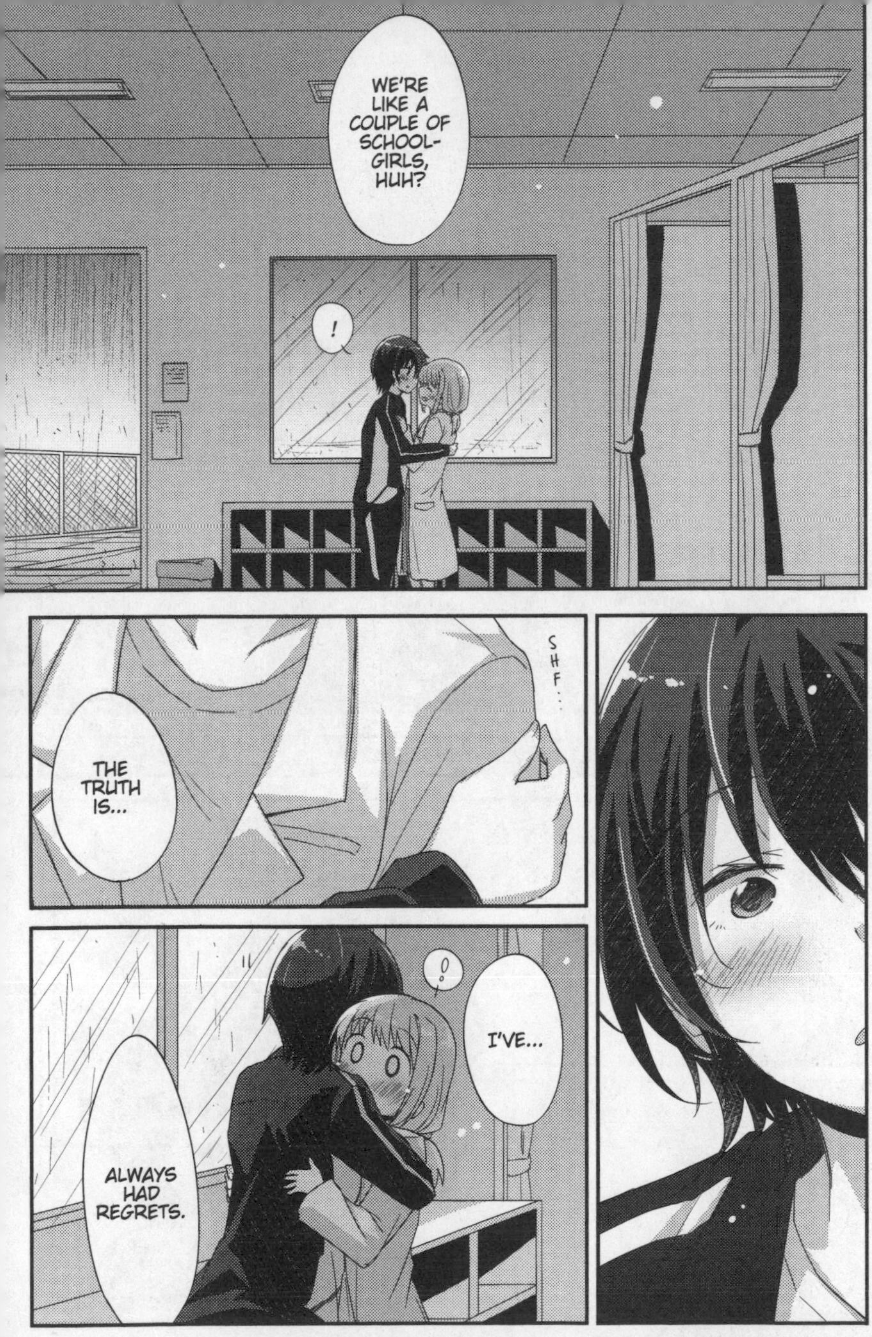
WE'RE LIKE A COUPLE OF SCHOOL-GIRLS, HUH?
!
SHF...
THE TRUTH IS...
!
I'VE...
ALWAYS HAD REGRETS.

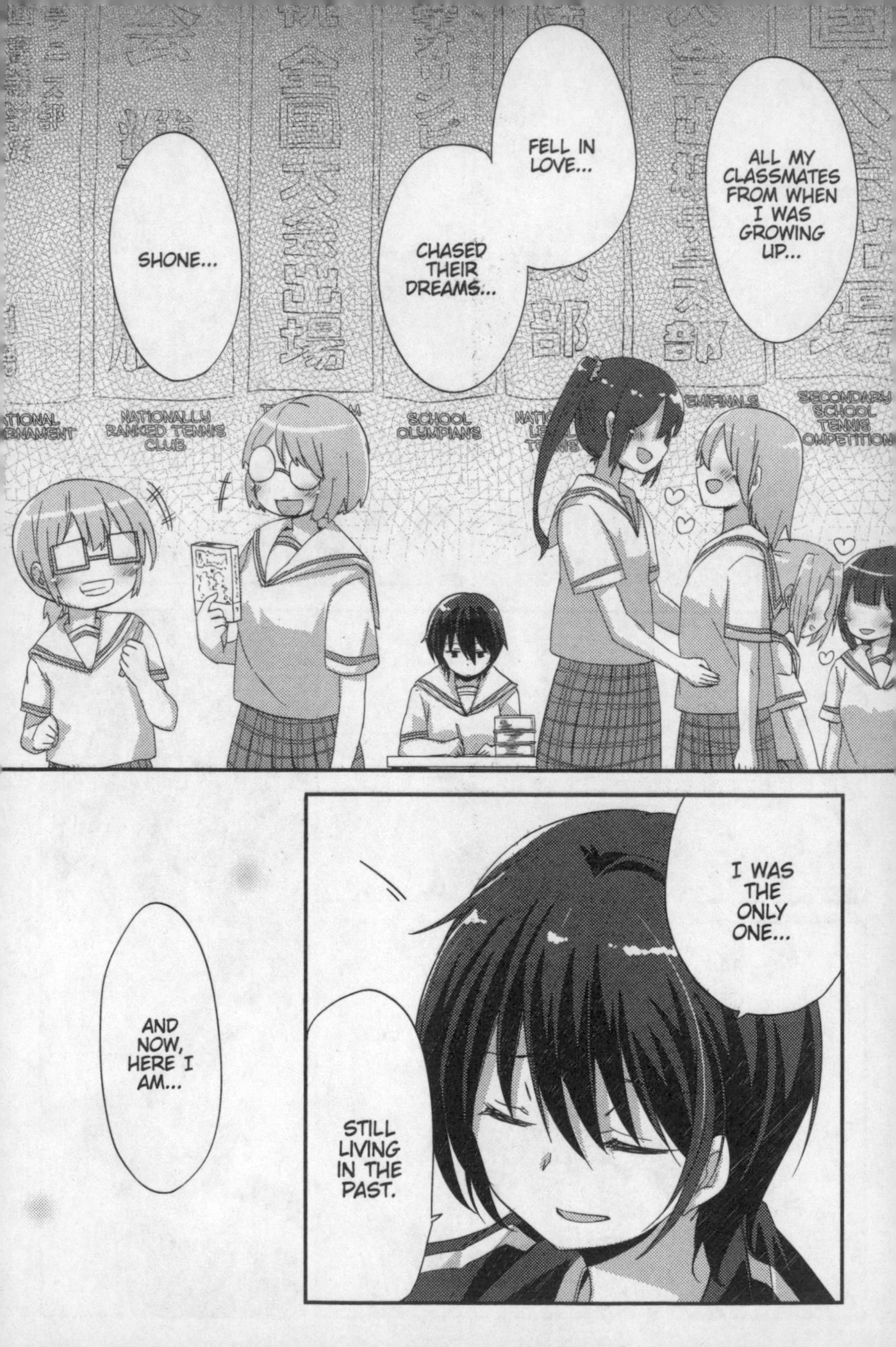
ALL MY CLASSMATES FROM WHEN I WAS GROWING UP...
FELL IN LOVE...
CHASED THEIR DREAMS...
SHONE...
SECONDARY SCHOOL TENNIS COMPETITION
SCHOOL OLYMPIANS
NATIONALLY RANKED TENNIS CLUB
I WAS THE ONLY ONE...
AND NOW, HERE I AM...
STILL LIVING IN THE PAST.

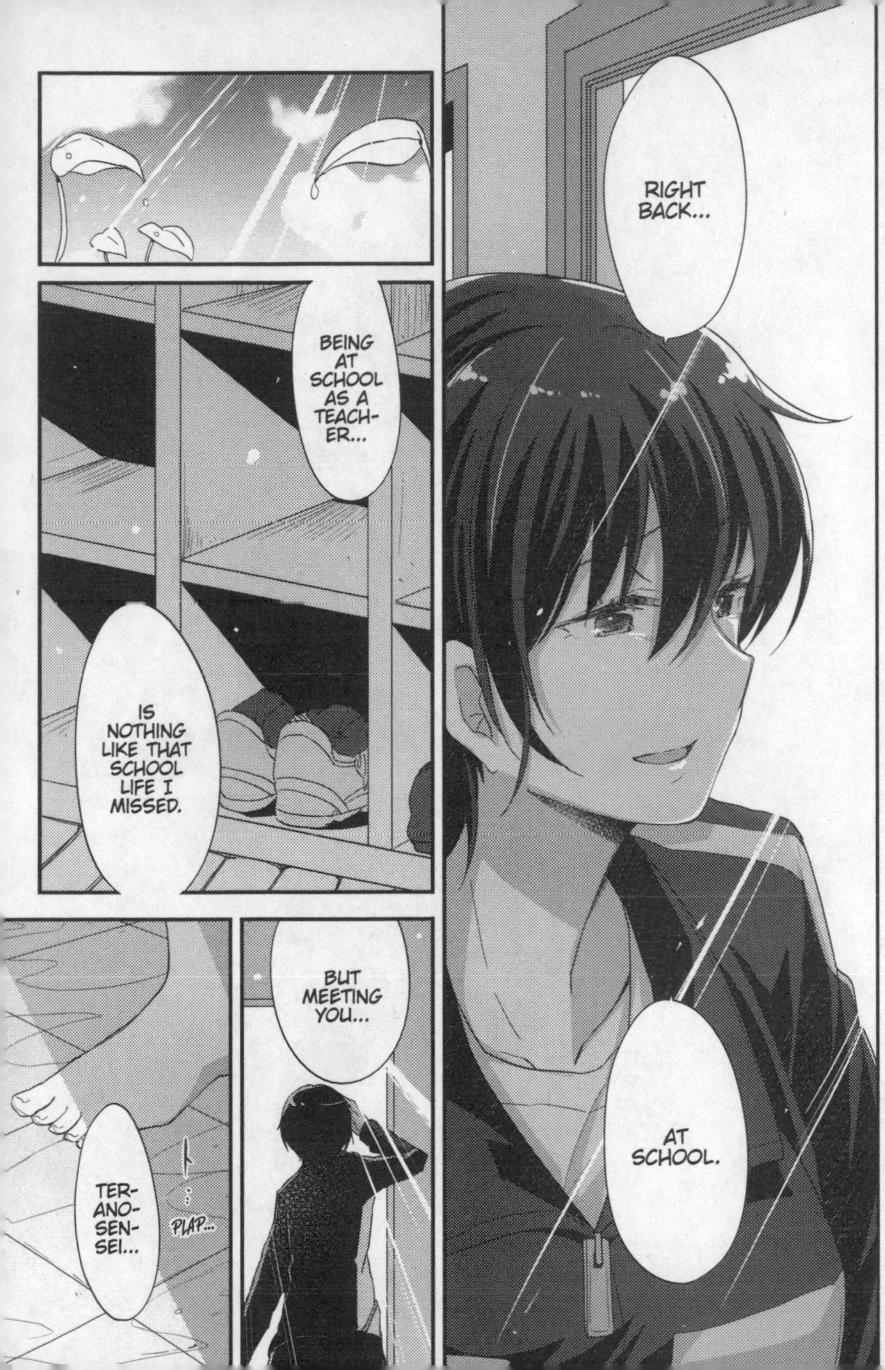
RIGHT BACK...
AT SCHOOL.
BEING AT SCHOOL AS A TEACHER...
IS NOTHING LIKE THAT SCHOOL LIFE I MISSED.
BUT MEETING YOU...
PLAP...
TERANO-SENSEI...

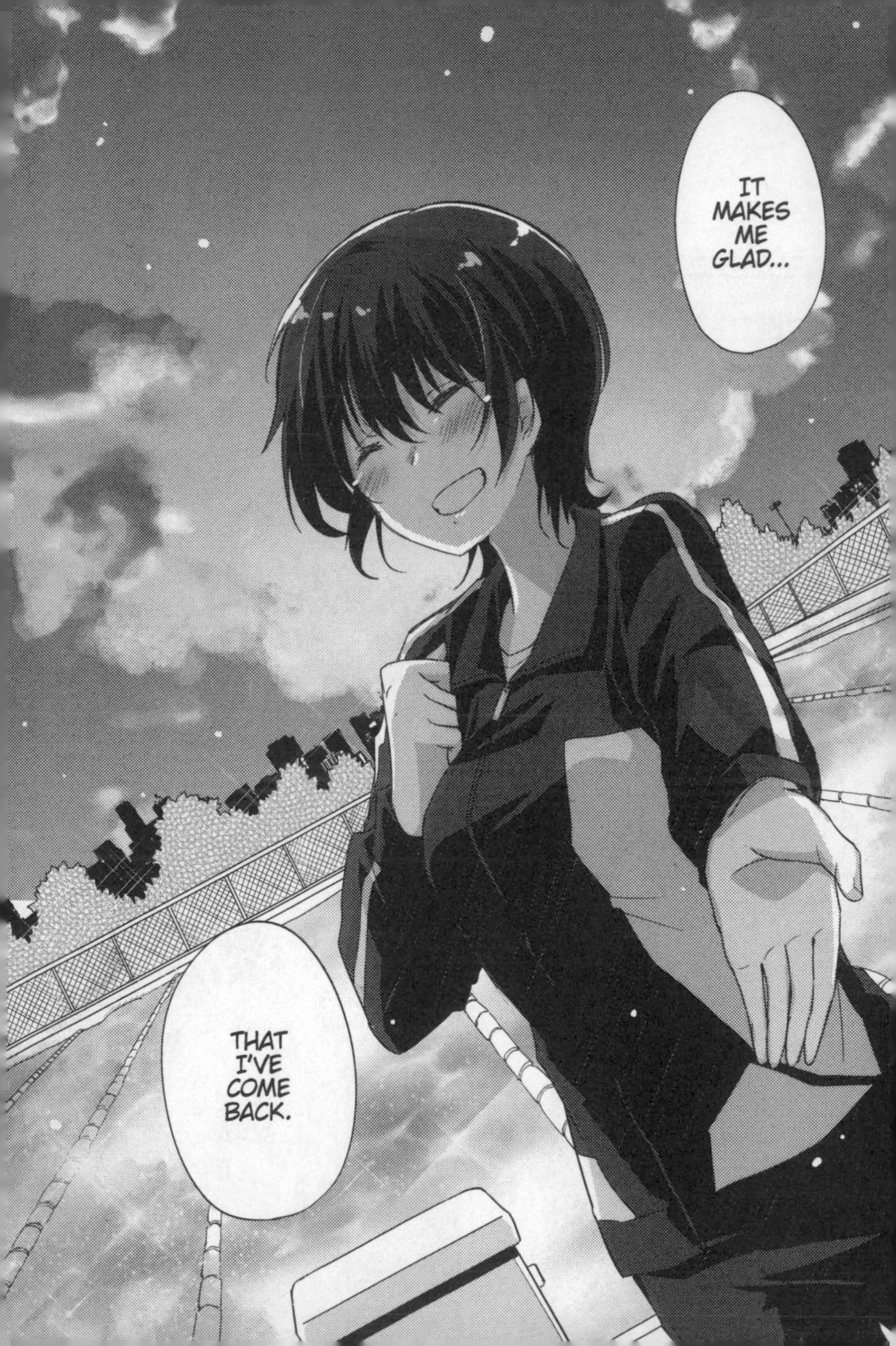
IT MAKES ME GLAD...
THAT I'VE COME BACK.

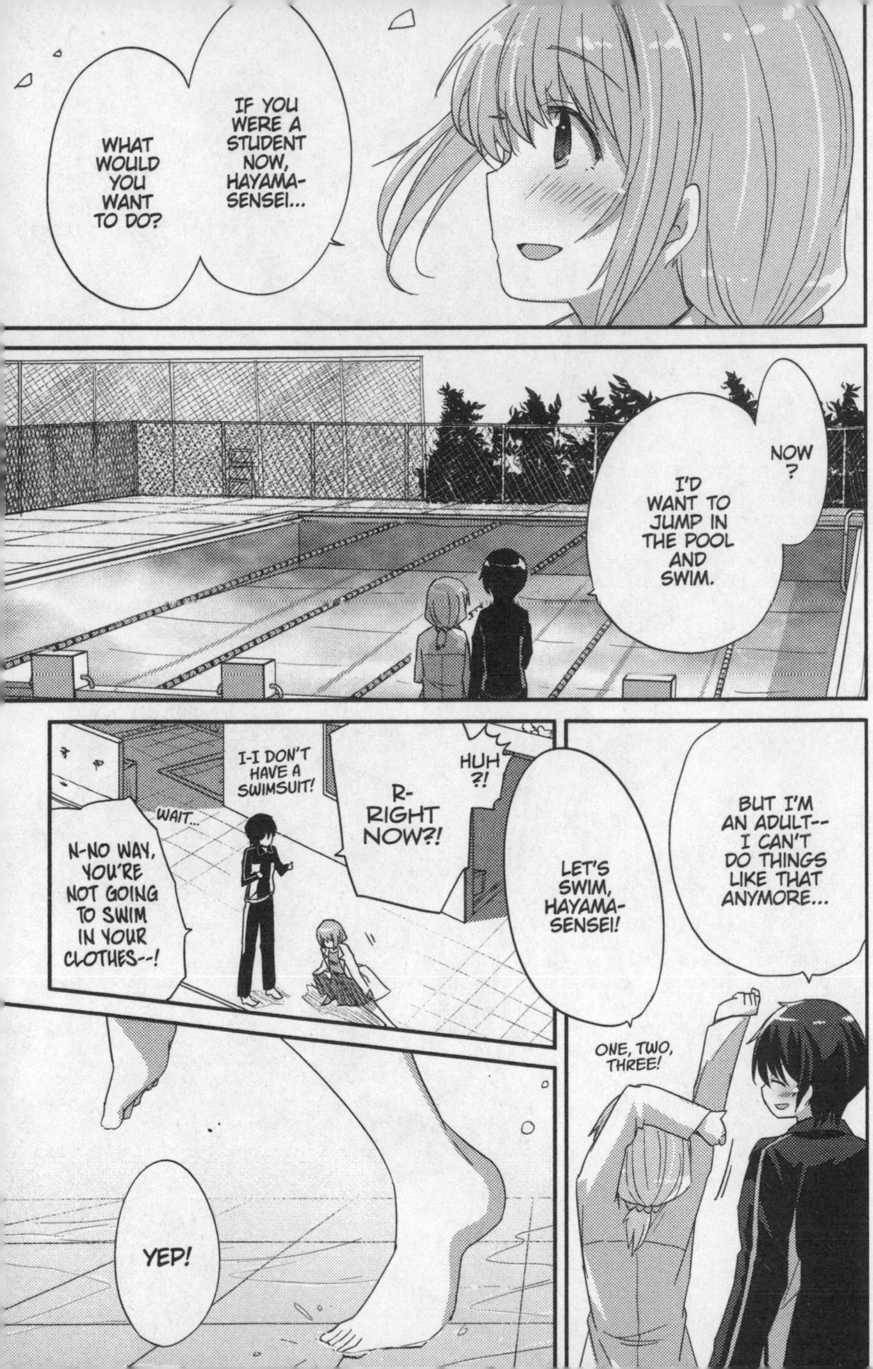
IF YOU WERE A STUDENT NOW, HAYAMA-SENSEI...
WHAT WOULD YOU WANT TO DO?
NOW?
I'D WANT TO JUMP IN THE POOL AND SWIM.
BUT I'M AN ADULT-- I CAN'T DO THINGS LIKE THAT ANYMORE...
LET'S SWIM, HAYAMA-SENSEI!
ONE, TWO, THREE!
HUH?!
R-RIGHT NOW?!
I-I DON'T HAVE A SWIMSUIT!
WAIT...
N-NO WAY, YOU'RE NOT GOING TO SWIM IN YOUR CLOTHES--!
YEP!

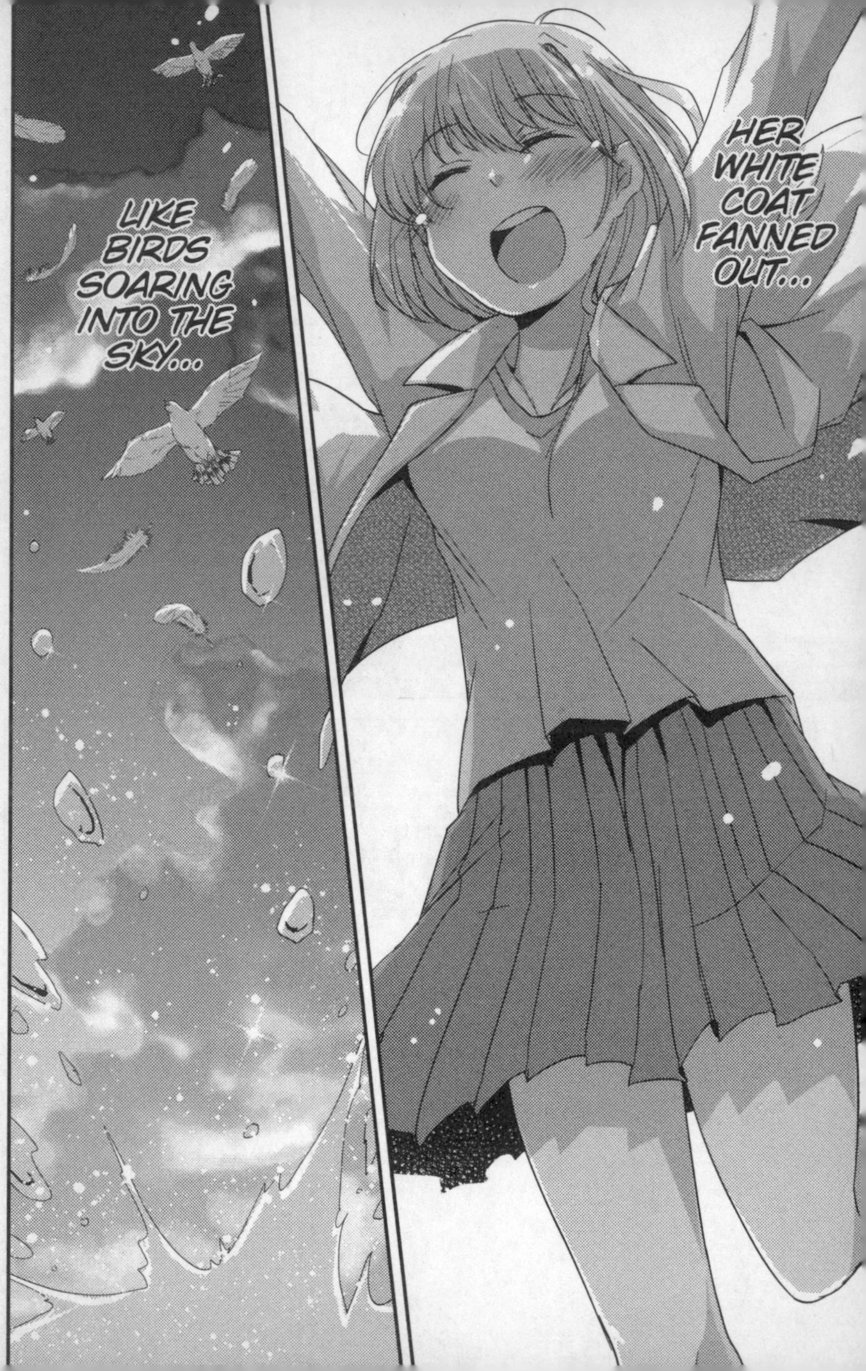
HER WHITE COAT FANNED OUT...
LIKE BIRDS SOARING INTO THE SKY...

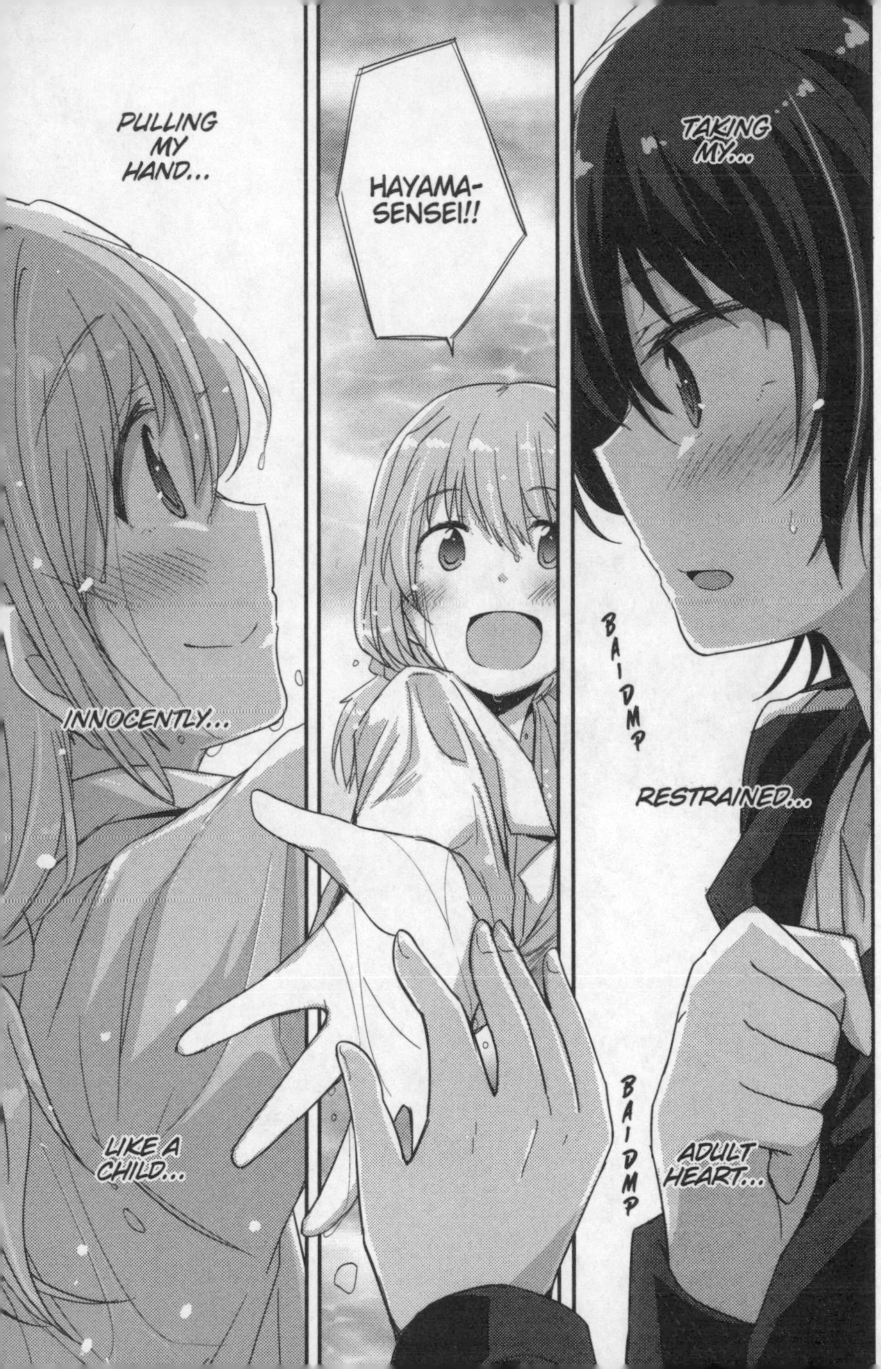
TAKING MY...
BA-DMP
RESTRAINED...
BA-DMP
ADULT HEART...
HAYAMA-SENSEI!!
PULLING MY HAND...
INNOCENTLY...
LIKE A CHILD...

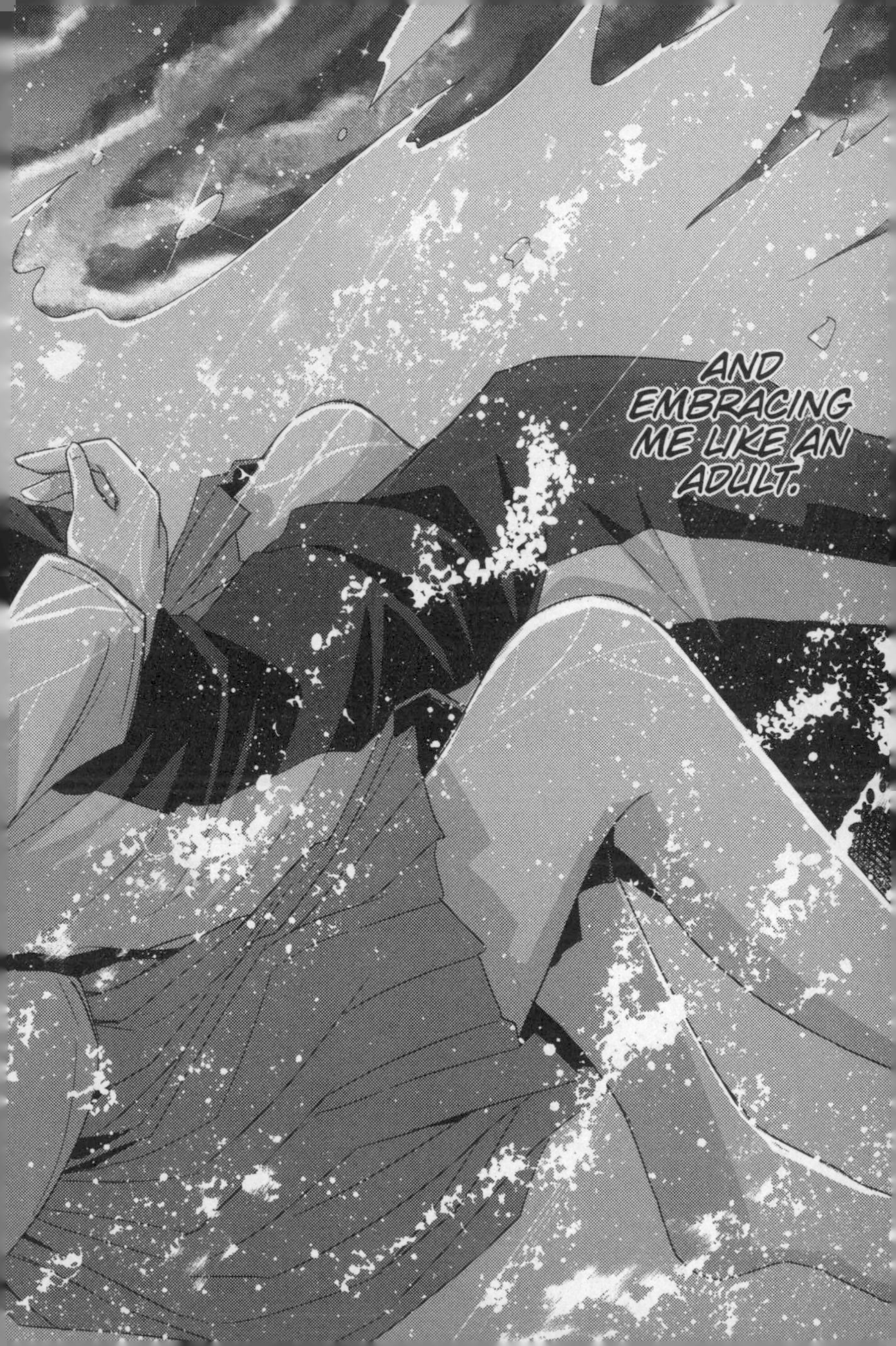
AND EMBRACING ME LIKE AN ADULT.

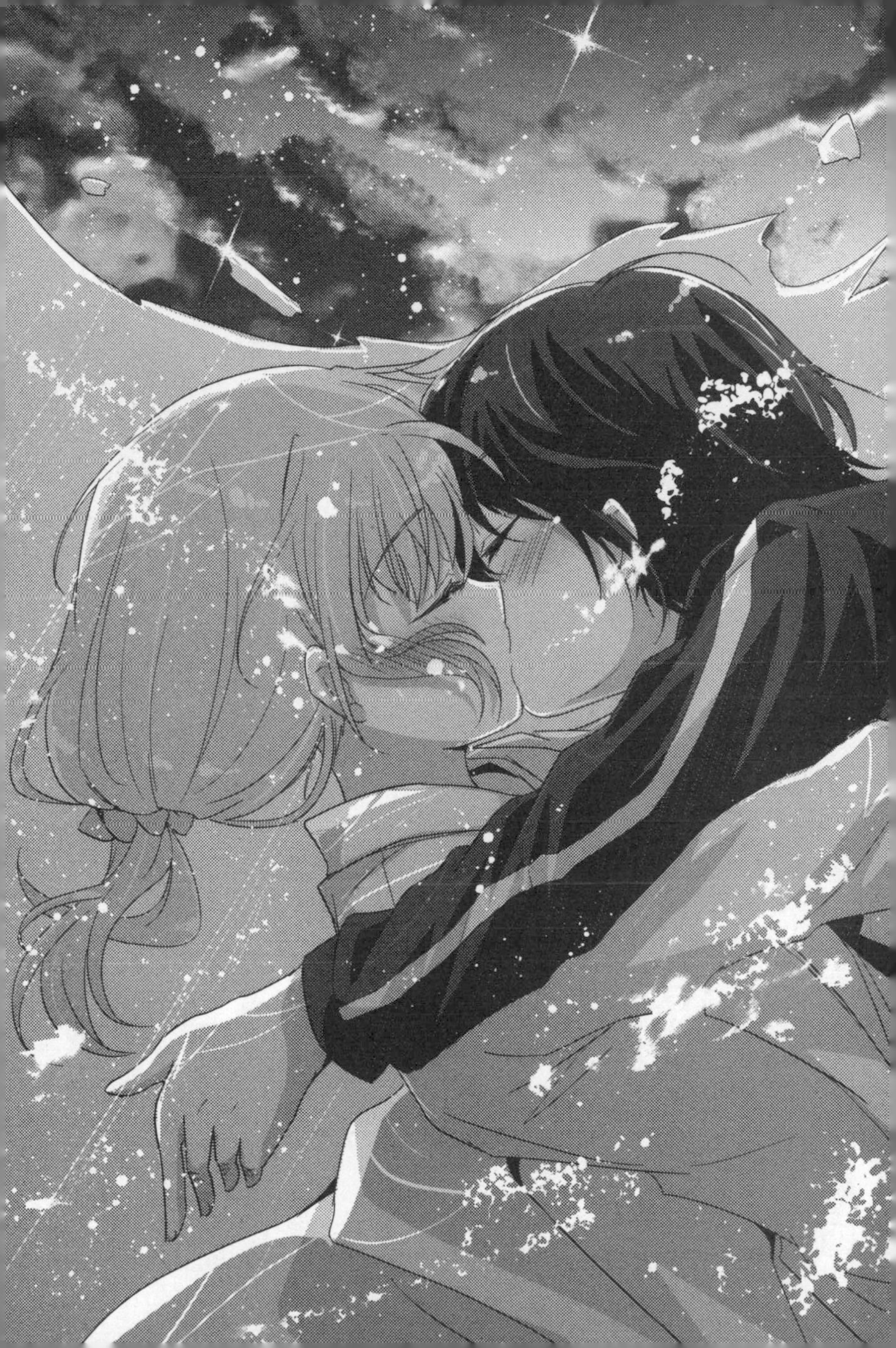

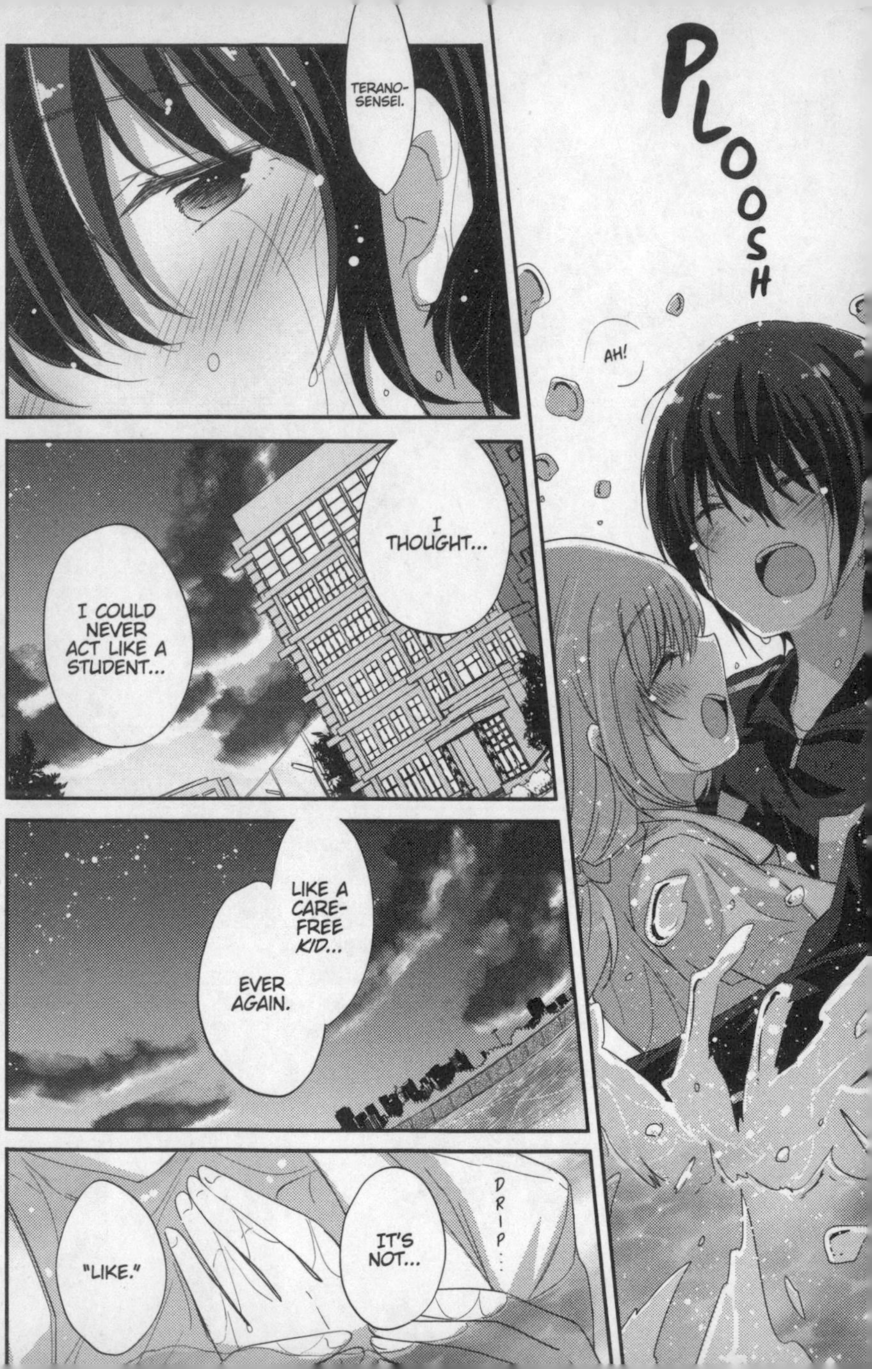
PLOOSH
AH!
TERANO-SENSEI.
I THOUGHT...
I COULD NEVER ACT LIKE A STUDENT...
LIKE A CARE-FREE KID...
EVER AGAIN.
DRIP...
IT'S NOT...
"LIKE."

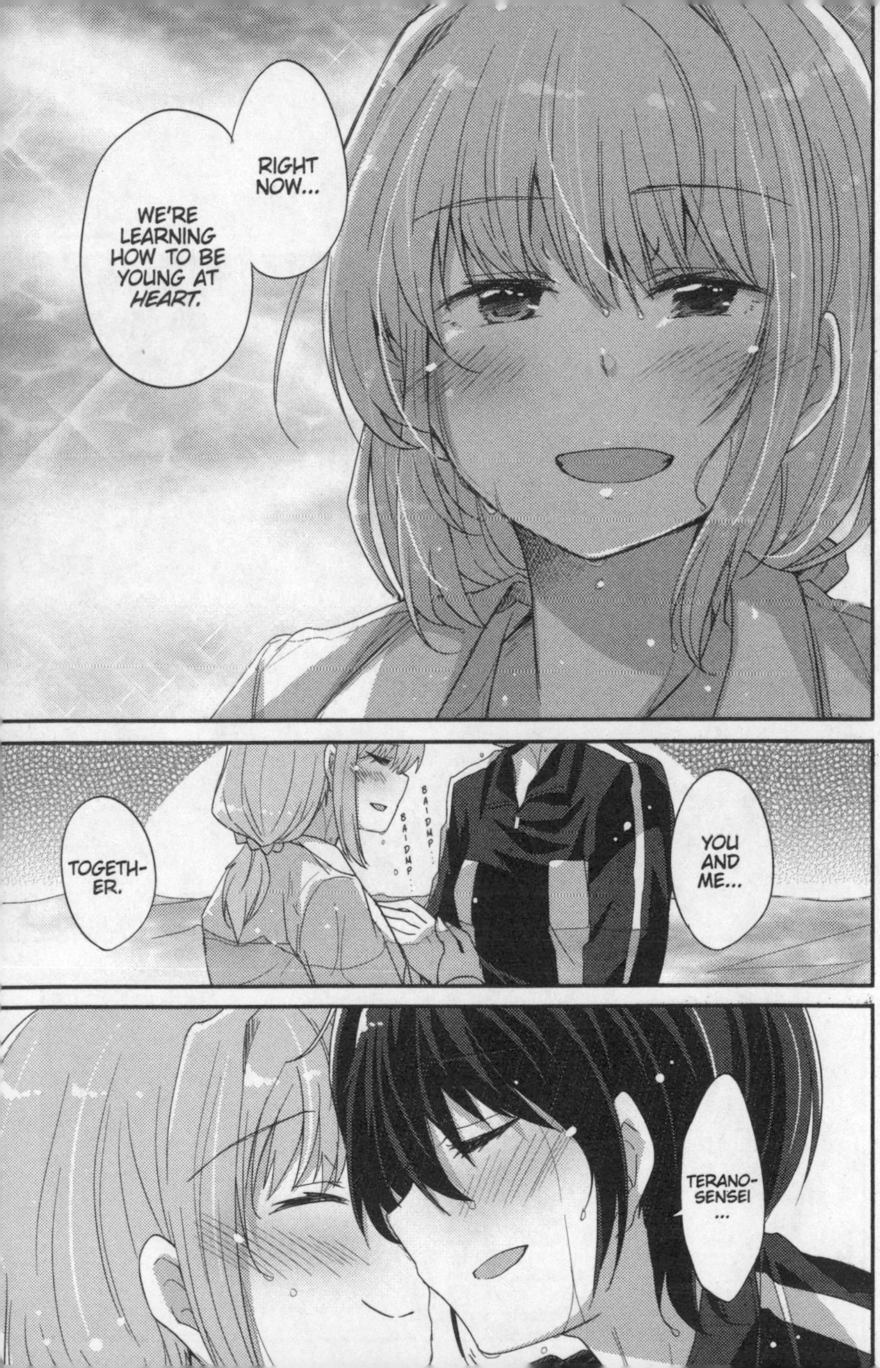
RIGHT NOW...
WE'RE LEARNING HOW TO BE YOUNG AT *HEART.*
YOU AND ME...
BA-DMP...
BA-DMP...
TOGETH-ER.
TERANO-SENSEI ...

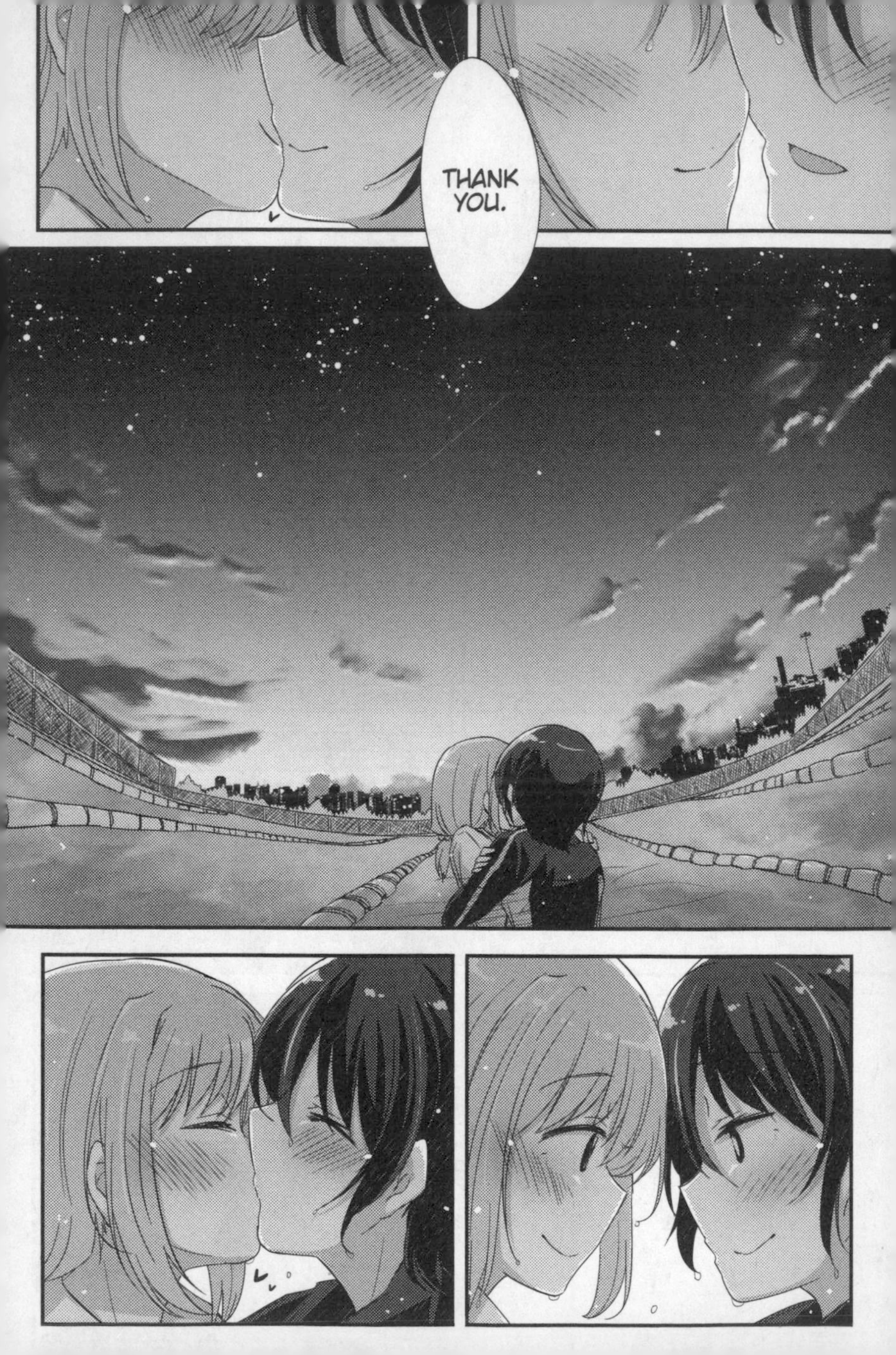
THANK YOU.

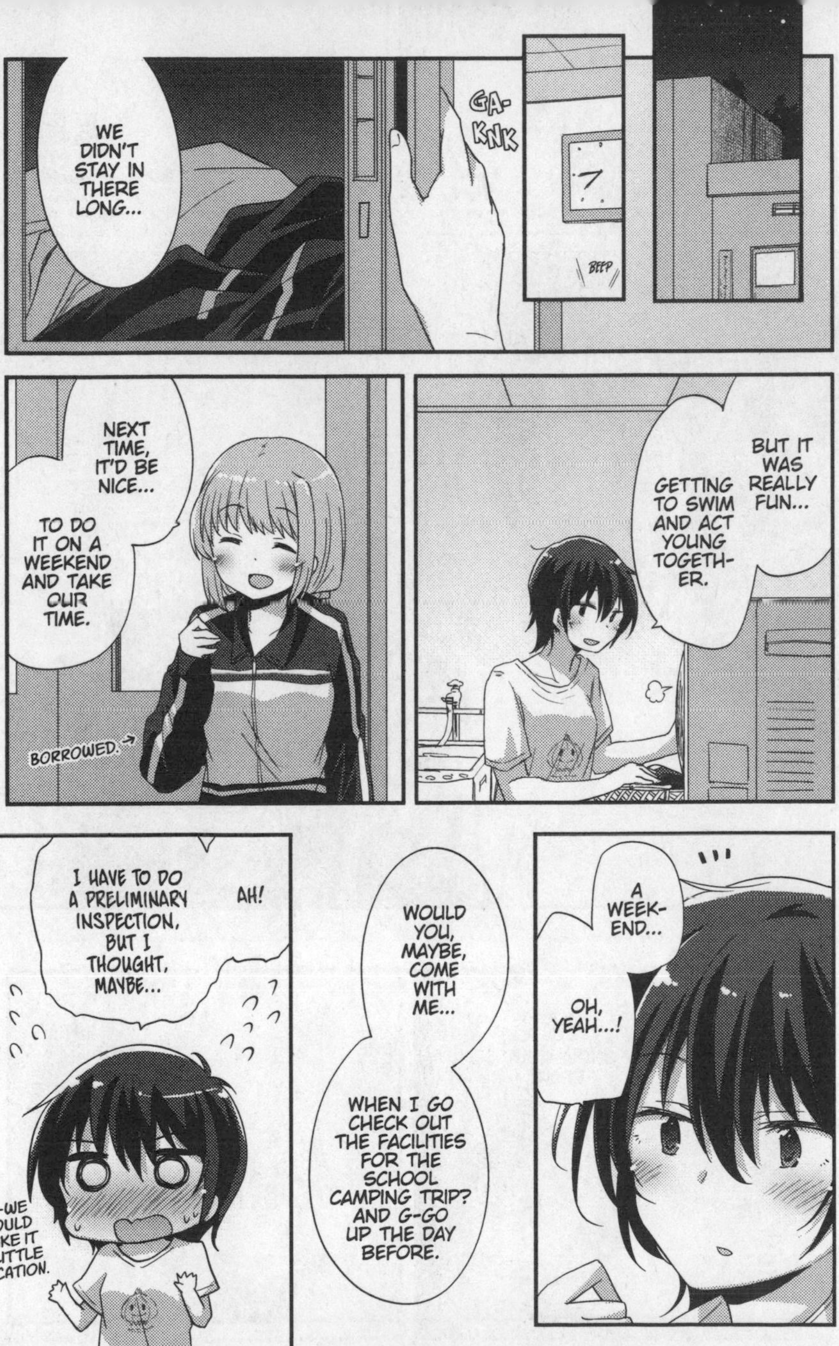
BEEP
GA-KNK
WE DIDN'T STAY IN THERE LONG...
BUT IT WAS REALLY FUN...
GETTING TO SWIM AND ACT YOUNG TOGETH-ER.
NEXT TIME, IT'D BE NICE...
TO DO IT ON A WEEKEND AND TAKE OUR TIME.
BORROWED.
A WEEK-END...
OH, YEAH...!
AH!
I HAVE TO DO A PRELIMINARY INSPECTION, BUT I THOUGHT, MAYBE...
WOULD YOU, MAYBE, COME WITH ME...
WHEN I GO CHECK OUT THE FACILITIES FOR THE SCHOOL CAMPING TRIP? AND G-GO UP THE DAY BEFORE.
W-WE COULD MAKE IT A LITTLE VACATION.

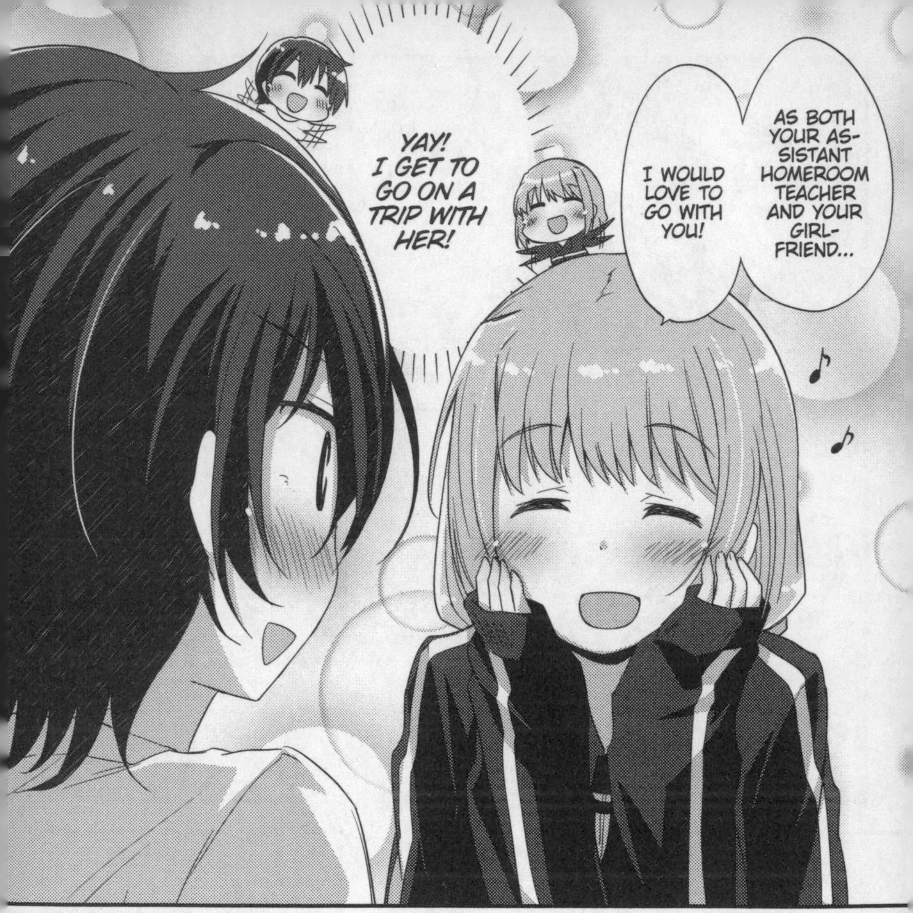
AS BOTH YOUR AS-SISTANT HOMEROOM TEACHER AND YOUR GIRL-FRIEND...
I WOULD LOVE TO GO WITH YOU!
YAY! I GET TO GO ON A TRIP WITH HER!

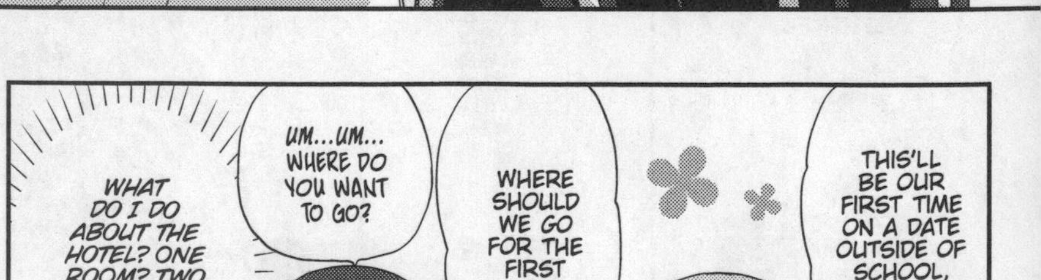
THIS'LL BE OUR FIRST TIME ON A DATE OUTSIDE OF SCHOOL, HUH?
YAY!
YAY!
WHERE SHOULD WE GO FOR THE FIRST DAY?
UM...UM... WHERE DO YOU WANT TO GO?
WHAT DO I DO ABOUT THE HOTEL? ONE ROOM? TWO BEDS? ONE? DO I NEED A SLEEPING BAG?
FRET
FRET

HANG IN THERE, HAYAMA.

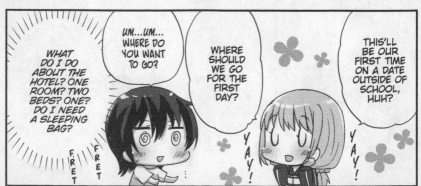

HAYAMA PLANNING THE DATE.

THIS PLACE LOOKS GOOD FOR LUNCH...

MAYBE WE CAN CHECK OUT THE NATURAL HISTORY MUSEUM, TOO?

OUR TEACHERS ARE DATING

Our Teachers are Dating!

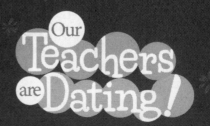

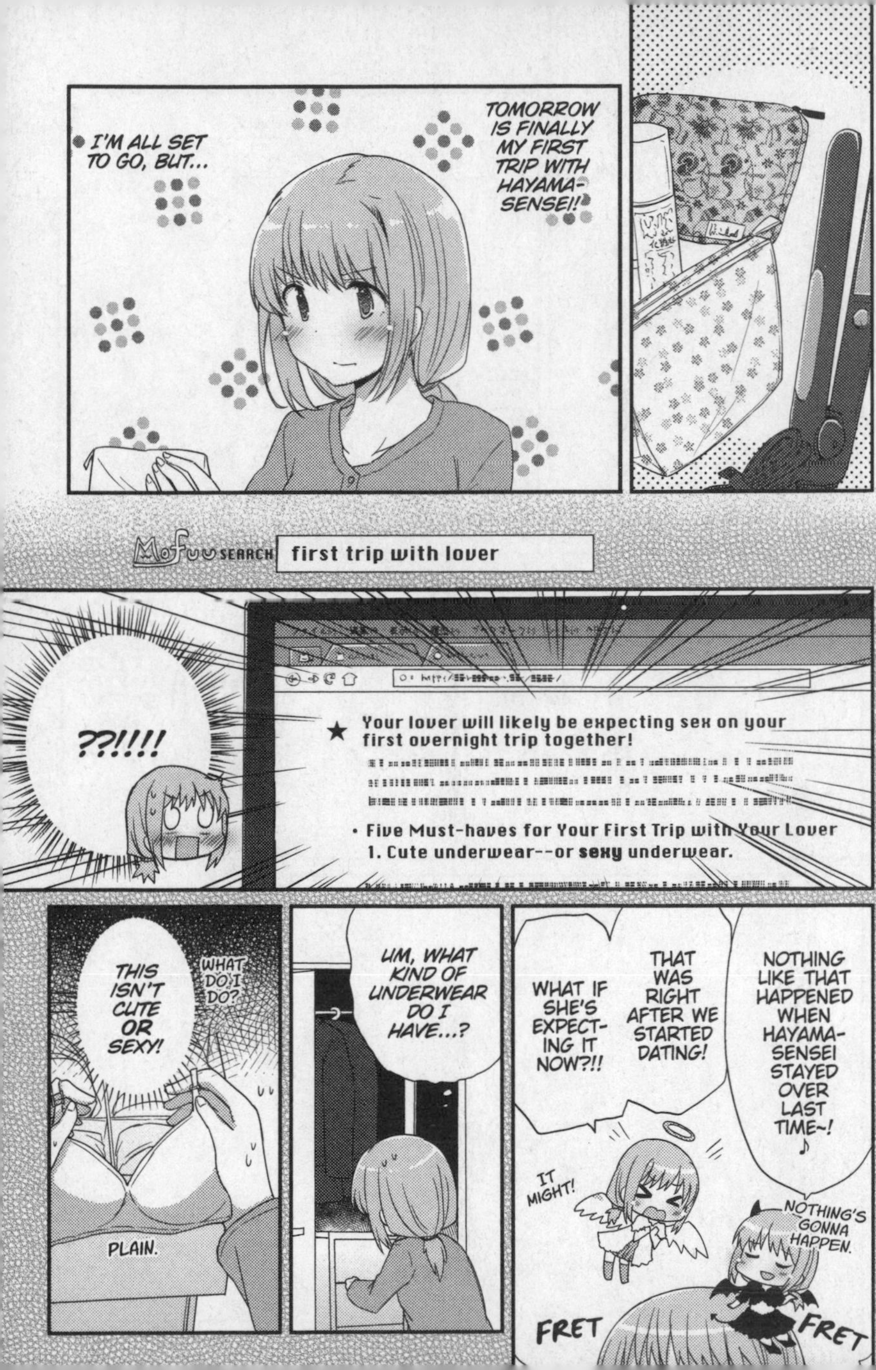
TOMORROW IS FINALLY MY FIRST TRIP WITH HAYAMA-SENSEI!!
I'M ALL SET TO GO, BUT...
MOFUU SEARCH
first trip with lover
★ Your lover will likely be expecting sex on your first overnight trip together!
• Five Must-haves for Your First Trip with Your Lover
1. Cute underwear--or sexy underwear.
??!!!!
NOTHING LIKE THAT HAPPENED WHEN HAYAMA-SENSEI STAYED OVER LAST TIME~! ♪
THAT WAS RIGHT AFTER WE STARTED DATING!
WHAT IF SHE'S EXPECTING IT NOW?!!
NOTHING'S GONNA HAPPEN.
IT MIGHT!
FRET
FRET
UM, WHAT KIND OF UNDERWEAR DO I HAVE...?
WHAT DO I DO?
THIS ISN'T CUTE OR SEXY!
PLAIN.

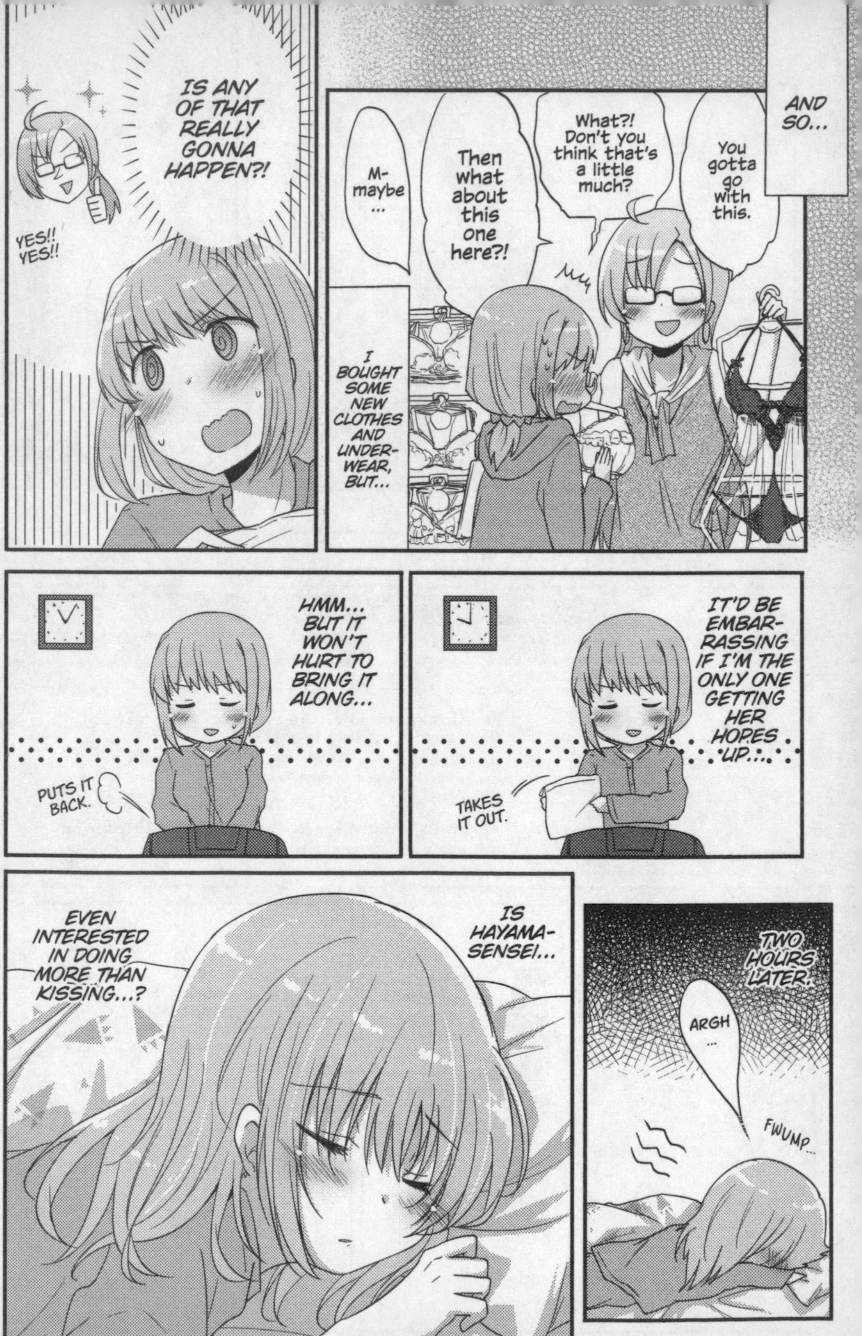

AND SO...
You gotta go with this.
What?! Don't you think that's a little much?
Then what about this one here?!
M-maybe...
I BOUGHT SOME NEW CLOTHES AND UNDER-WEAR, BUT...
IS ANY OF THAT REALLY GONNA HAPPEN?!
YES!! YES!!
IT'D BE EMBAR-RASSING IF I'M THE ONLY ONE GETTING HER HOPES UP...
TAKES IT OUT.
HMM... BUT IT WON'T HURT TO BRING IT ALONG...
PUTS IT BACK.
TWO HOURS LATER.
ARGH...
FWUMP...
IS HAYAMA-SENSEI...
EVEN INTERESTED IN DOING MORE THAN KISSING...?

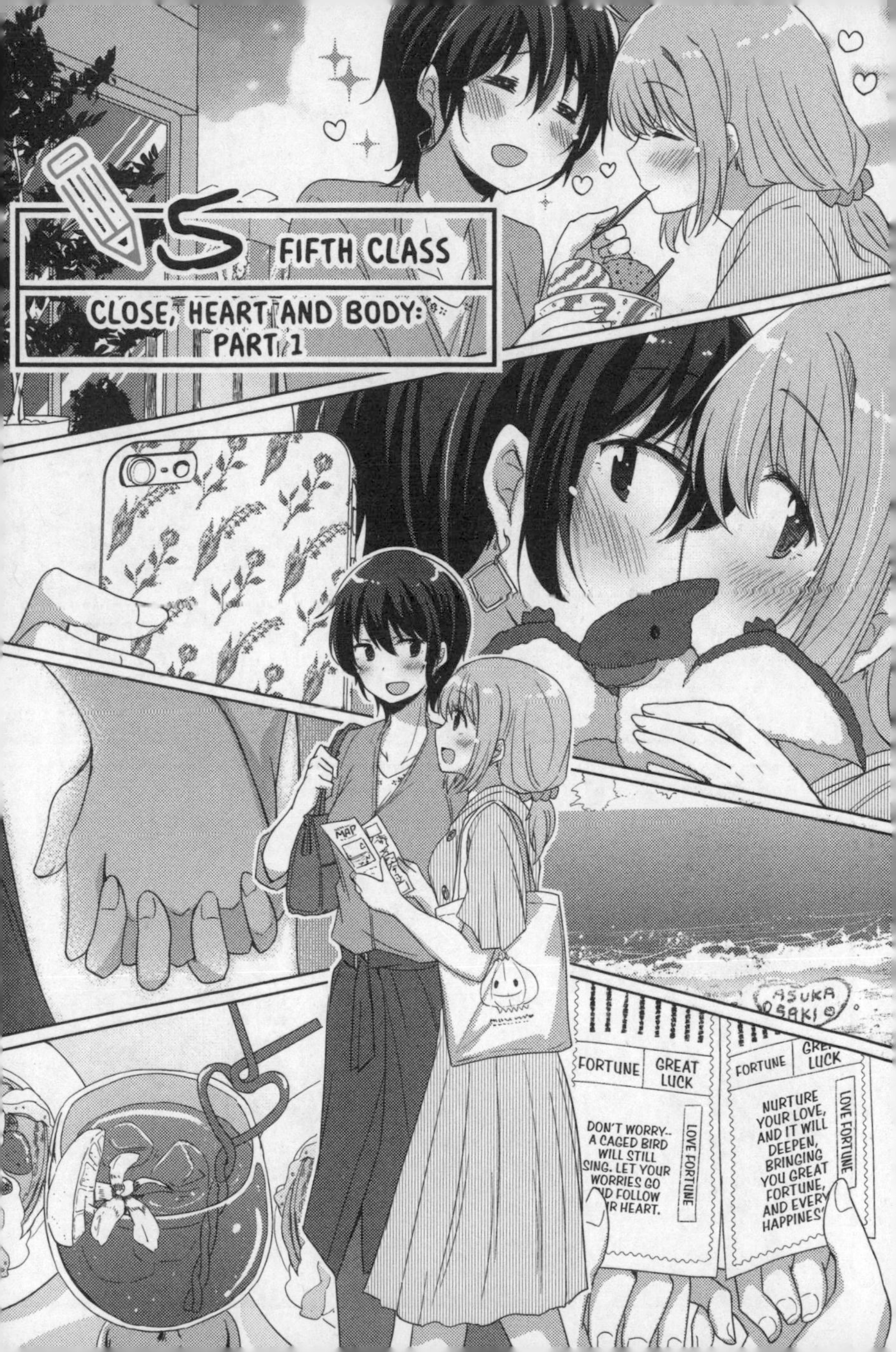
5 FIFTH CLASS
CLOSE, HEART AND BODY: PART 1
MAP
ASUKA OSAKI
FORTUNE
LUCK
LOVE FORTUNE
NURTURE YOUR LOVE, AND IT WILL DEEPEN, BRINGING YOU GREAT FORTUNE, AND EVERY HAPPINES
FORTUNE
GREAT LUCK
LOVE FORTUNE
DON'T WORRY-- A CAGED BIRD WILL STILL SING. LET YOUR WORRIES GO
D FOLLOW
R HEART.

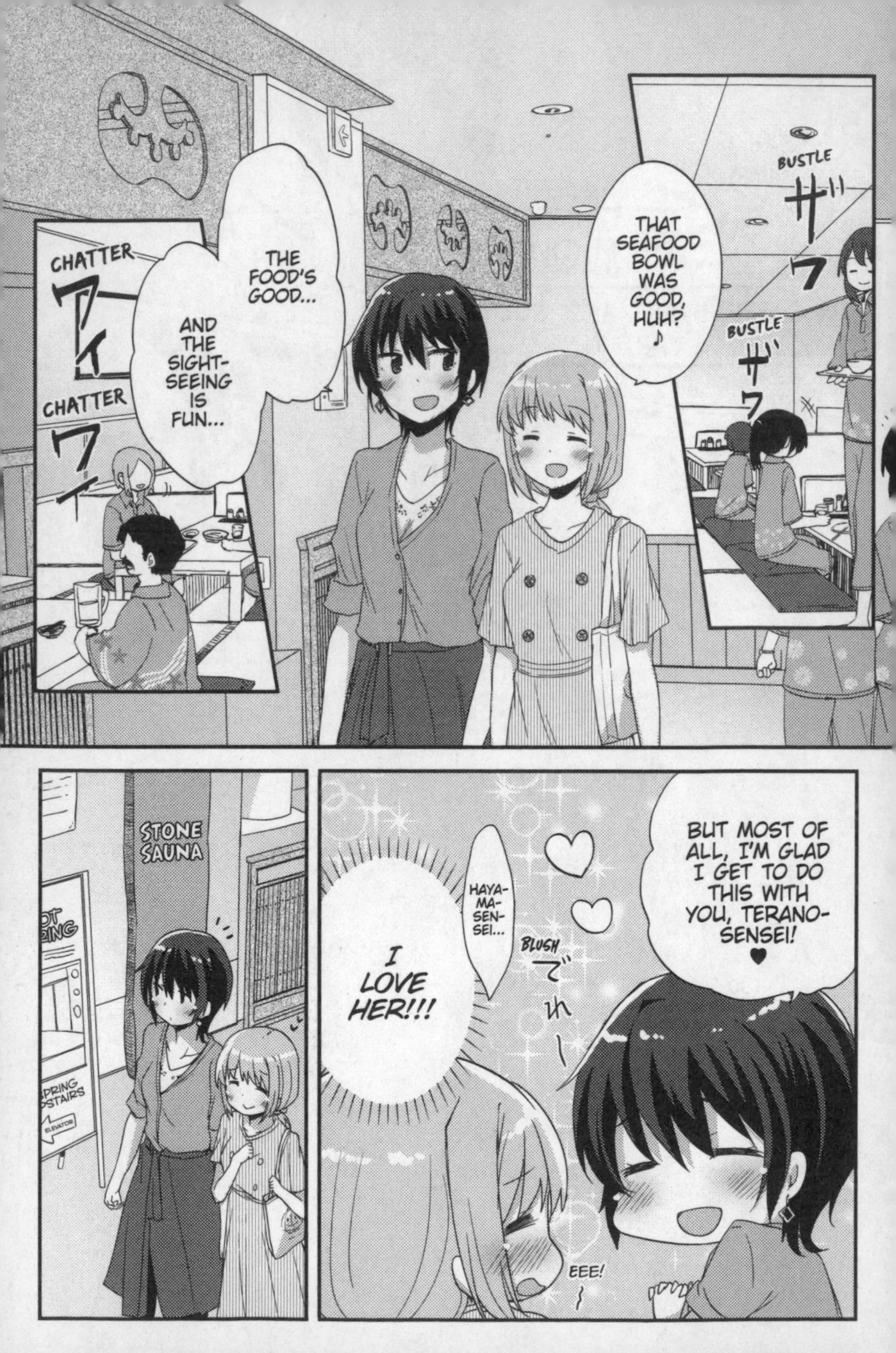
BUSTLE
BUSTLE
THAT SEAFOOD BOWL WAS GOOD, HUH? ♪
THE FOOD'S GOOD...
AND THE SIGHT-SEEING IS FUN...
CHATTER
CHATTER
BUT MOST OF ALL, I'M GLAD I GET TO DO THIS WITH YOU, TERANO-SENSEI! ♥
HAYA-MA-SEN-SEI...
BLUSH
I LOVE HER!!!
EEE!
STONE SAUNA
ELEVATOR

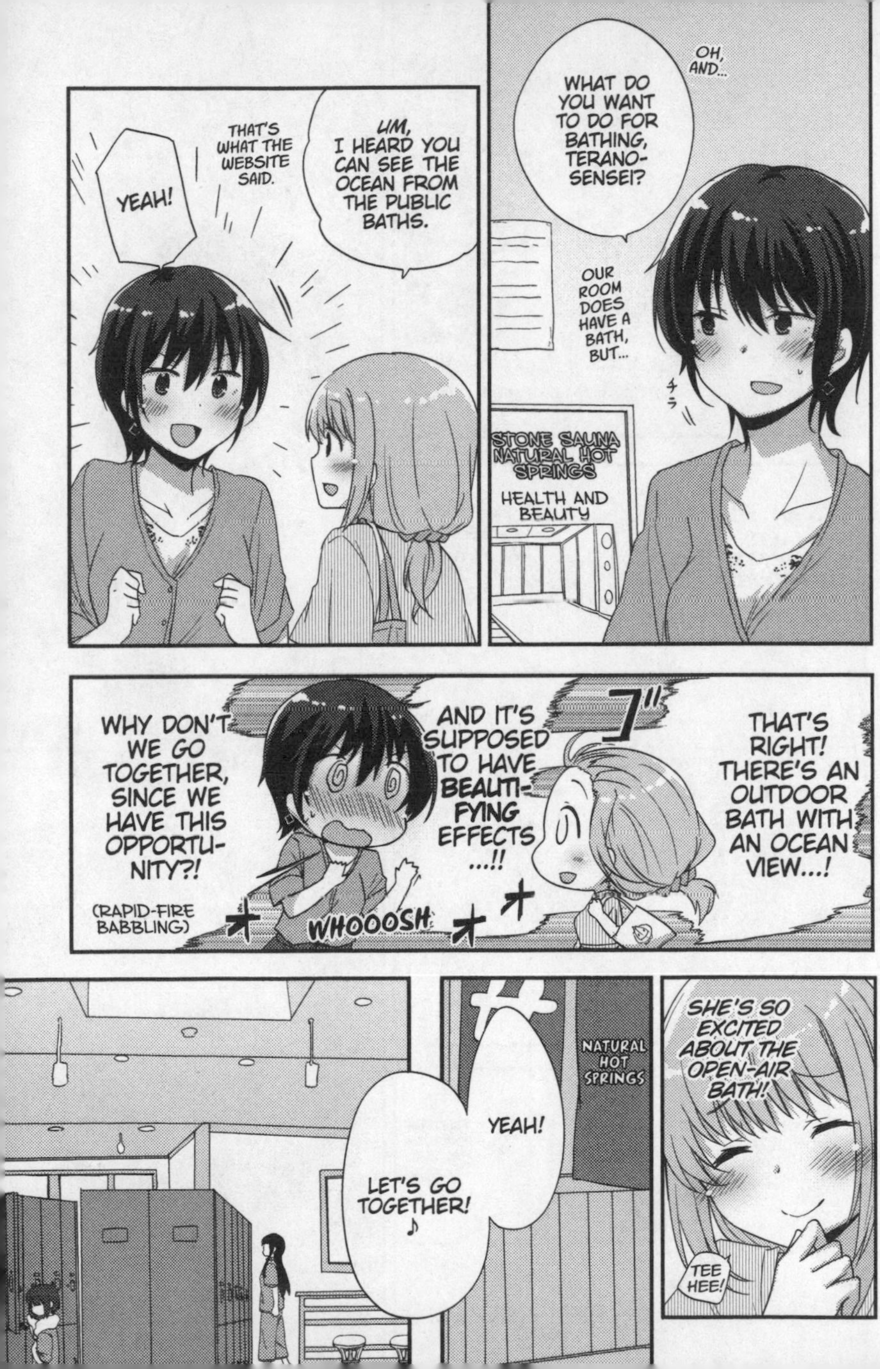
OH, AND...
WHAT DO YOU WANT TO DO FOR BATHING, TERANO-SENSEI?
OUR ROOM DOES HAVE A BATH, BUT...
チラ
STONE SAUNA NATURAL HOT SPRINGS
HEALTH AND BEAUTY
UM, I HEARD YOU CAN SEE THE OCEAN FROM THE PUBLIC BATHS.
THAT'S WHAT THE WEBSITE SAID.
YEAH!
THAT'S RIGHT! THERE'S AN OUTDOOR BATH WITH AN OCEAN VIEW...!
AND IT'S SUPPOSED TO HAVE BEAUTIFYING EFFECTS...!!
WHY DON'T WE GO TOGETHER, SINCE WE HAVE THIS OPPORTUNITY?!
(RAPID-FIRE BABBLING)
WHOOOSH
SHE'S SO EXCITED ABOUT THE OPEN-AIR BATH!
TEE HEE!
NATURAL HOT SPRINGS
YEAH!
LET'S GO TOGETHER! ♪

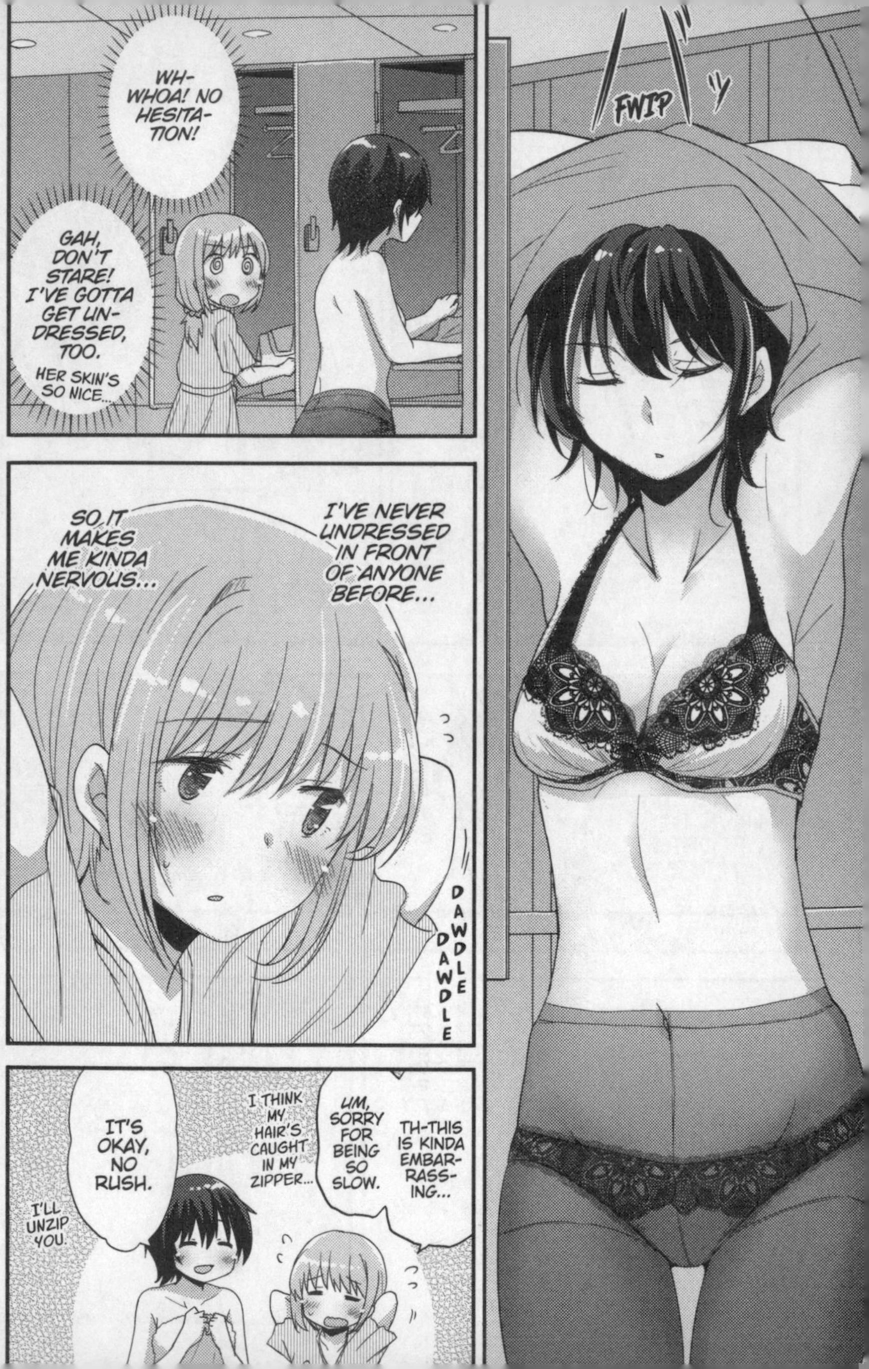
FWIP
WH-WHOA! NO HESITATION!
GAH, DON'T STARE! I'VE GOTTA GET UNDRESSED, TOO.
HER SKIN'S SO NICE...
I'VE NEVER UNDRESSED IN FRONT OF ANYONE BEFORE...
SO IT MAKES ME KINDA NERVOUS...
DAWDLE DAWDLE
TH-THIS IS KINDA EMBARRASSING...
UM, SORRY FOR BEING SO SLOW.
I THINK MY HAIR'S CAUGHT IN MY ZIPPER...
IT'S OKAY, NO RUSH.
I'LL UNZIP YOU.

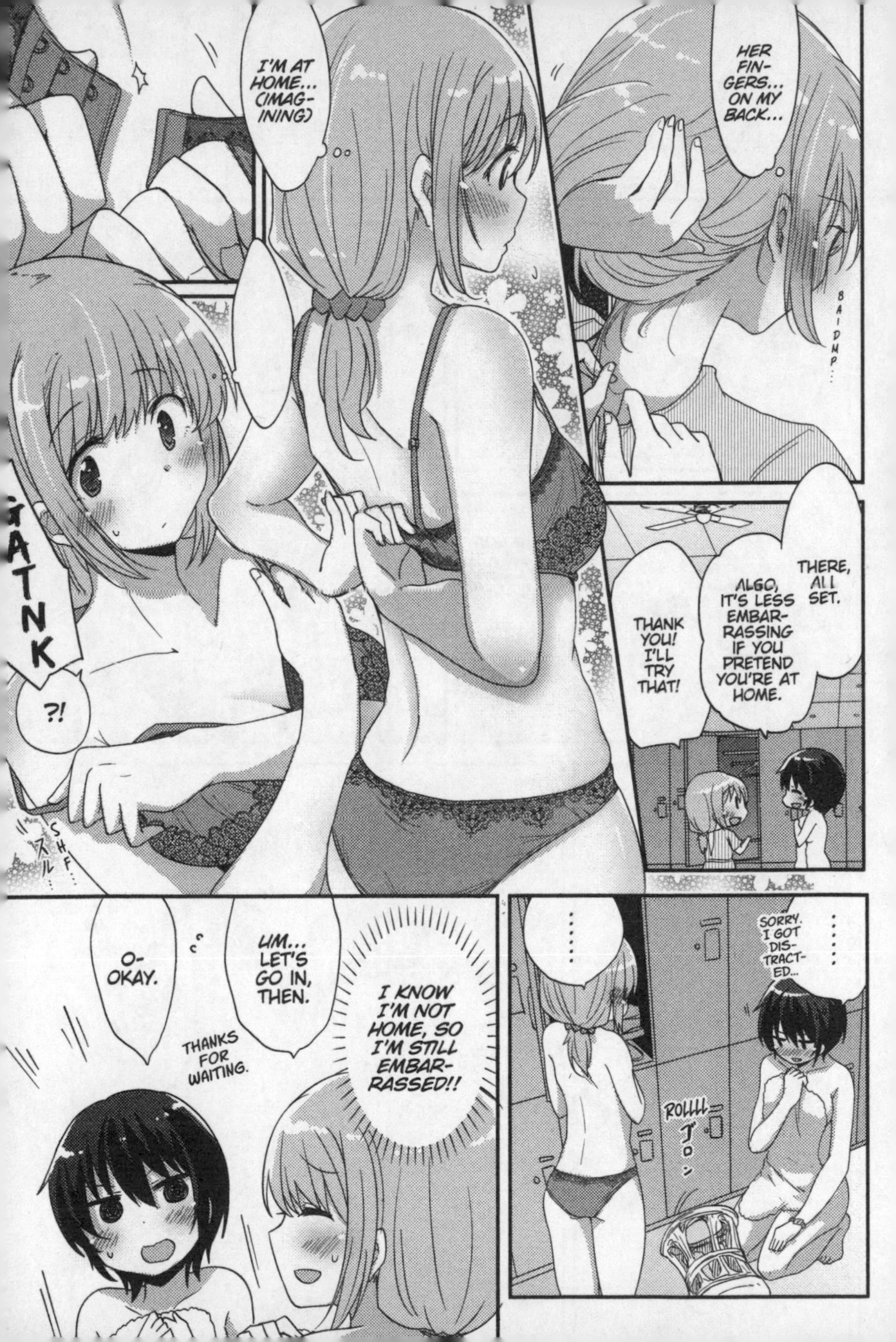
HER FIN-GERS... ON MY BACK...
BA-DMP...
THERE, ALL SET.
ALSO, IT'S LESS EMBAR-RASSING IF YOU PRETEND YOU'RE AT HOME.
THANK YOU! I'LL TRY THAT!
I'M AT HOME... (IMAG-INING)
GATNK
?!
SHF...
......
SORRY. I GOT DIS-TRACT-ED...
......
ROLLLL
UM... LET'S GO IN, THEN.
I KNOW I'M NOT HOME, SO I'M STILL EMBAR-RASSED!!
O-OKAY.
THANKS FOR WAITING.

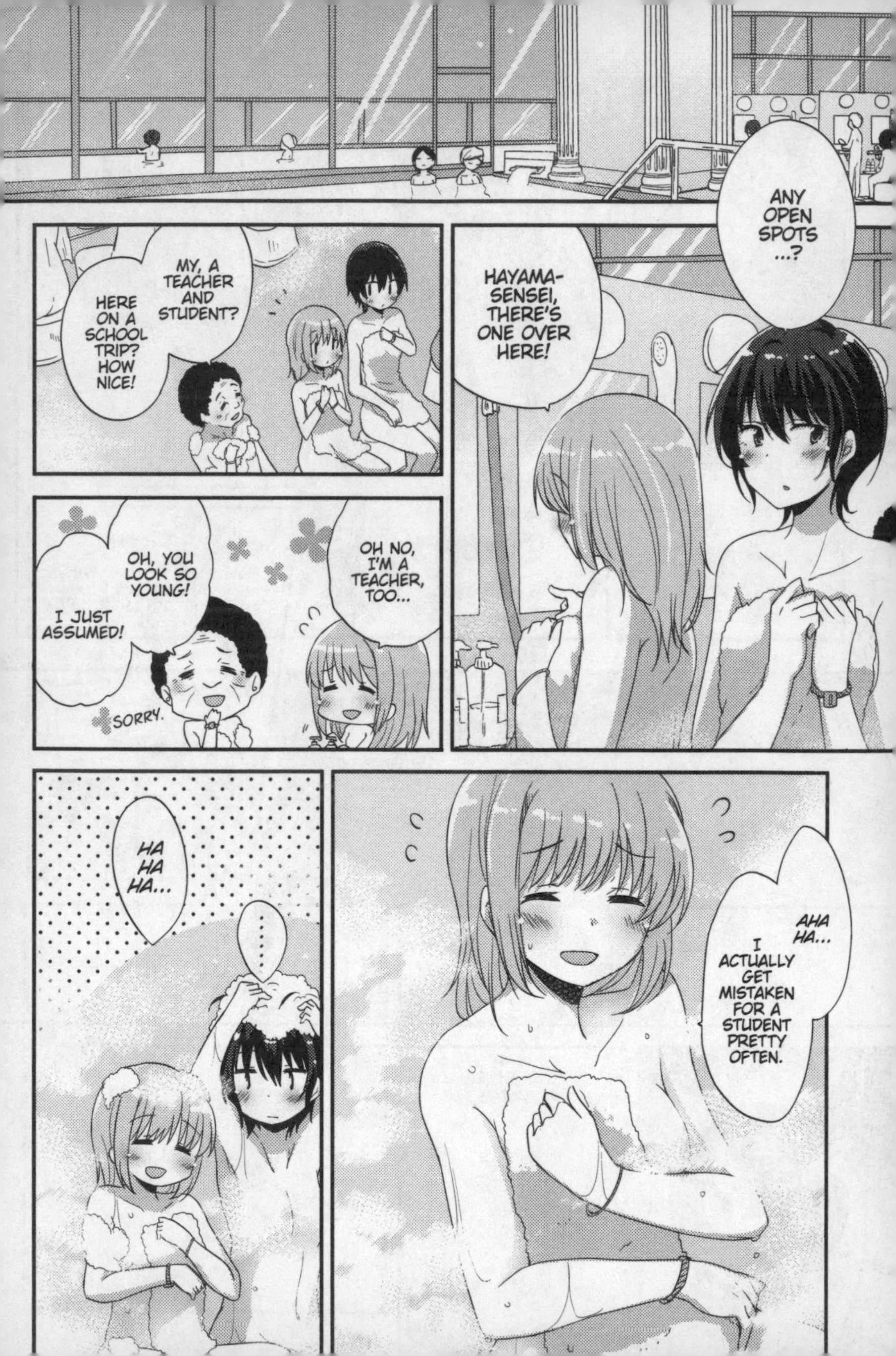
ANY OPEN SPOTS ...?
HAYAMA-SENSEI, THERE'S ONE OVER HERE!
MY, A TEACHER AND STUDENT?
HERE ON A SCHOOL TRIP? HOW NICE!
OH NO, I'M A TEACHER, TOO...
OH, YOU LOOK SO YOUNG!
I JUST ASSUMED!
SORRY.
AHA HA...
I ACTUALLY GET MISTAKEN FOR A STUDENT PRETTY OFTEN.
HA HA HA...
...

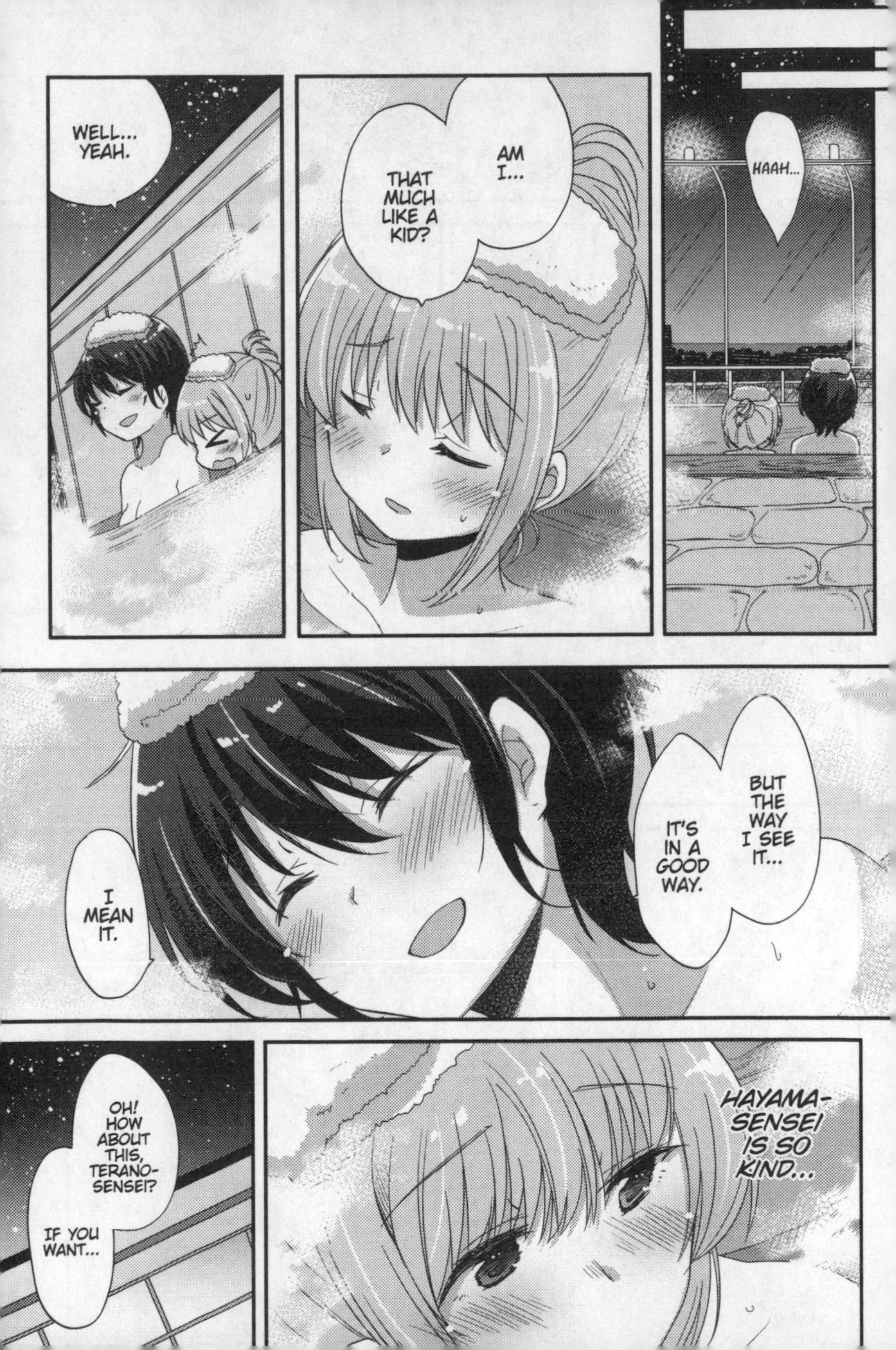
HAAH...
AM I... THAT MUCH LIKE A KID?
WELL... YEAH.
BUT THE WAY I SEE IT... IT'S IN A GOOD WAY.
I MEAN IT.
HAYAMA-SENSEI IS SO KIND...
OH! HOW ABOUT THIS, TERANO-SENSEI?
IF YOU WANT...

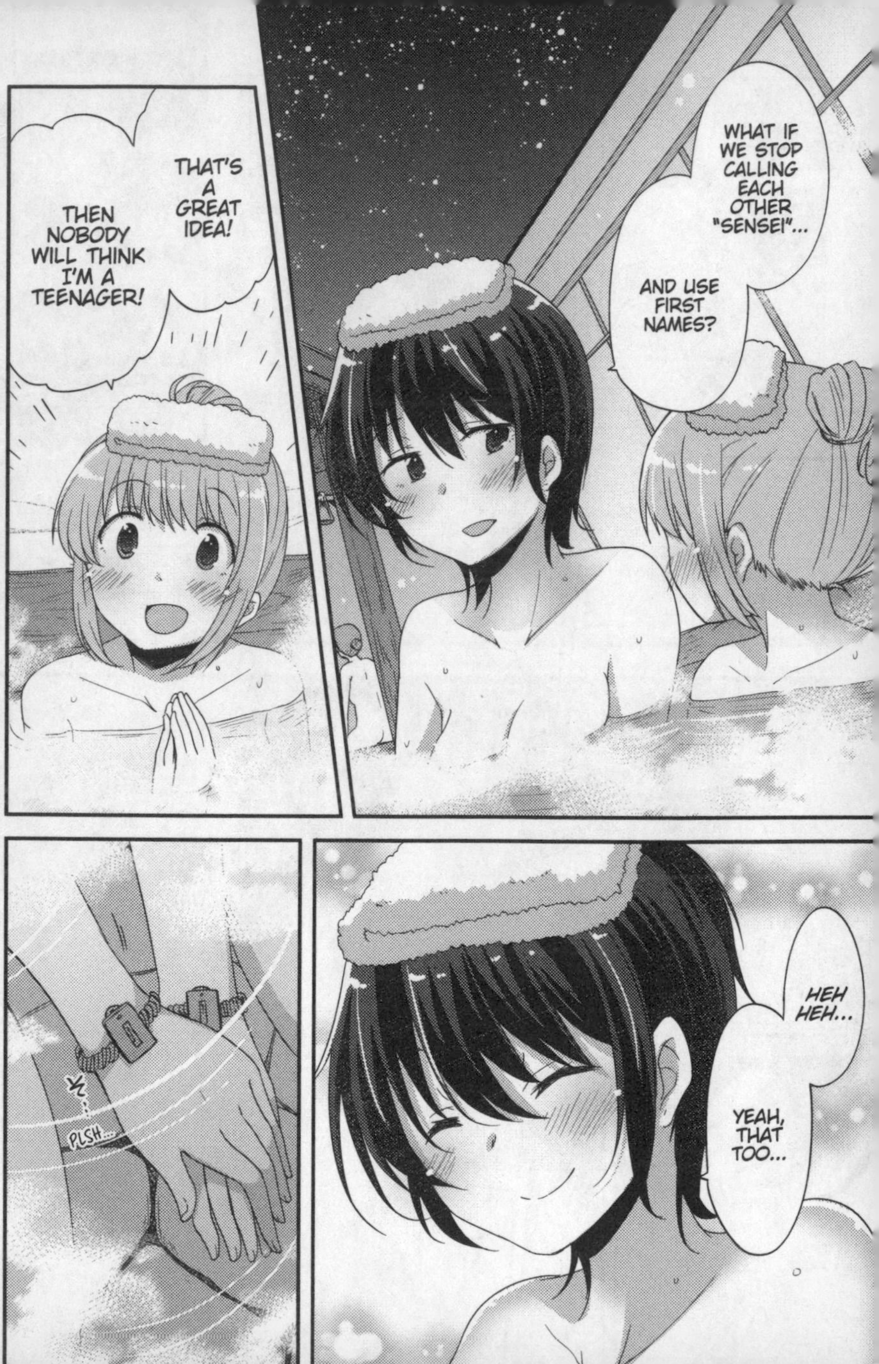
WHAT IF WE STOP CALLING EACH OTHER "SENSEI"...
AND USE FIRST NAMES?
THAT'S A GREAT IDEA!
THEN NOBODY WILL THINK I'M A TEENAGER!
HEH HEH...
YEAH, THAT TOO...
PLSH...

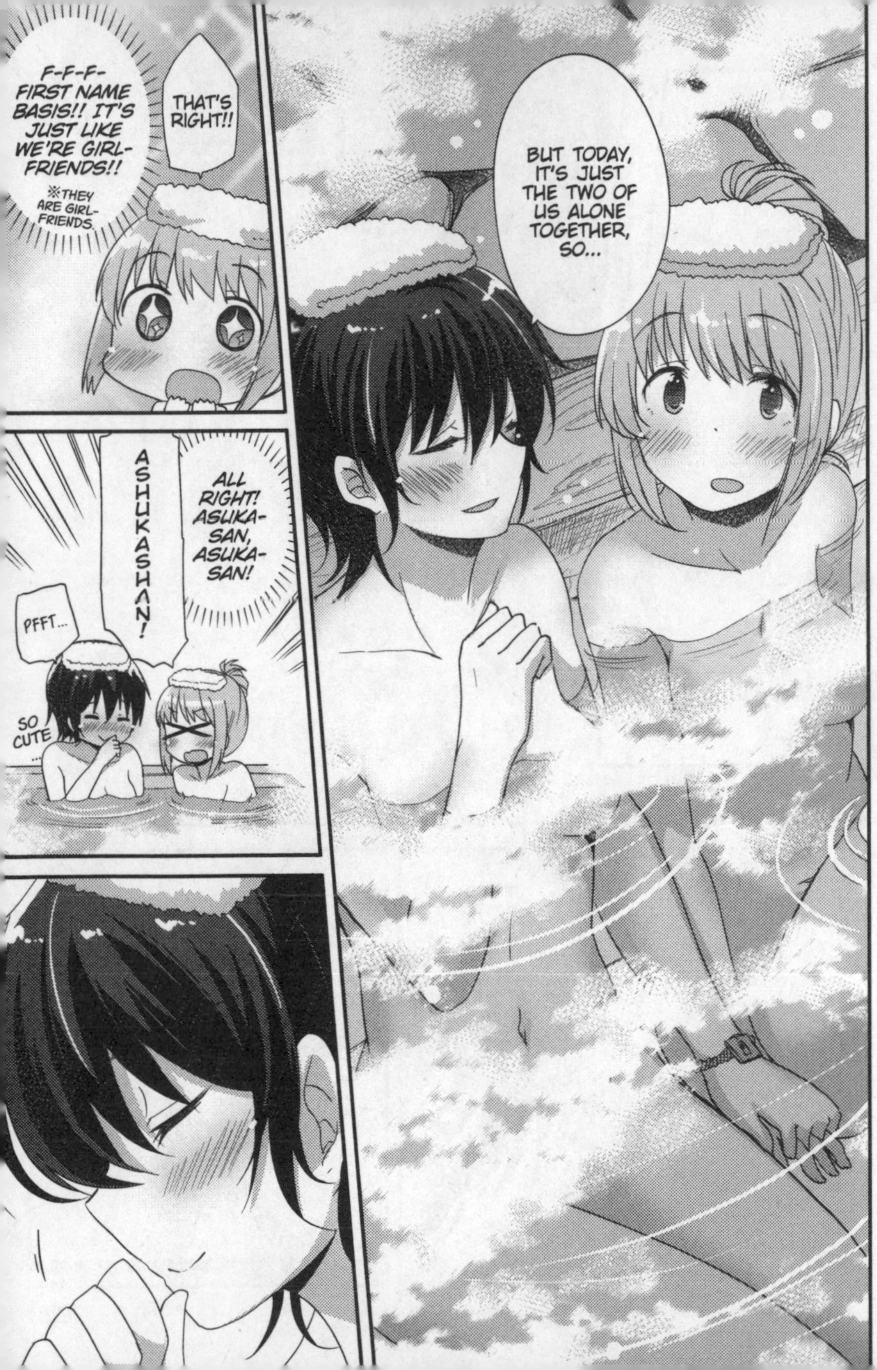
BUT TODAY, IT'S JUST THE TWO OF US ALONE TOGETHER, SO...
THAT'S RIGHT!!
F-F-F-FIRST NAME BASIS!! IT'S JUST LIKE WE'RE GIRL-FRIENDS!!
※THEY ARE GIRL-FRIENDS.
ALL RIGHT! ASUKA-SAN, ASUKA-SAN!
ASHUKASHAN!
PFFT...
SO CUTE...

THMP

HYAH...

SAKI-SAN.

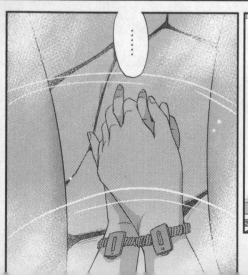

.....

IT'S NICE WE GET TO BE IN THE HOT SPRING TOGETHER, SINCE WE'RE BOTH WOMEN, HUH?

Y-YEAH... I'M GLAD.

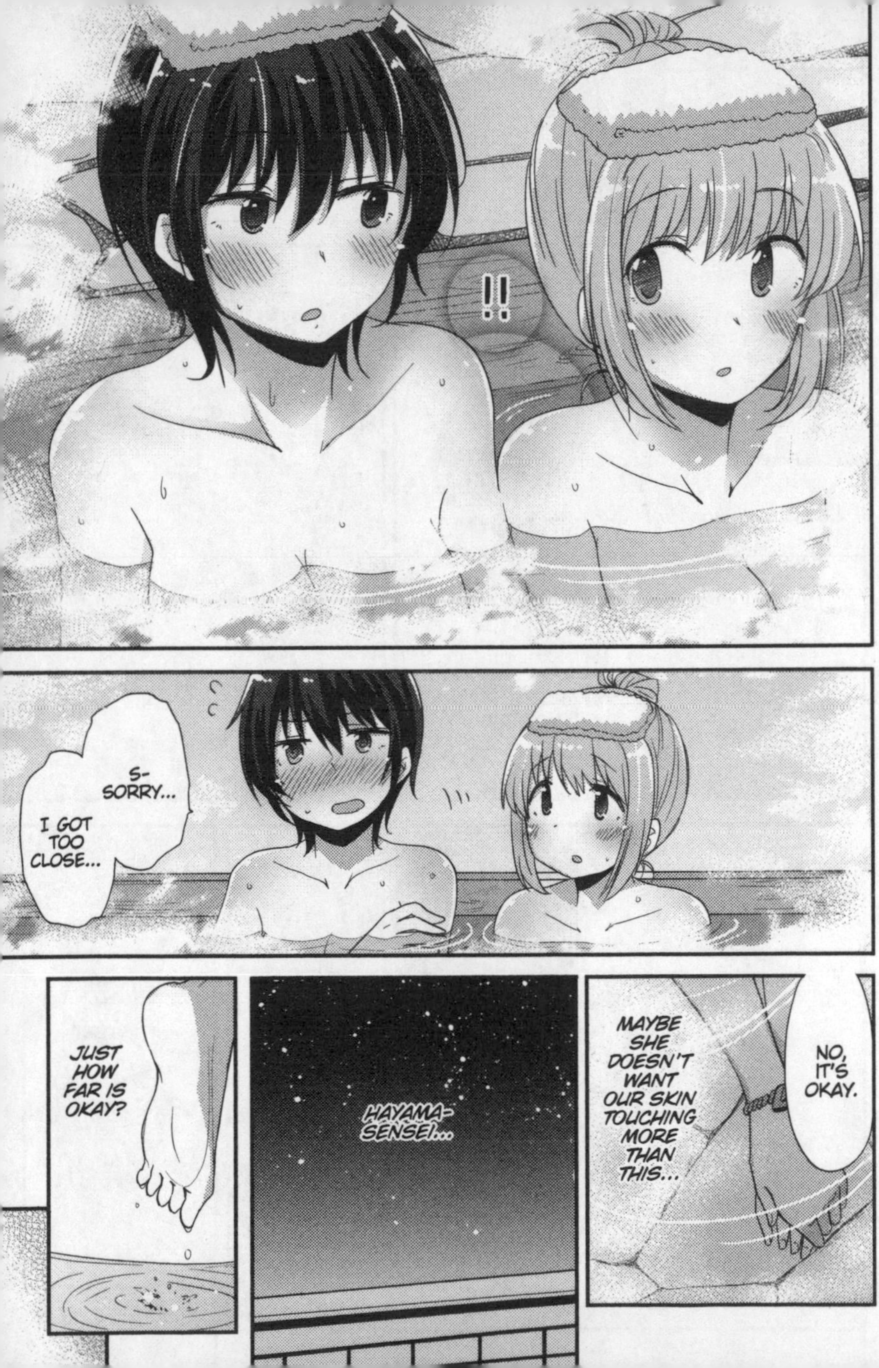
!!
S-SORRY...
I GOT TOO CLOSE...
NO, IT'S OKAY.
MAYBE SHE DOESN'T WANT OUR SKIN TOUCHING MORE THAN THIS...
HAYAMA-SENSEI...
JUST HOW FAR IS OKAY?

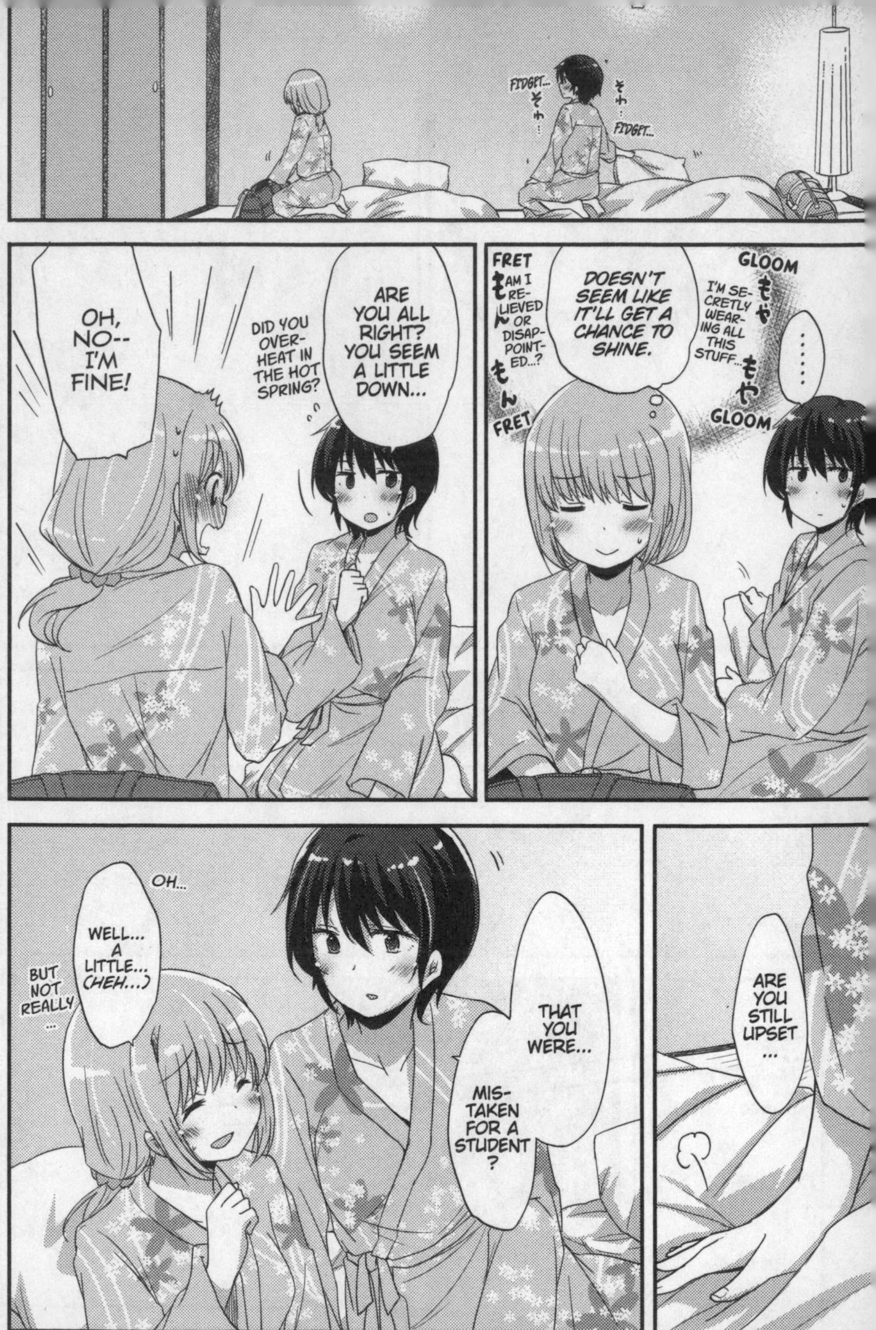
FIDGET...
そわ...
そわ...
FIDGET...
GLOOM
もや
I'M SECRETLY WEARING ALL THIS STUFF...
もや
GLOOM
......
DOESN'T SEEM LIKE IT'LL GET A CHANCE TO SHINE.
FRET
もん
AM I RELIEVED OR DISAPPOINTED...?
もん
FRET
ARE YOU ALL RIGHT? YOU SEEM A LITTLE DOWN...
DID YOU OVERHEAT IN THE HOT SPRING?
OH, NO-- I'M FINE!
ARE YOU STILL UPSET...
THAT YOU WERE...
MISTAKEN FOR A STUDENT?
OH...
WELL... A LITTLE... (HEH...)
BUT NOT REALLY...

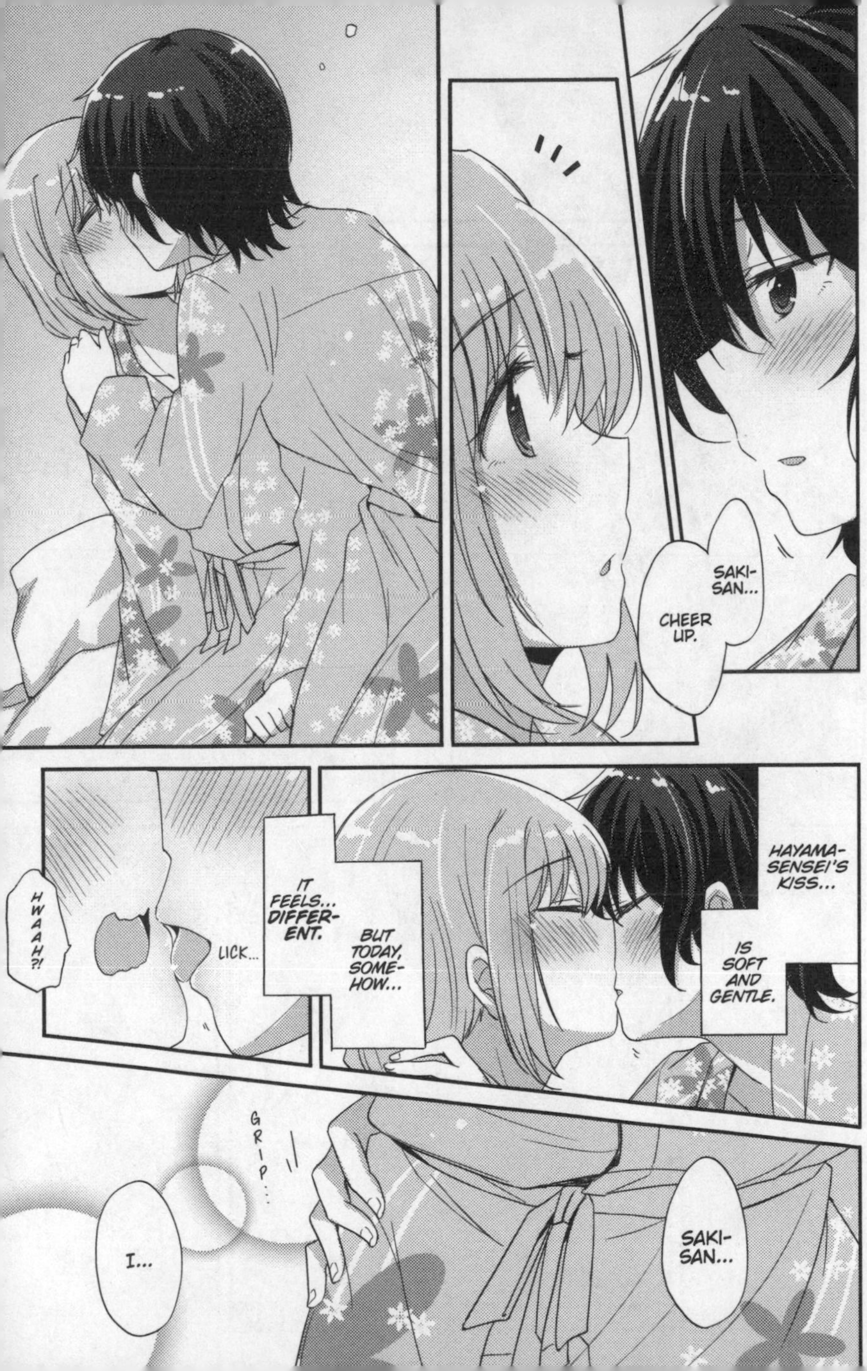
SAKI-SAN...
CHEER UP.
HAYAMA-SENSEI'S KISS...
IS SOFT AND GENTLE.
BUT TODAY, SOMEHOW...
IT FEELS... DIFFER-ENT.
LICK...
HWAAAH?!
SAKI-SAN...
GRIP...
I...

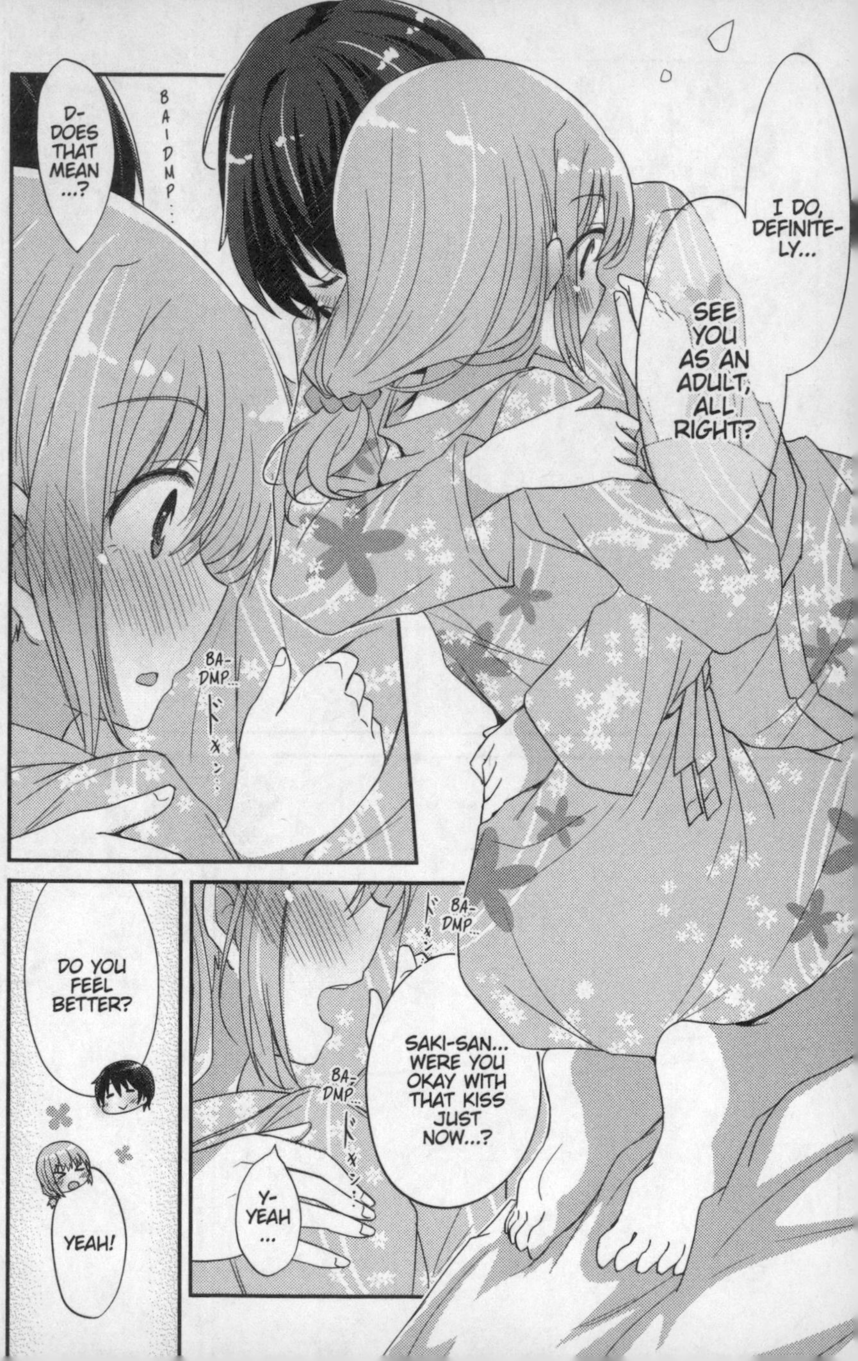
I DO, DEFINITELY...
SEE YOU AS AN ADULT, ALL RIGHT?
BA-DMP...
D-DOES THAT MEAN...?
BA-DMP...
ドキン…
BA-DMP...
ドキン…
SAKI-SAN... WERE YOU OKAY WITH THAT KISS JUST NOW...?
BA-DMP...
ドキン…
Y-YEAH...
DO YOU FEEL BETTER?
YEAH!

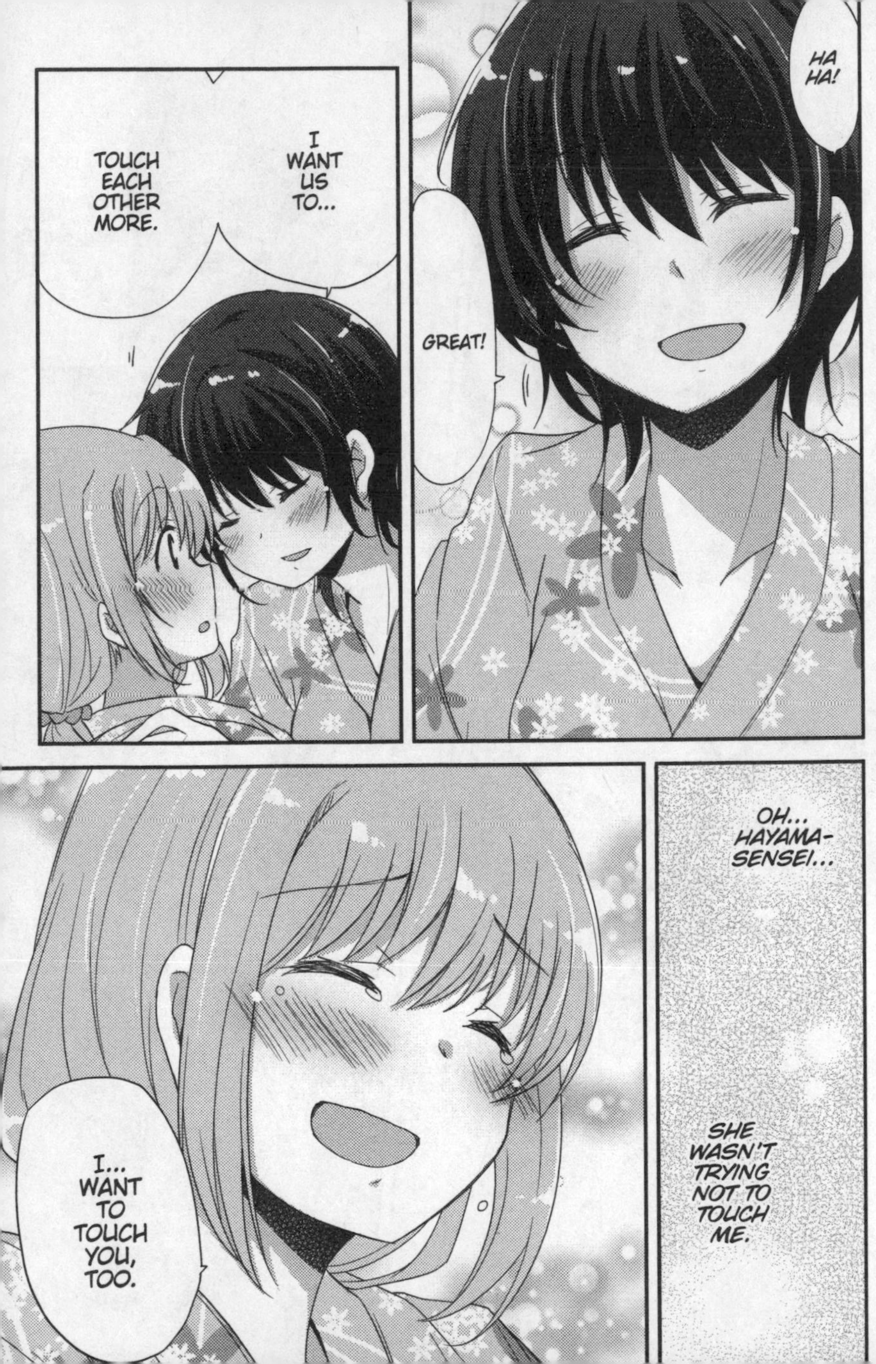
HA HA!
GREAT!
I WANT US TO...
TOUCH EACH OTHER MORE.
OH... HAYAMA-SENSEI...
SHE WASN'T TRYING NOT TO TOUCH ME.
I... WANT TO TOUCH YOU, TOO.

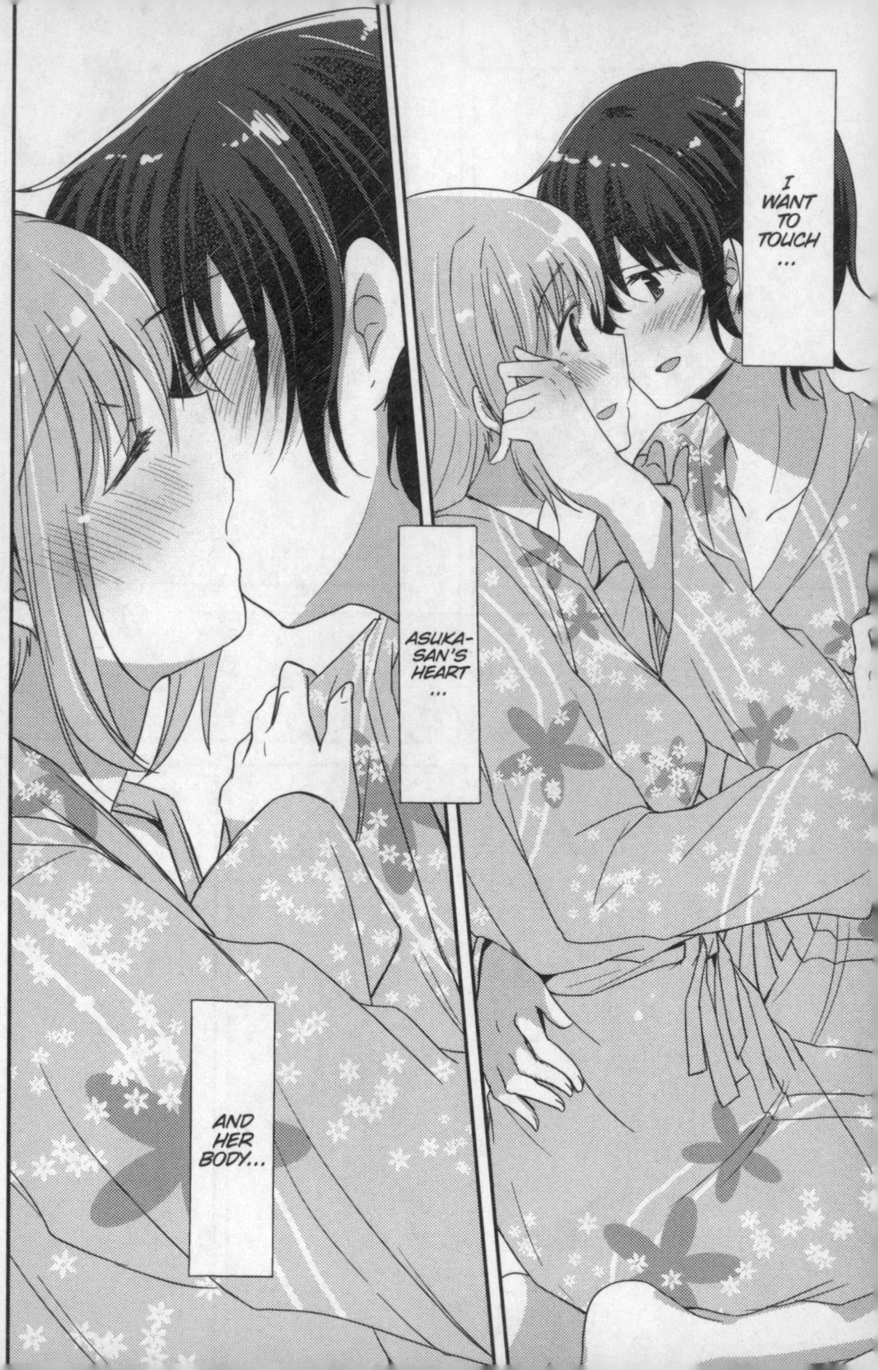
I WANT TO TOUCH ...
ASUKA-SAN'S HEART ...
AND HER BODY...

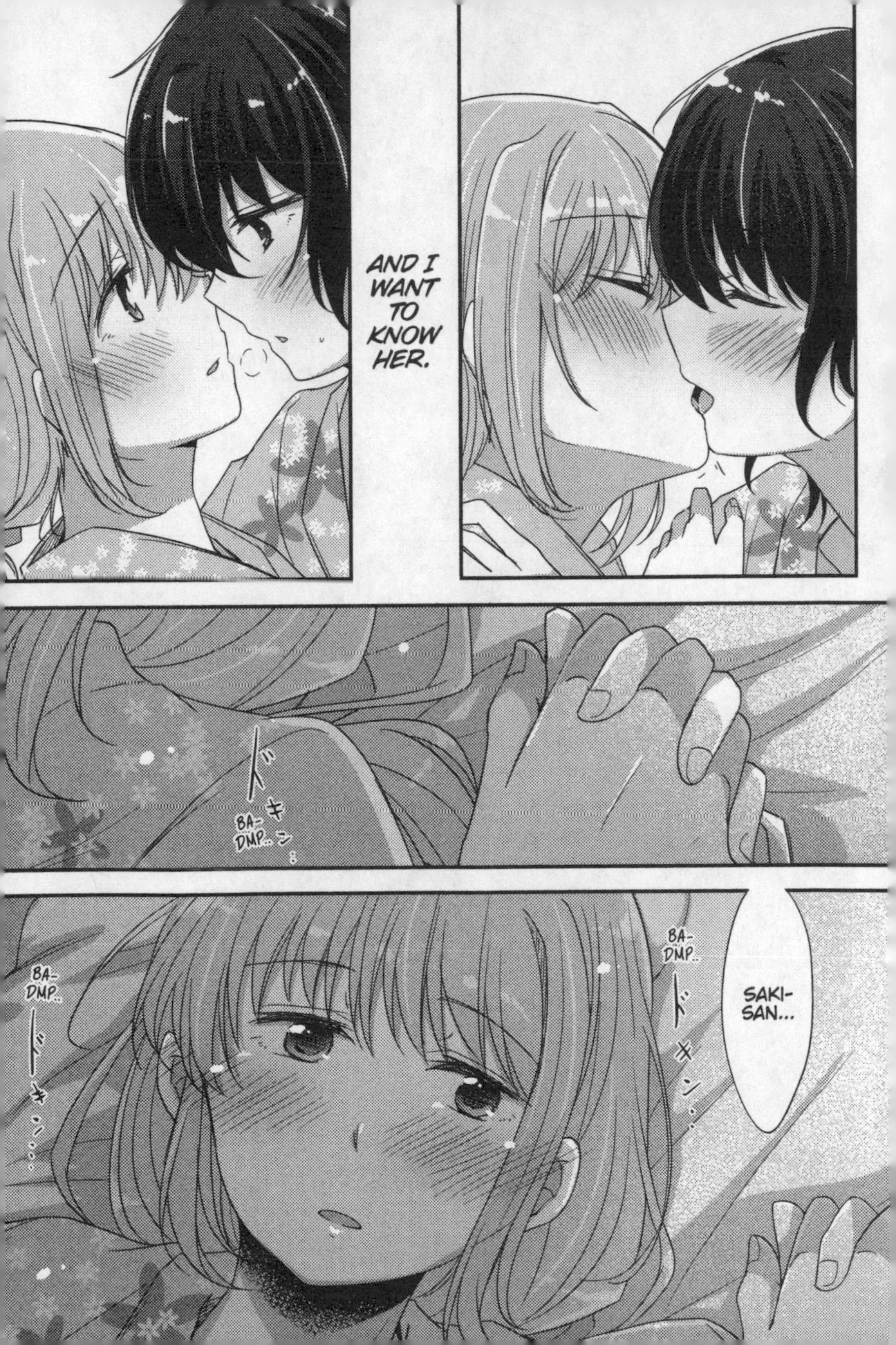
AND I WANT TO KNOW HER.
ドキン…
BA-DMP…
SAKI-SAN...
BA-DMP..
ドキン・・
BA-DMP..
ドキン・・・

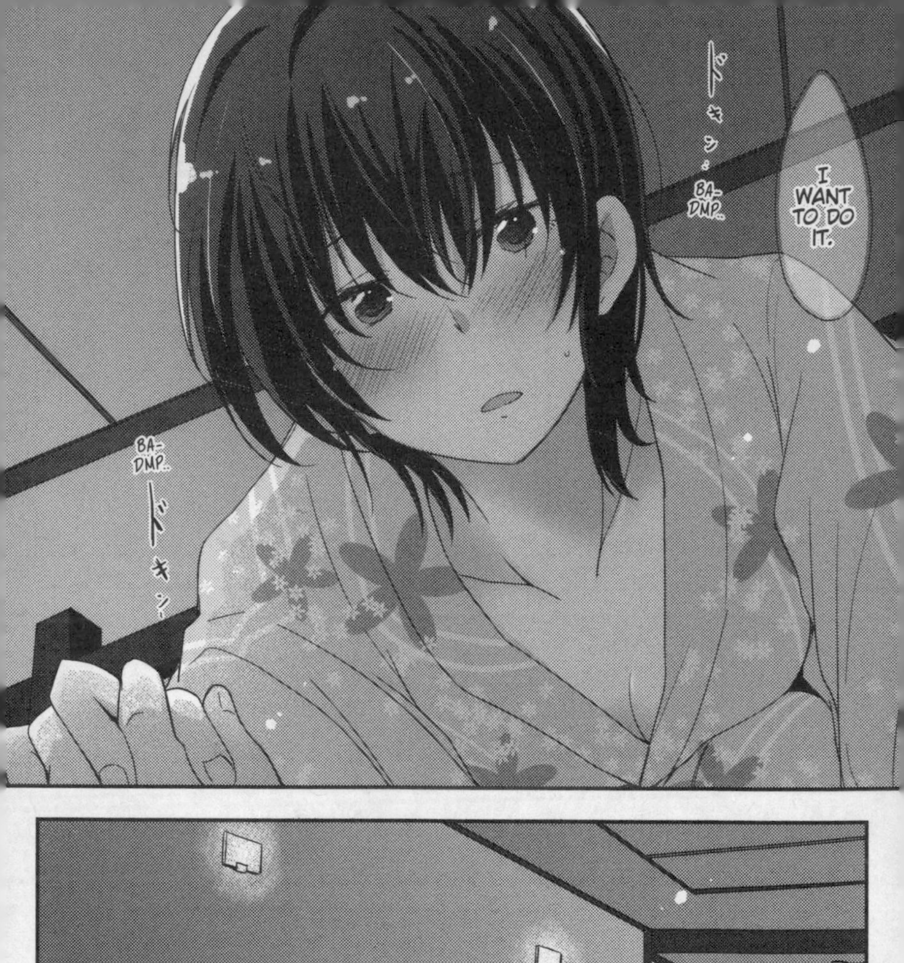
I WANT TO DO IT.
ドキン
BA-DMP...
BA-DMP...
ドキン

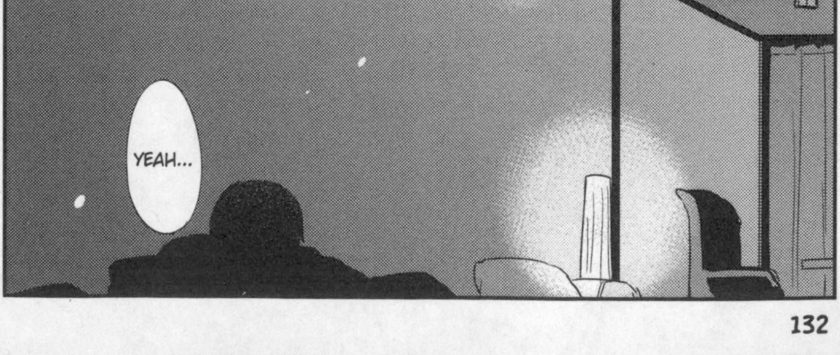
YEAH...

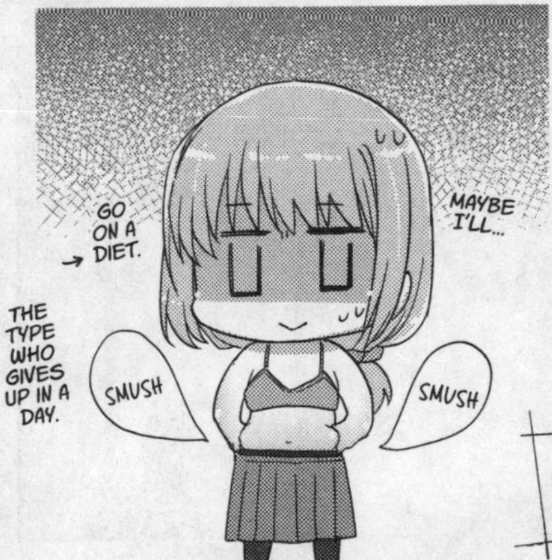
MAYBE I'LL...
GO ON A DIET.
SMUSH
SMUSH
THE TYPE WHO GIVES UP IN A DAY.

OUR TEACHERS ARE DATING

Our Teachers are Dating!

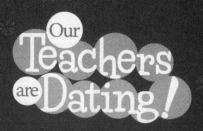

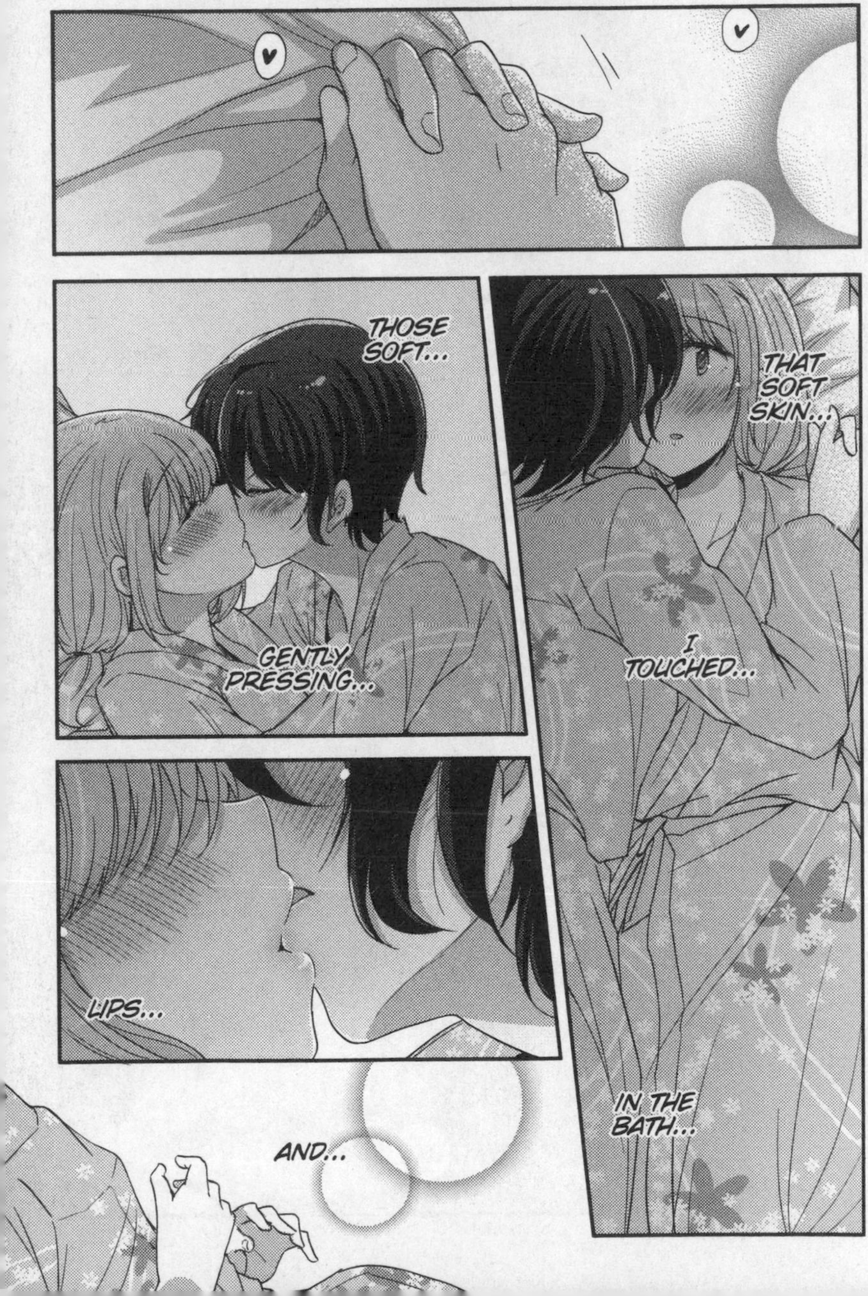
THAT SOFT SKIN...
I TOUCHED...
IN THE BATH...
THOSE SOFT...
GENTLY PRESSING...
LIPS...
AND...

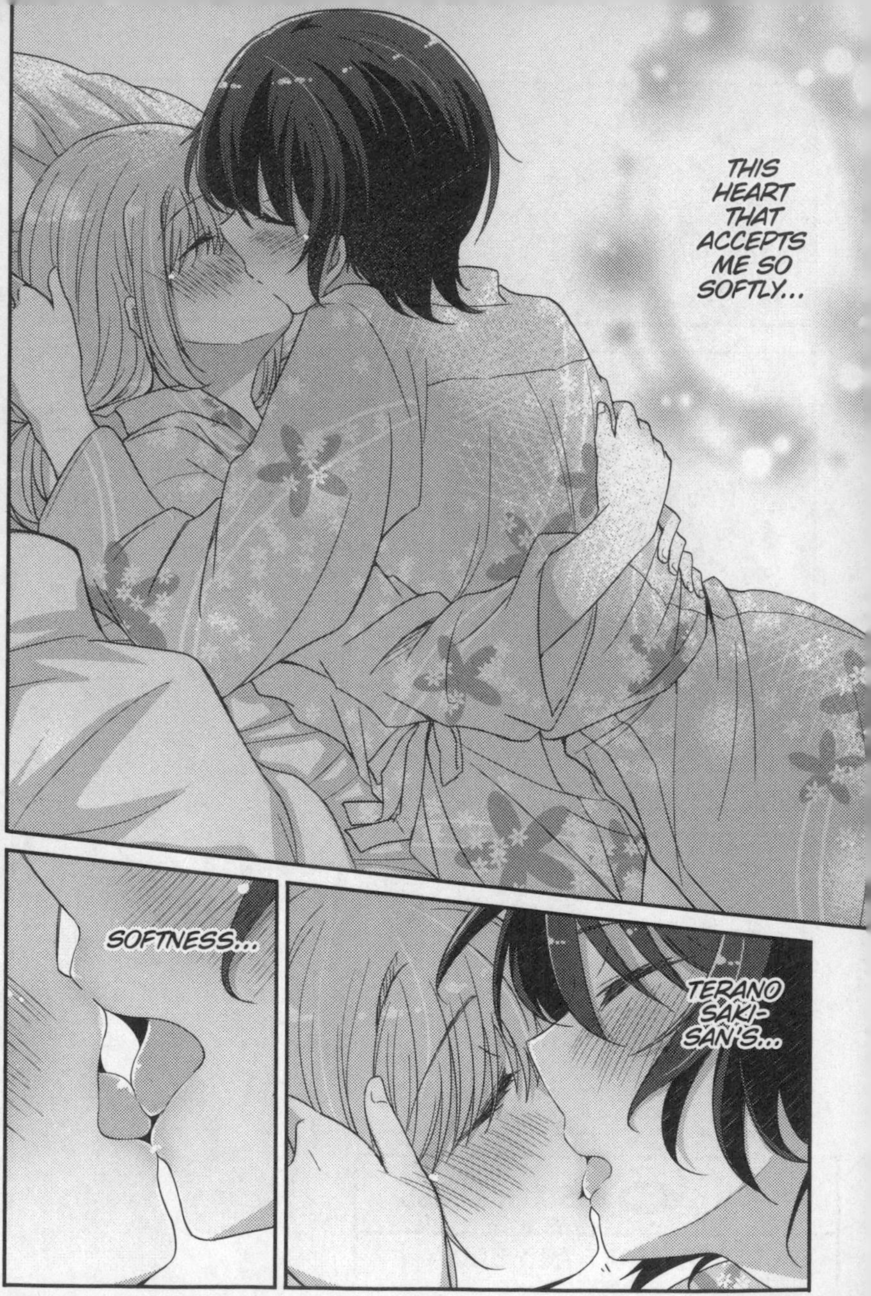
THIS HEART THAT ACCEPTS ME SO SOFTLY...
TERANO SAKI-SAN'S...
SOFTNESS...

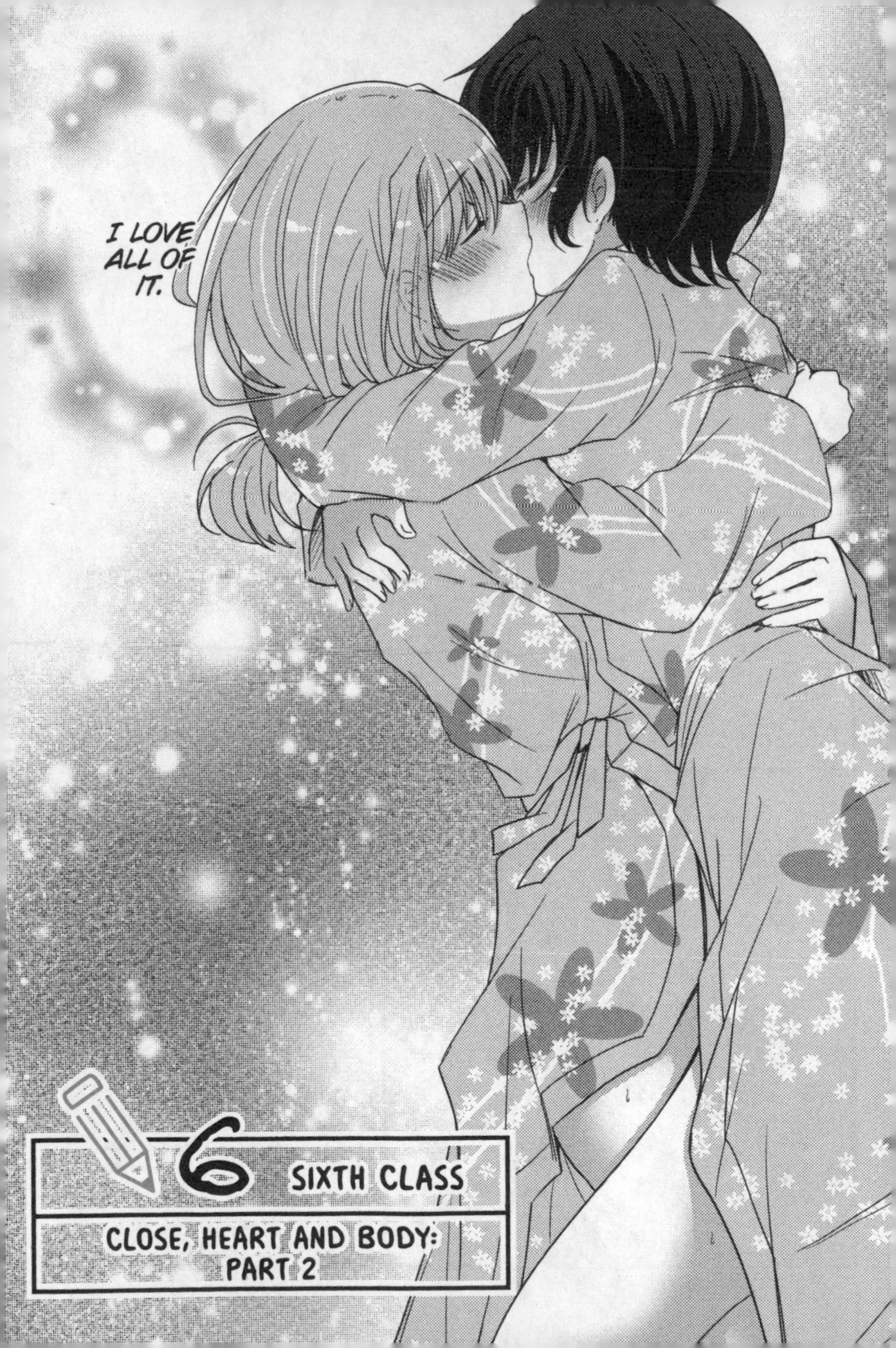
I LOVE ALL OF IT.
6 SIXTH CLASS
CLOSE, HEART AND BODY: PART 2

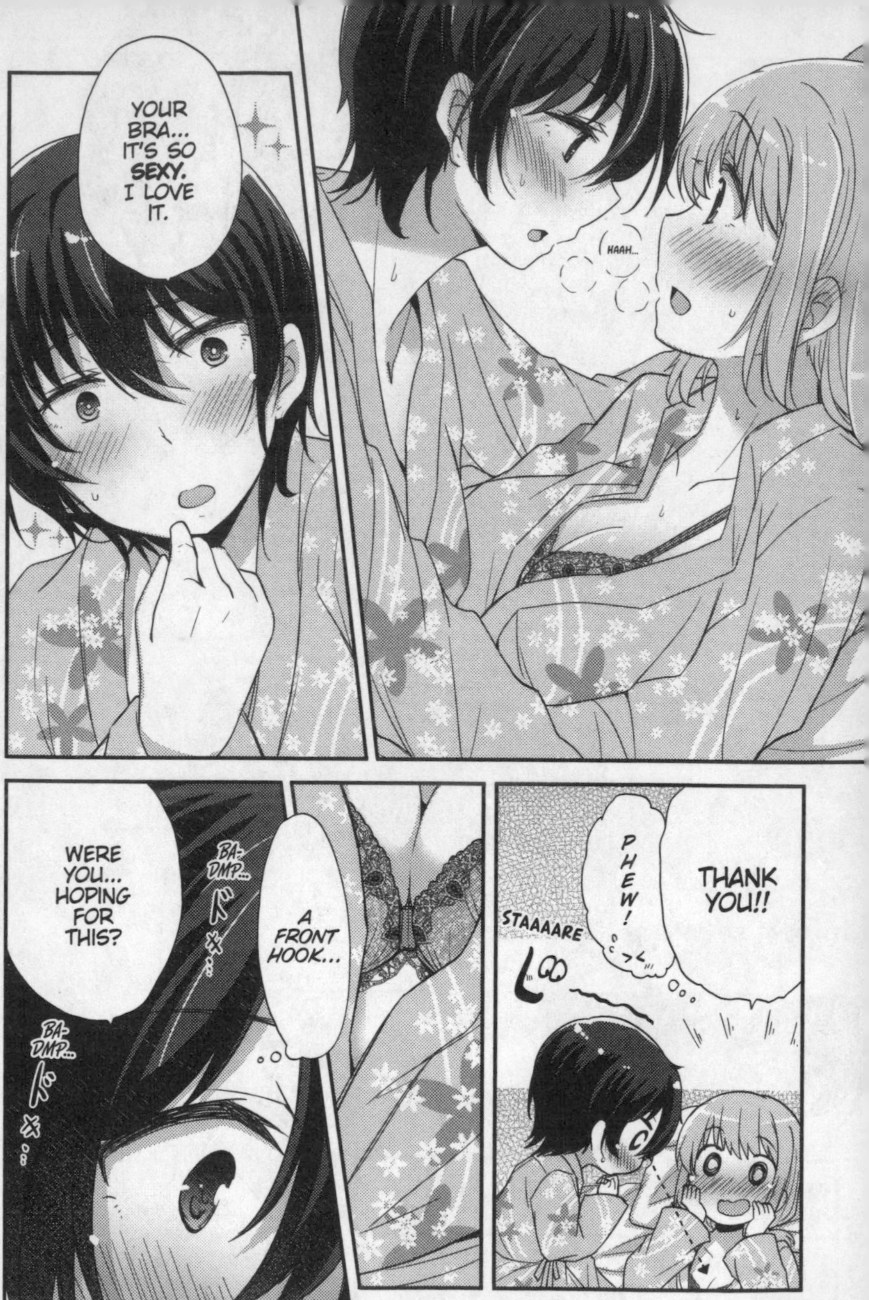
HAAH...
YOUR BRA... IT'S SO SEXY. I LOVE IT.
THANK YOU!!
PHEW! >_<
STAAAARE
A FRONT HOOK...
BA-DMP... ドキ…
WERE YOU... HOPING FOR THIS?
BA-DMP... ドキ…

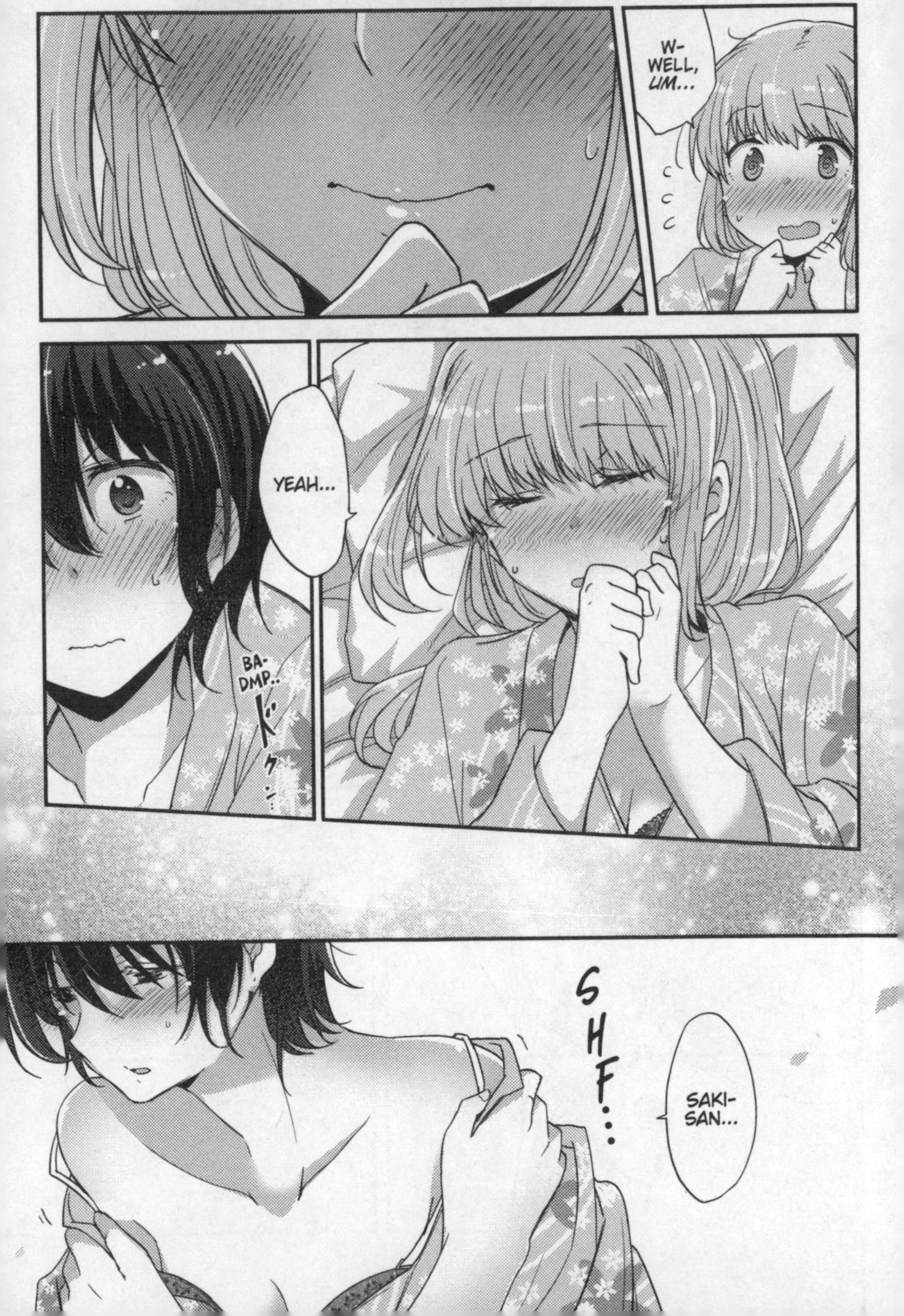
W-WELL, UM...
YEAH...
BA-DMP..
SHF...
SAKI-SAN...

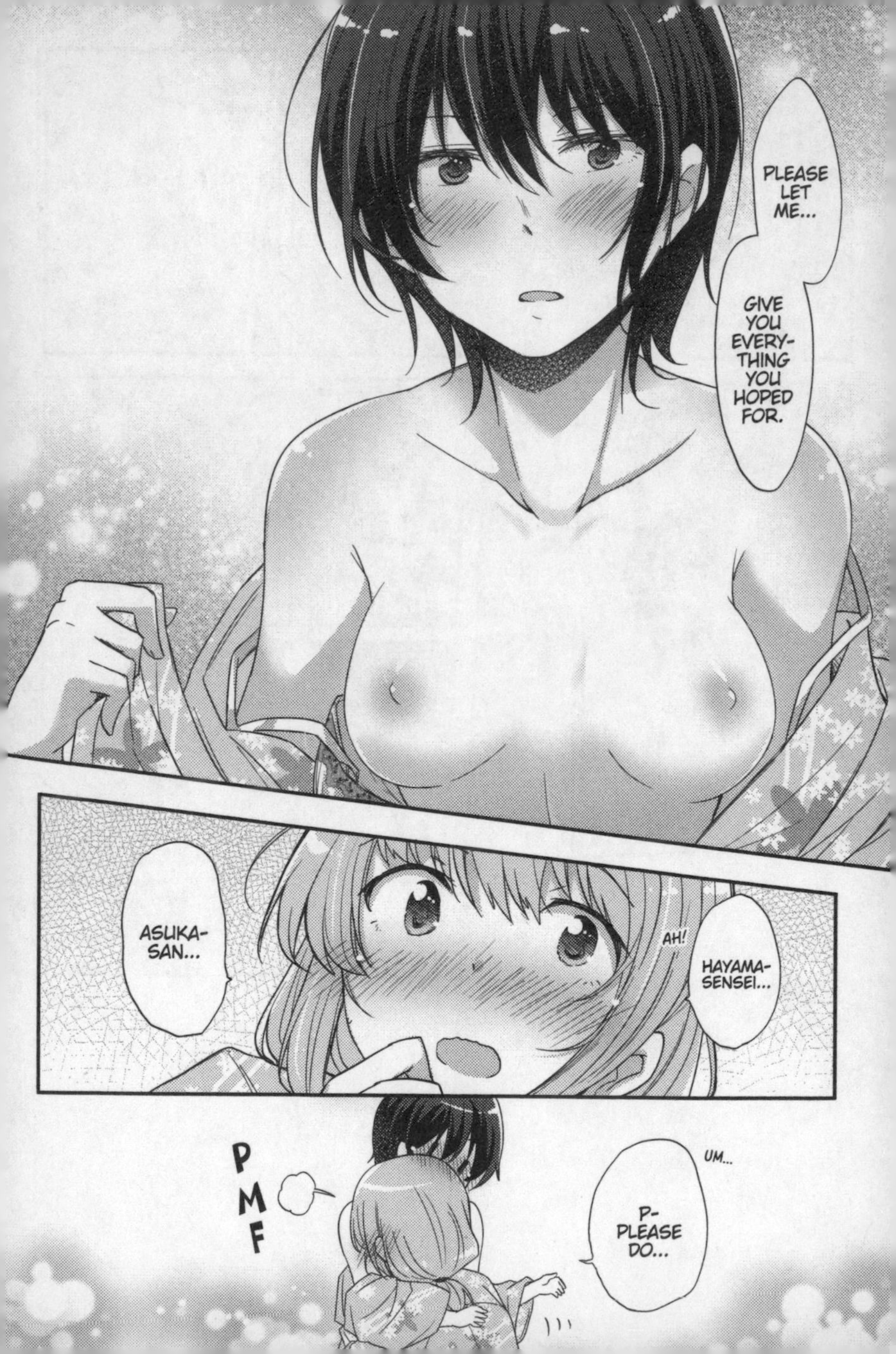
PLEASE LET ME...
GIVE YOU EVERY-THING YOU HOPED FOR.
AH!
HAYAMA-SENSEI...
ASUKA-SAN...
UM...
P-PLEASE DO...
PMF

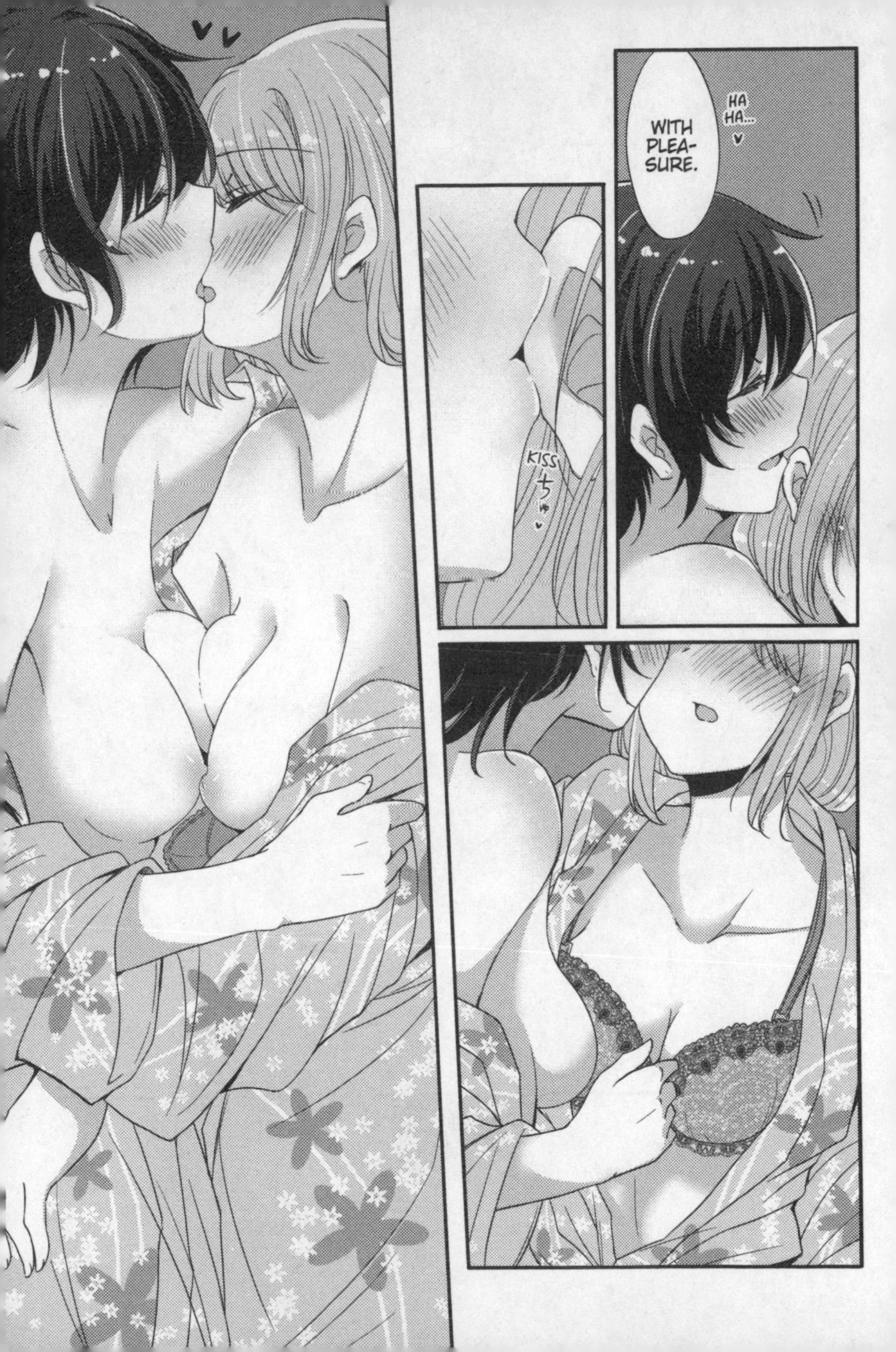
HA HA... ♥
WITH PLEASURE.
KISS ちゅ ♥

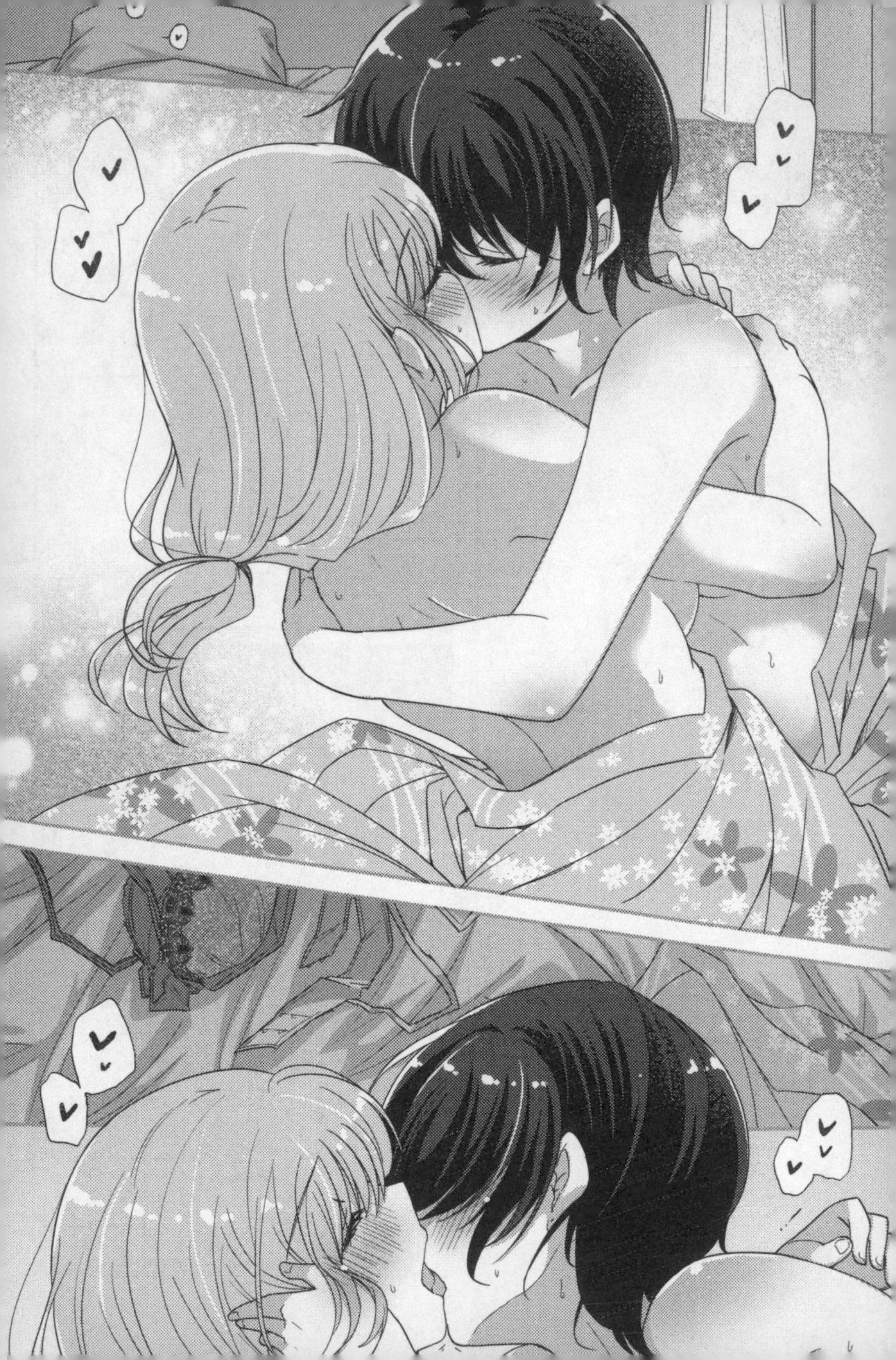

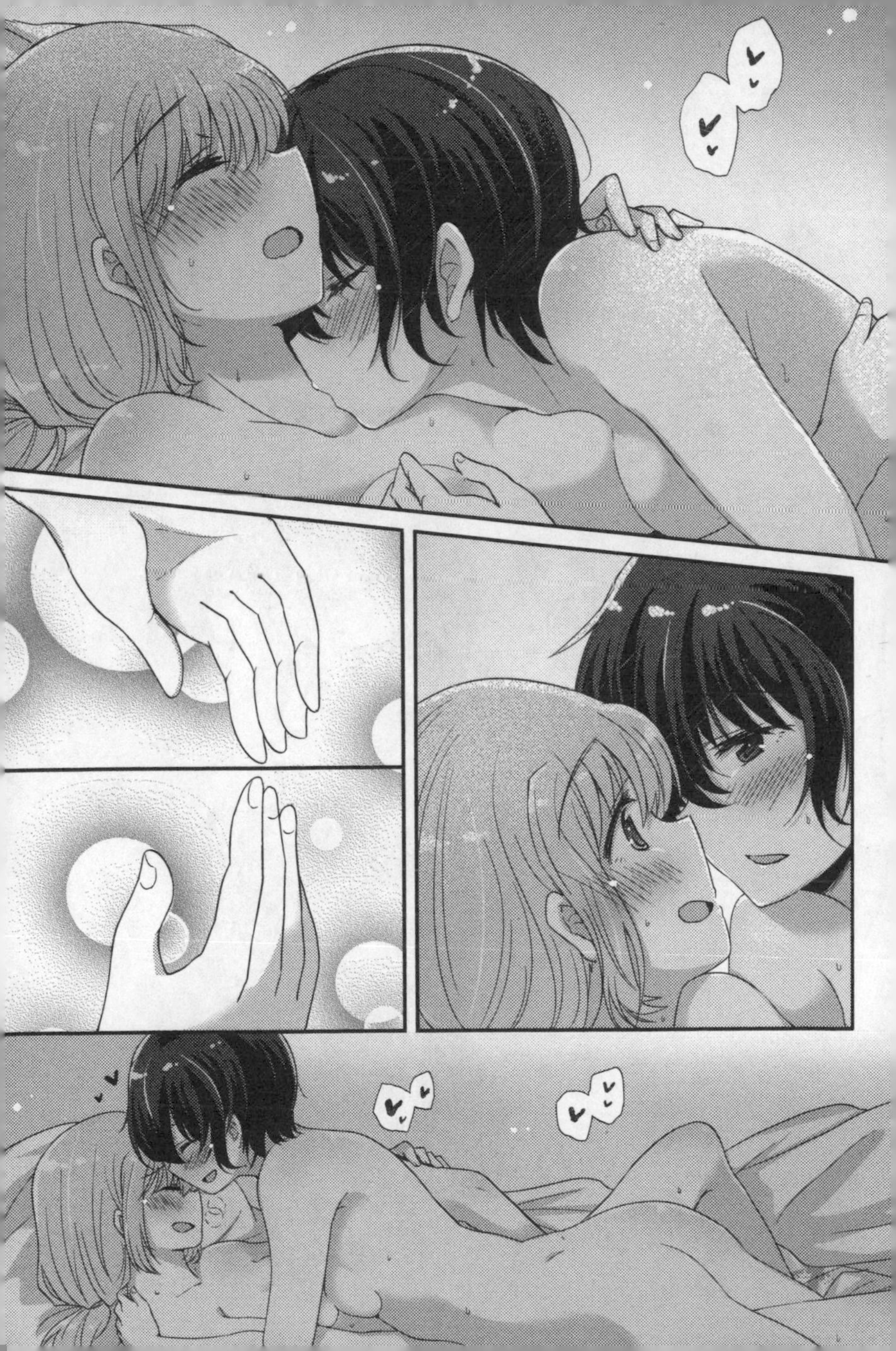

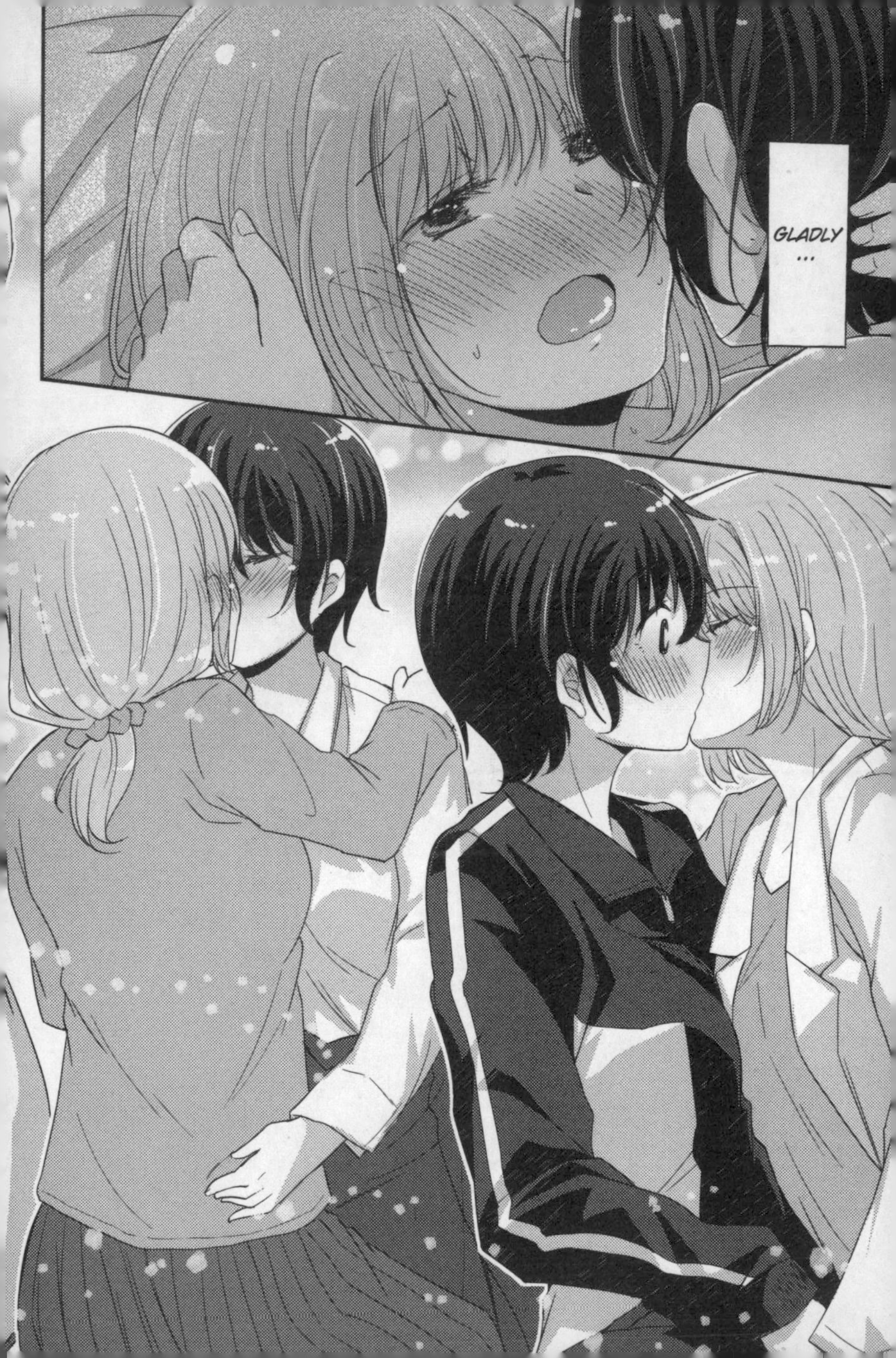
GLADLY ...

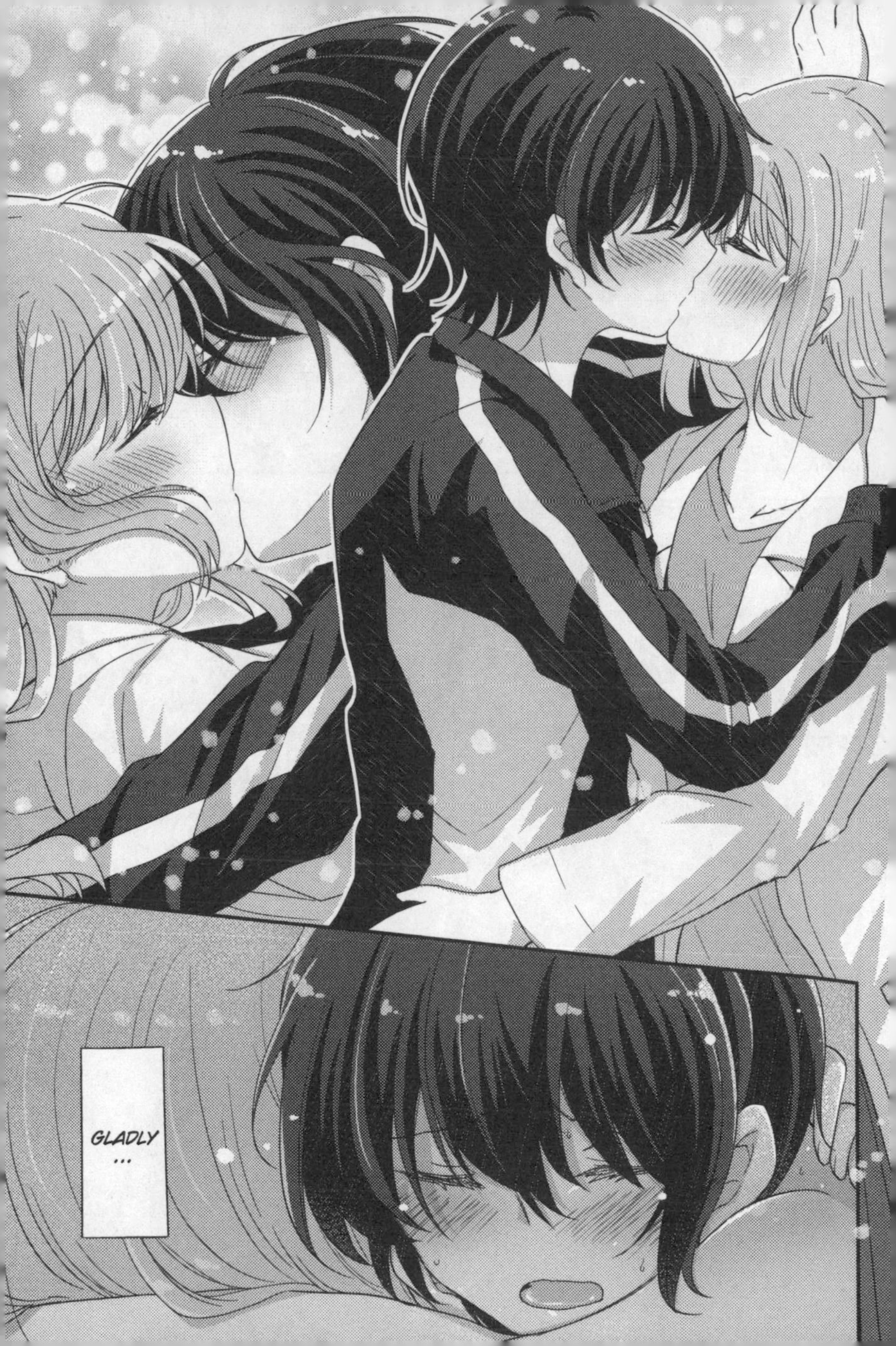
GLADLY
...

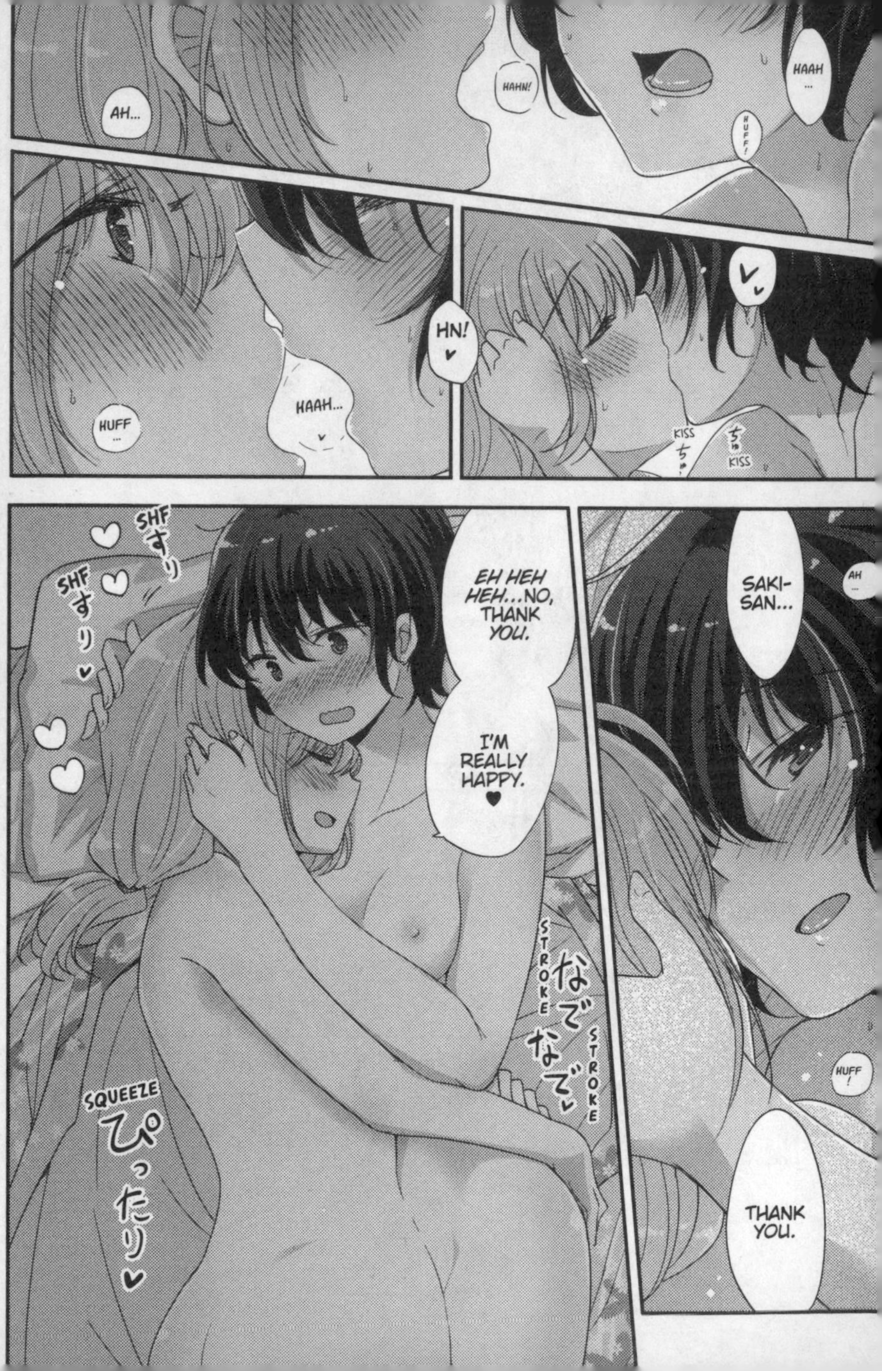
HAAH ...
HUFF!
HAHN!
AH...
HN! ♥
KISS ちゅ
ちゅ KISS
HAAH... ♥
HUFF ...
SAKI-SAN...
AH ...
HUFF!
THANK YOU.
EH HEH HEH...NO, THANK YOU.
I'M REALLY HAPPY. ♥
SHF すり
SHF すりっ
STROKE なで
なで STROKE
SQUEEZE ぴったり

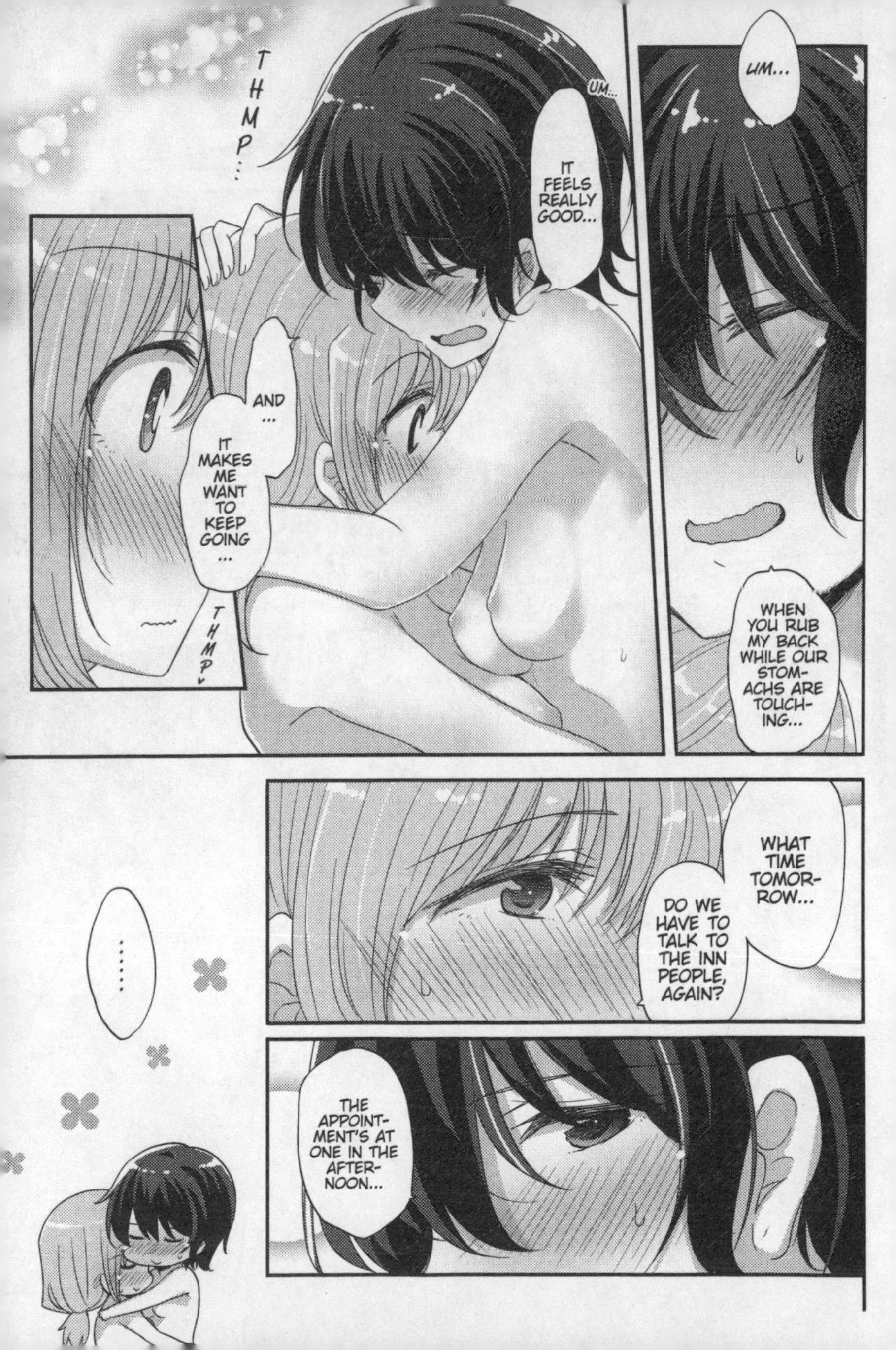

UM...
WHEN YOU RUB MY BACK WHILE OUR STOMACHS ARE TOUCHING...
UM...
IT FEELS REALLY GOOD...
THMP...
AND...
IT MAKES ME WANT TO KEEP GOING...
THMP
WHAT TIME TOMORROW...
DO WE HAVE TO TALK TO THE INN PEOPLE, AGAIN?
THE APPOINTMENT'S AT ONE IN THE AFTERNOON...
......

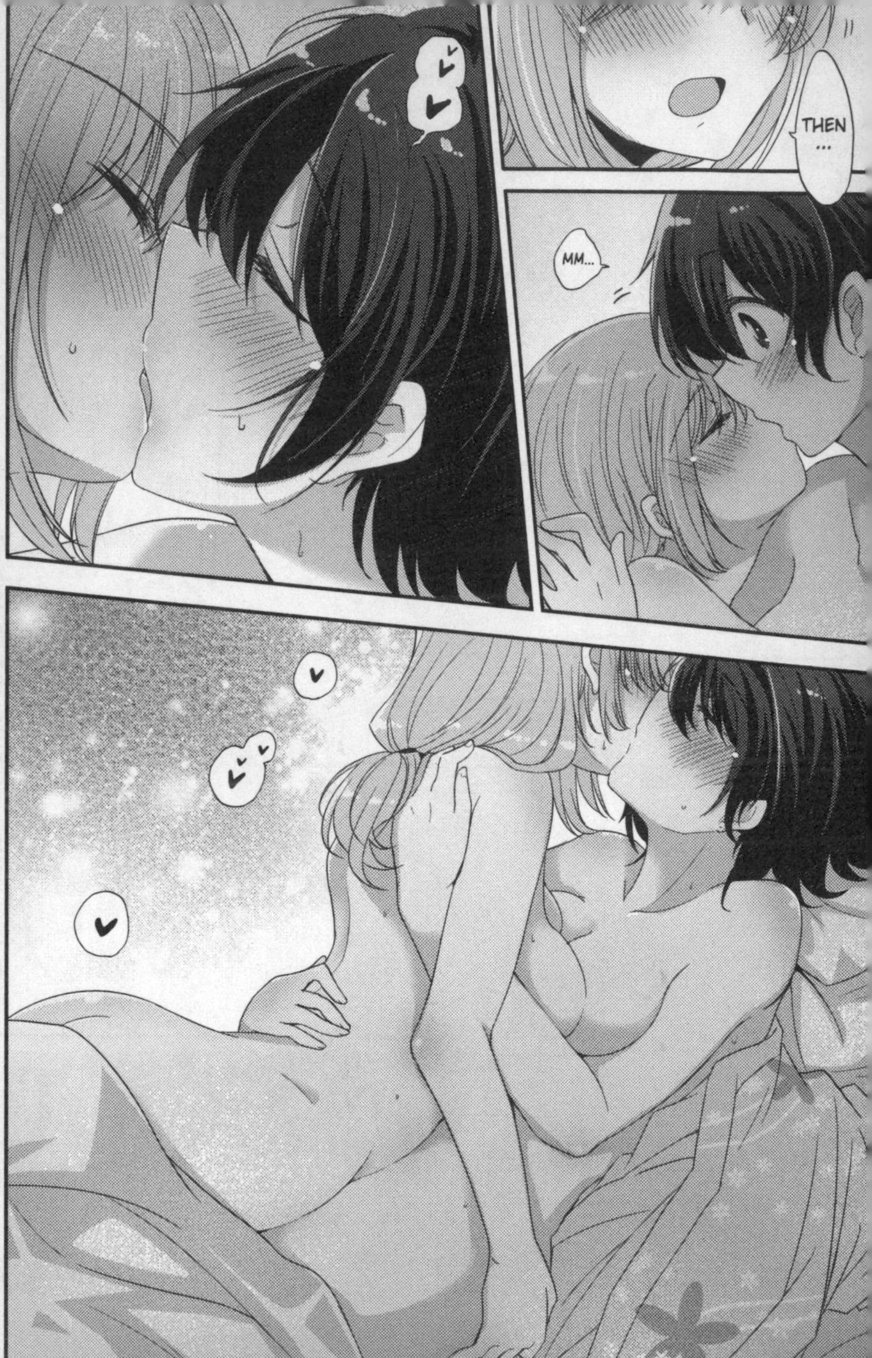
THEN ...
MM...

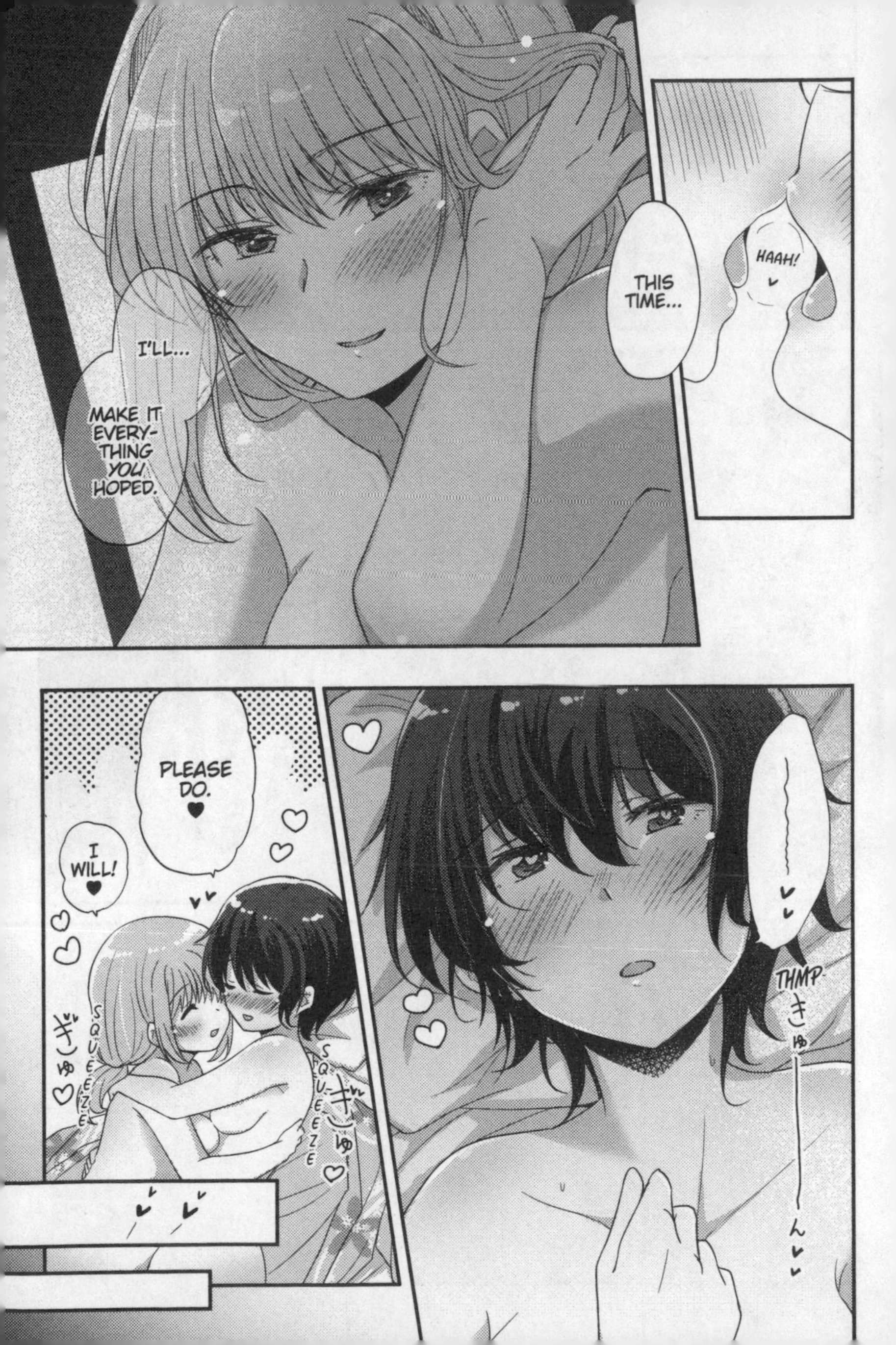
HAAH!
THIS TIME...
I'LL...
MAKE IT EVERYTHING YOU HOPED.
......
THMP
きゅーーん
PLEASE DO.
I WILL!
SQUEEZE
ぎゅ
SQUEEZE
ぎゅ

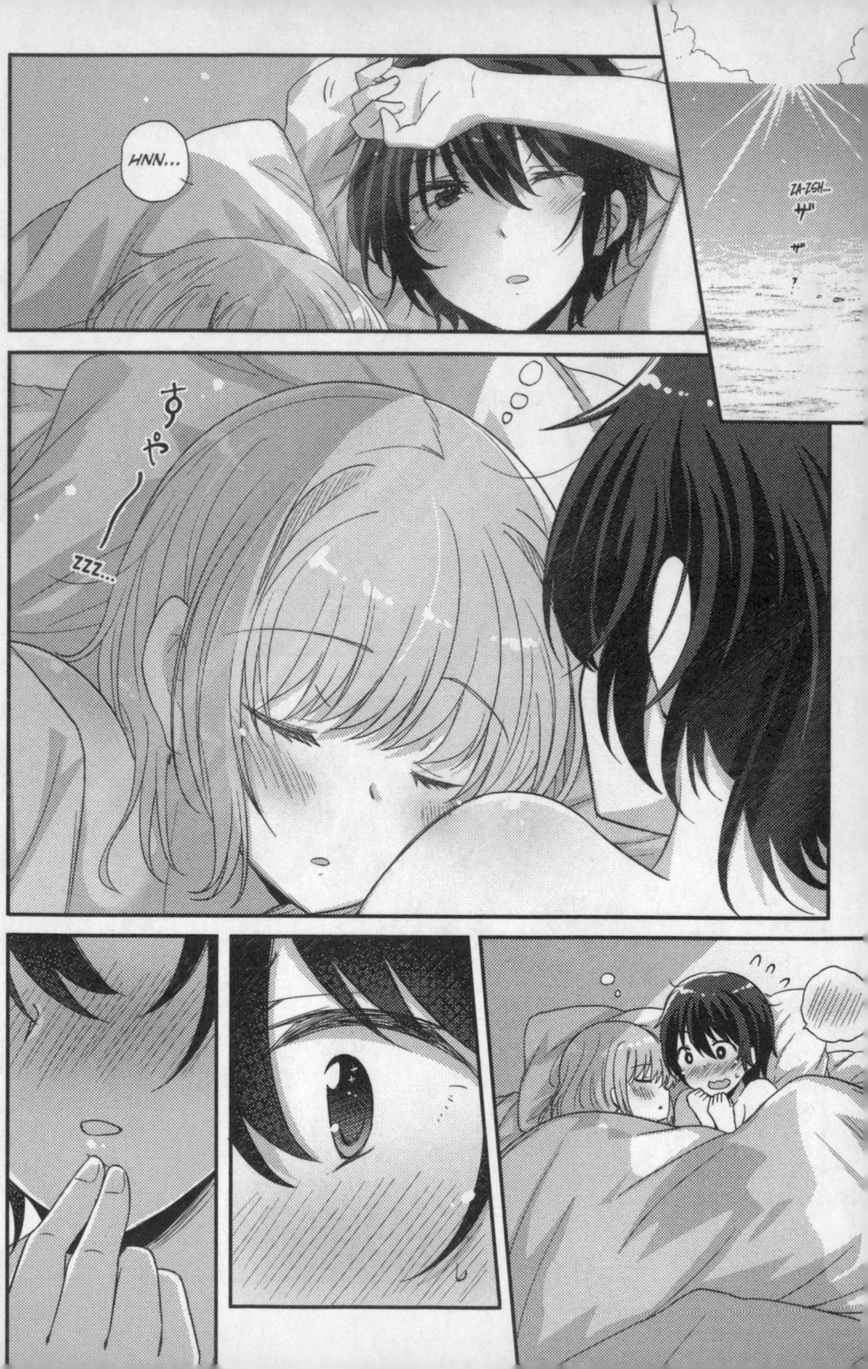
ZA-ZSH...
ザ
ザ
HNN...
すやーー
ZZZ...

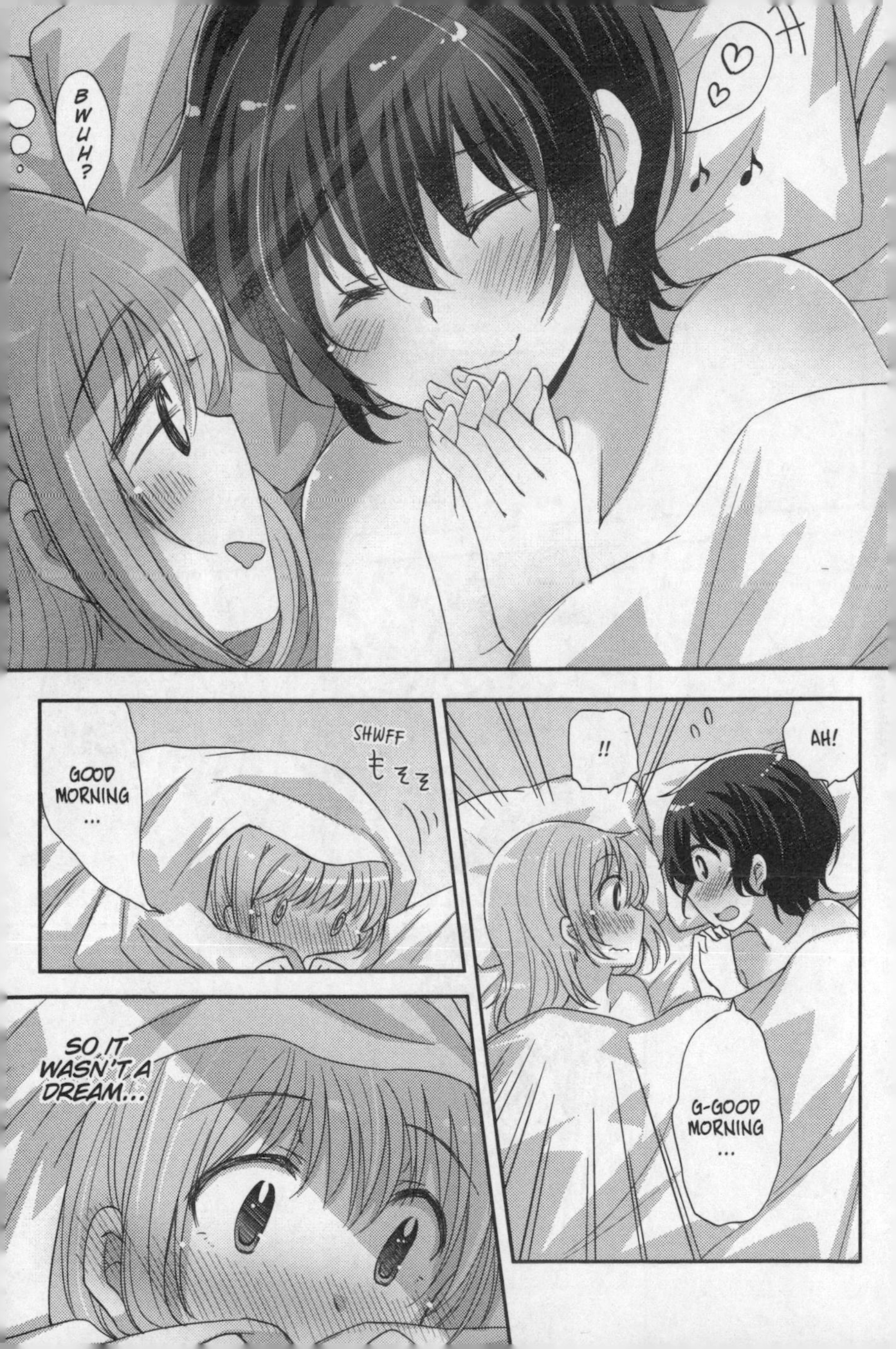

BWUH?
AH!
!!
G-GOOD MORNING ...
SHWFF
もぞぞ
GOOD MORNING ...
SO IT WASN'T A DREAM...

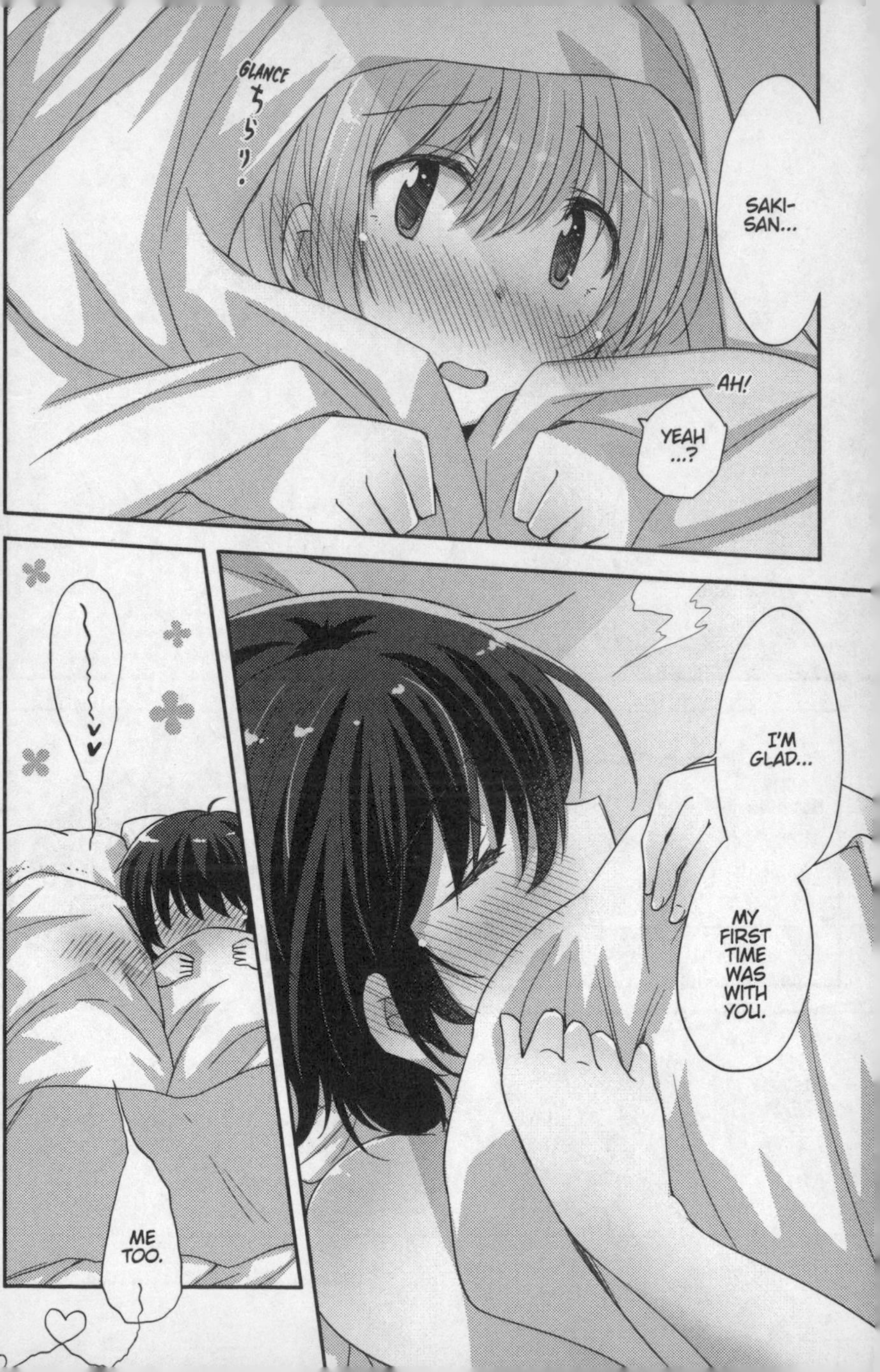
SAKI-SAN...
GLANCE
ちらり。
AH!
YEAH ...?
I'M GLAD...
MY FIRST TIME WAS WITH YOU.
ME TOO.

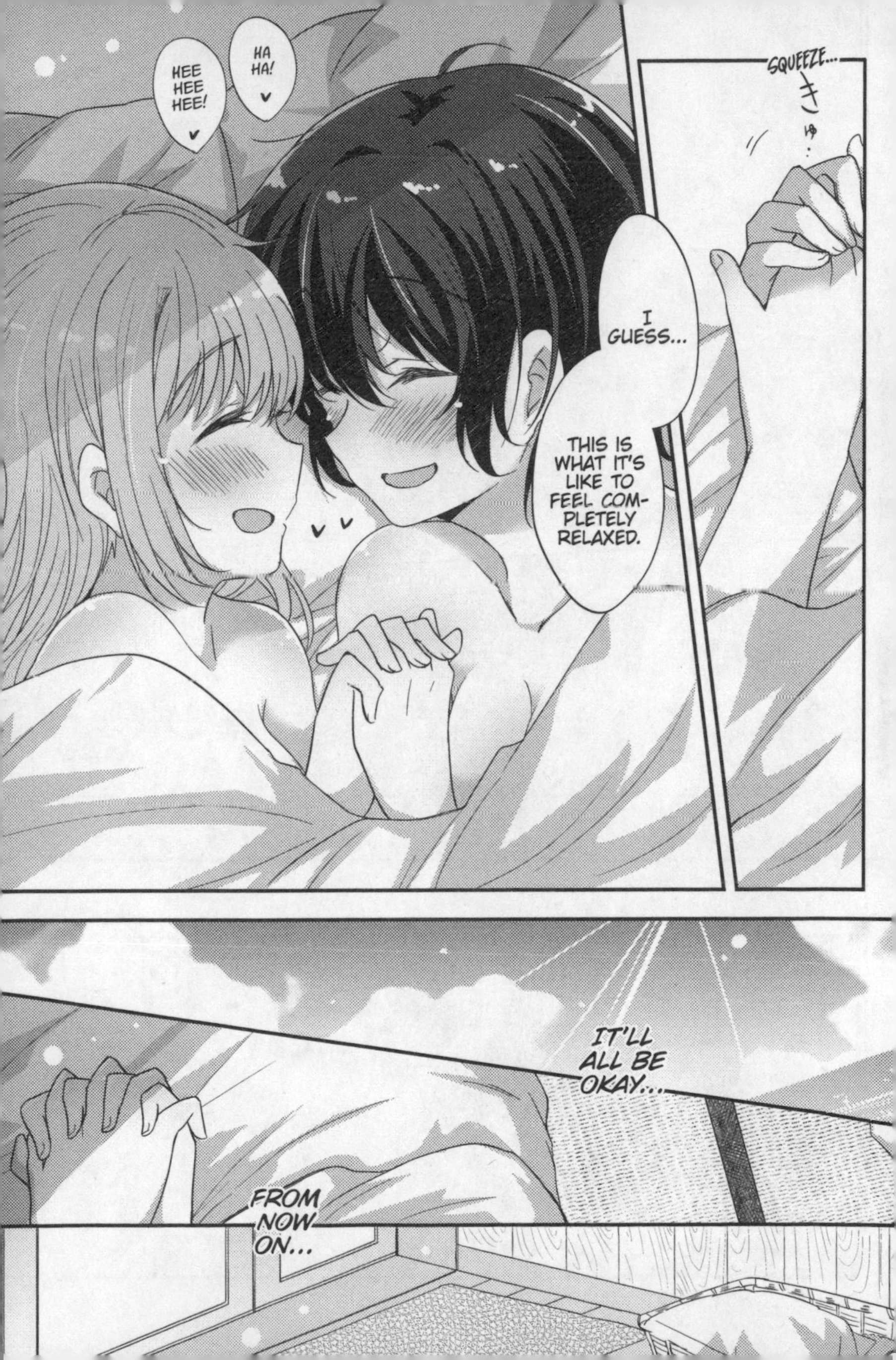
SQUEEZE...
きゅ…
HA HA!
HEE HEE HEE!
I GUESS...
THIS IS WHAT IT'S LIKE TO FEEL COMPLETELY RELAXED.
IT'LL ALL BE OKAY...
FROM NOW ON...

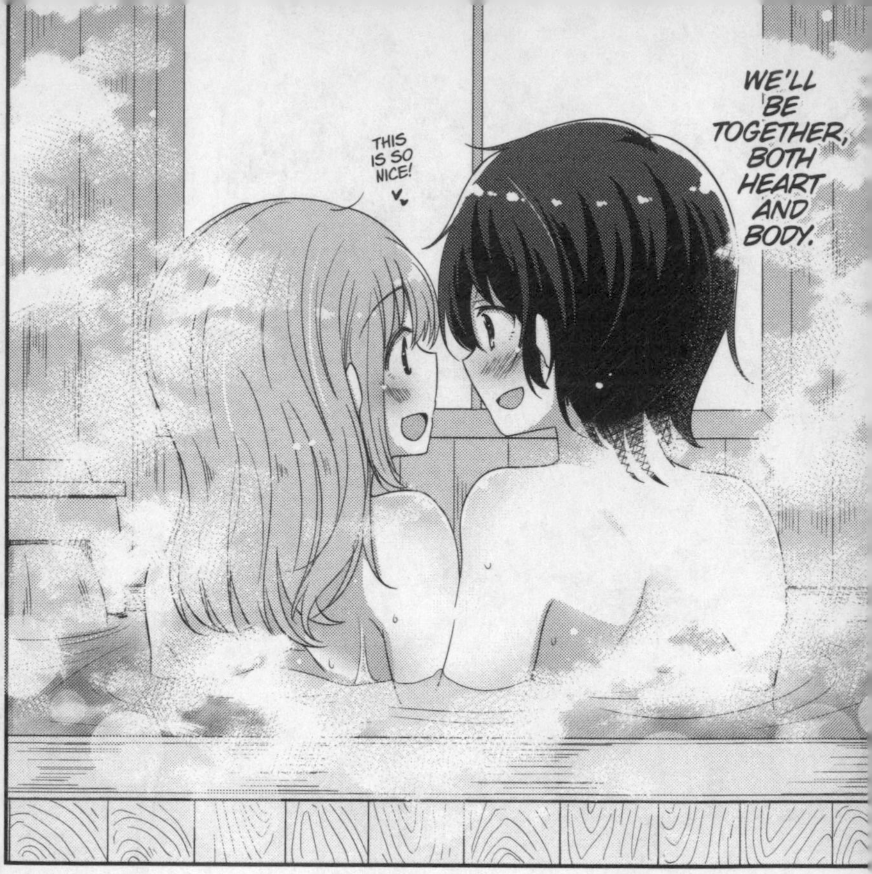
WE'LL BE TOGETHER, BOTH HEART AND BODY.
THIS IS SO NICE! ♥

OMAKE

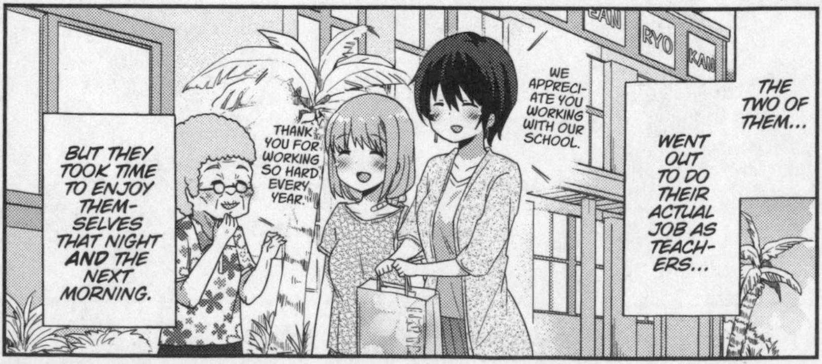
THE TWO OF THEM...
WENT OUT TO DO THEIR ACTUAL JOB AS TEACHERS...
WE APPRECIATE YOU WORKING WITH OUR SCHOOL.
THANK YOU FOR WORKING SO HARD EVERY YEAR.
BUT THEY TOOK TIME TO ENJOY THEMSELVES THAT NIGHT AND THE NEXT MORNING.

TO BE CONTINUED...

OUR TEACHERS
ARE DATING

Our Teachers are Dating!

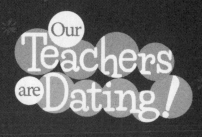

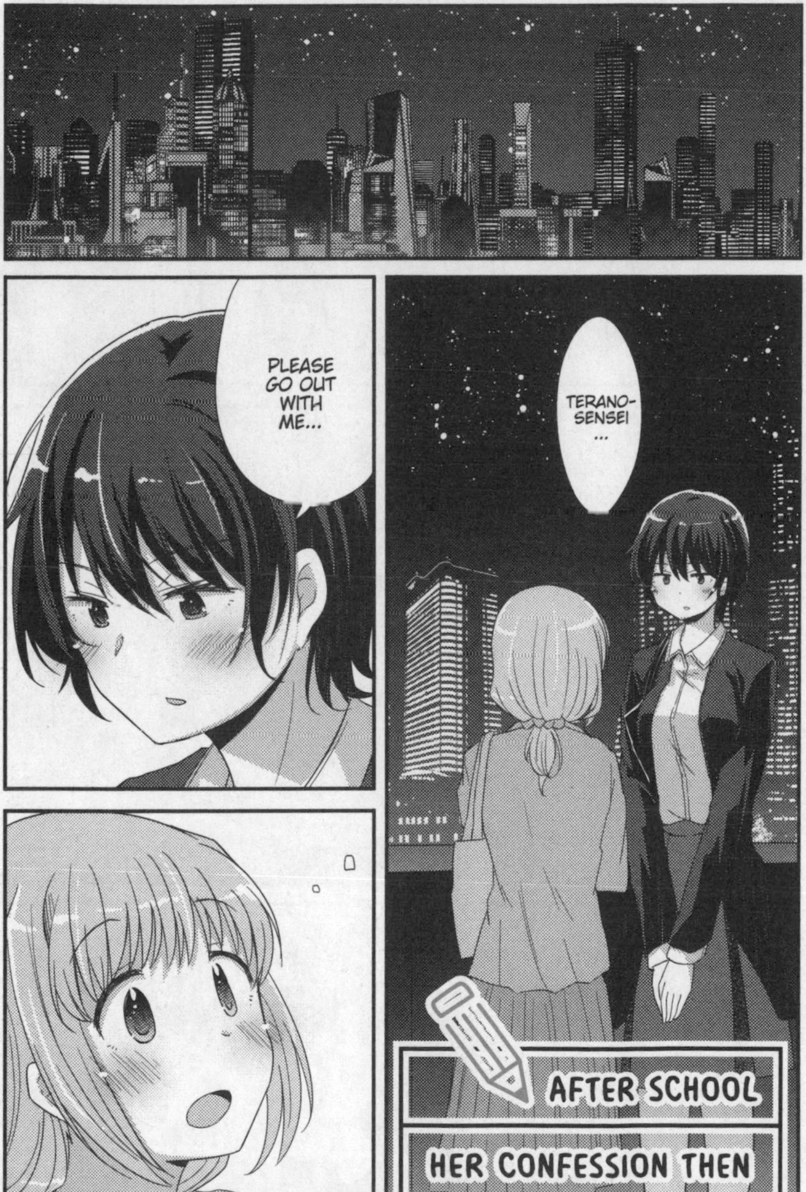
TERANO-SENSEI...
AFTER SCHOOL
HER CONFESSION THEN
PLEASE GO OUT WITH ME...

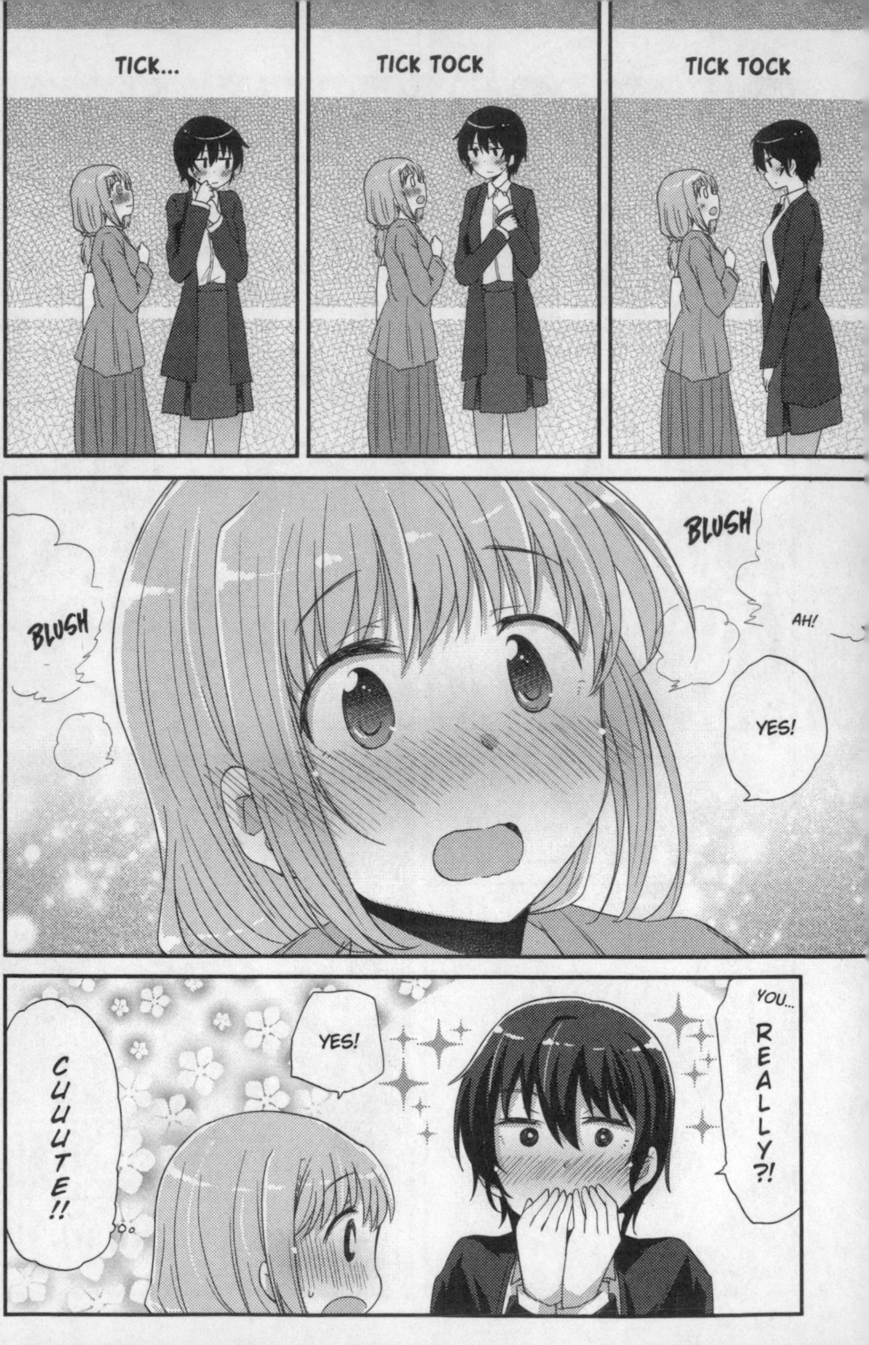
TICK TOCK
TICK TOCK
TICK...
BLUSH
AH!
YES!
BLUSH
YOU... REALLY?!
YES!
CUUUTE!!

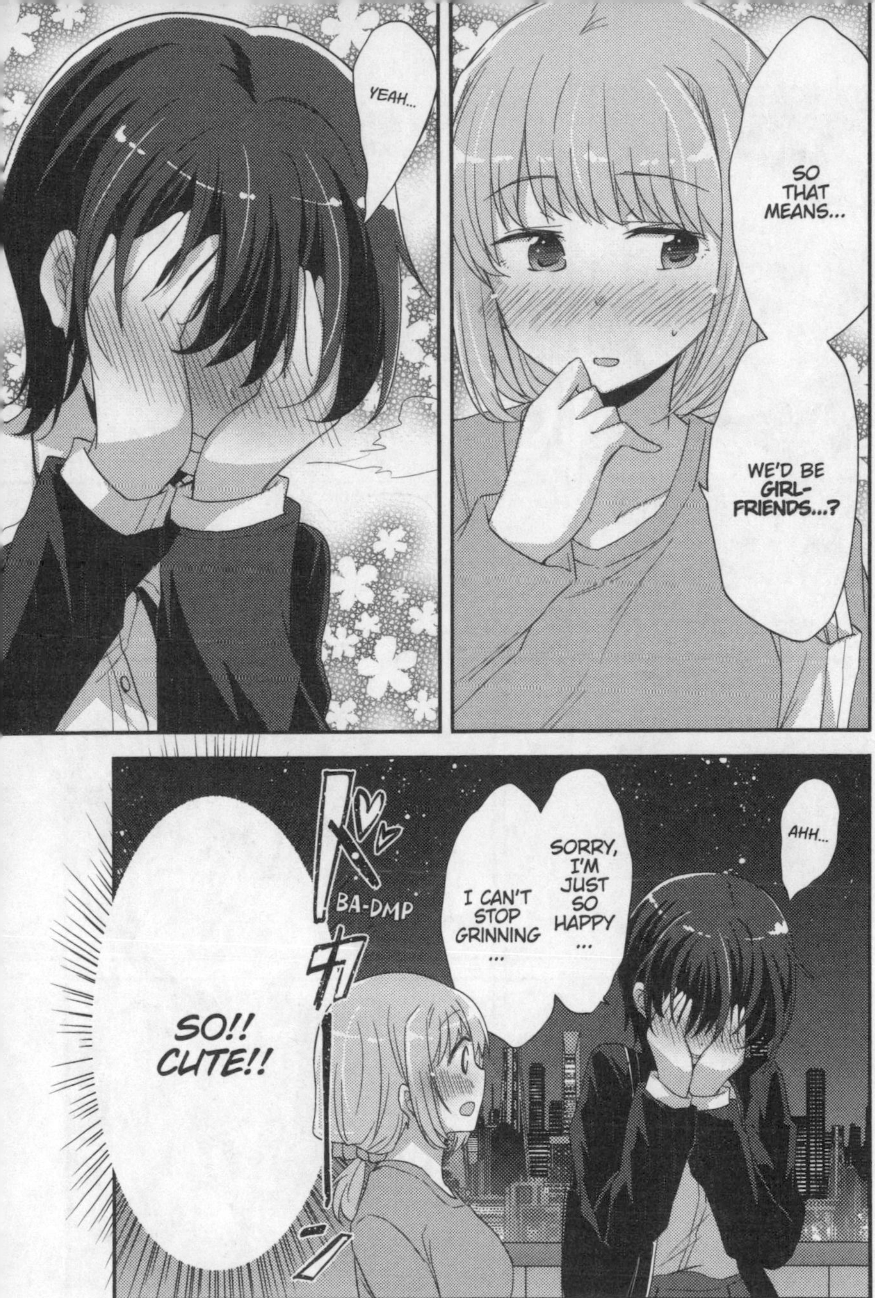
SO THAT MEANS...
WE'D BE GIRL-FRIENDS...?
YEAH...
AHH...
SORRY, I'M JUST SO HAPPY...
I CAN'T STOP GRINNING...
BA-DMP
SO!! CUTE!!

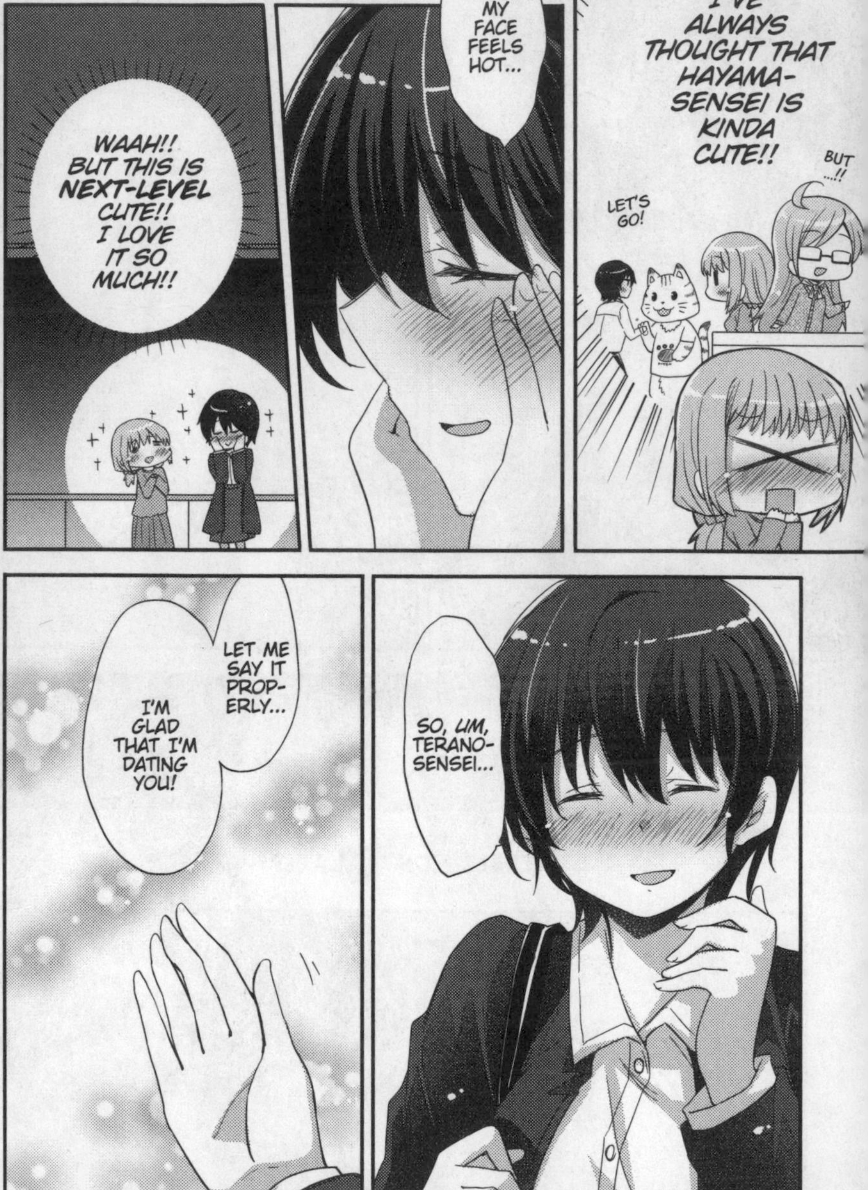
I'VE ALWAYS THOUGHT THAT HAYAMA-SENSEI IS KINDA CUTE!!
BUT ...!!
LET'S GO!
OH... MY FACE FEELS HOT...
WAAH!! BUT THIS IS NEXT-LEVEL CUTE!! I LOVE IT SO MUCH!!
SO, UM, TERANO-SENSEI...
LET ME SAY IT PROPERLY...
I'M GLAD THAT I'M DATING YOU!

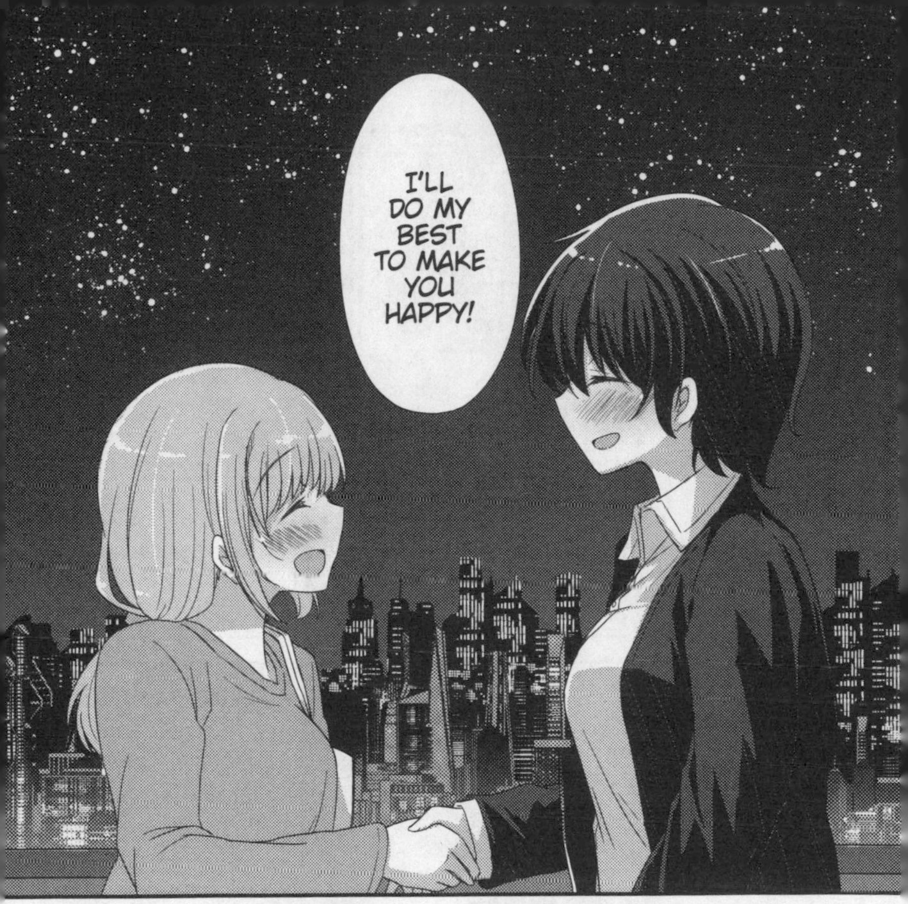
I'LL DO MY BEST TO MAKE YOU HAPPY!

~THREE MONTHS LATER~

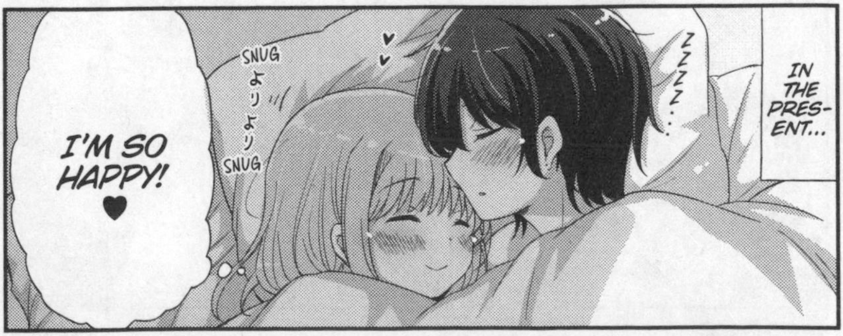
IN THE PRESENT...
ZZZZ...
SNUG
よりより
SNUG
I'M SO HAPPY! ♥

(※Initial draft.)

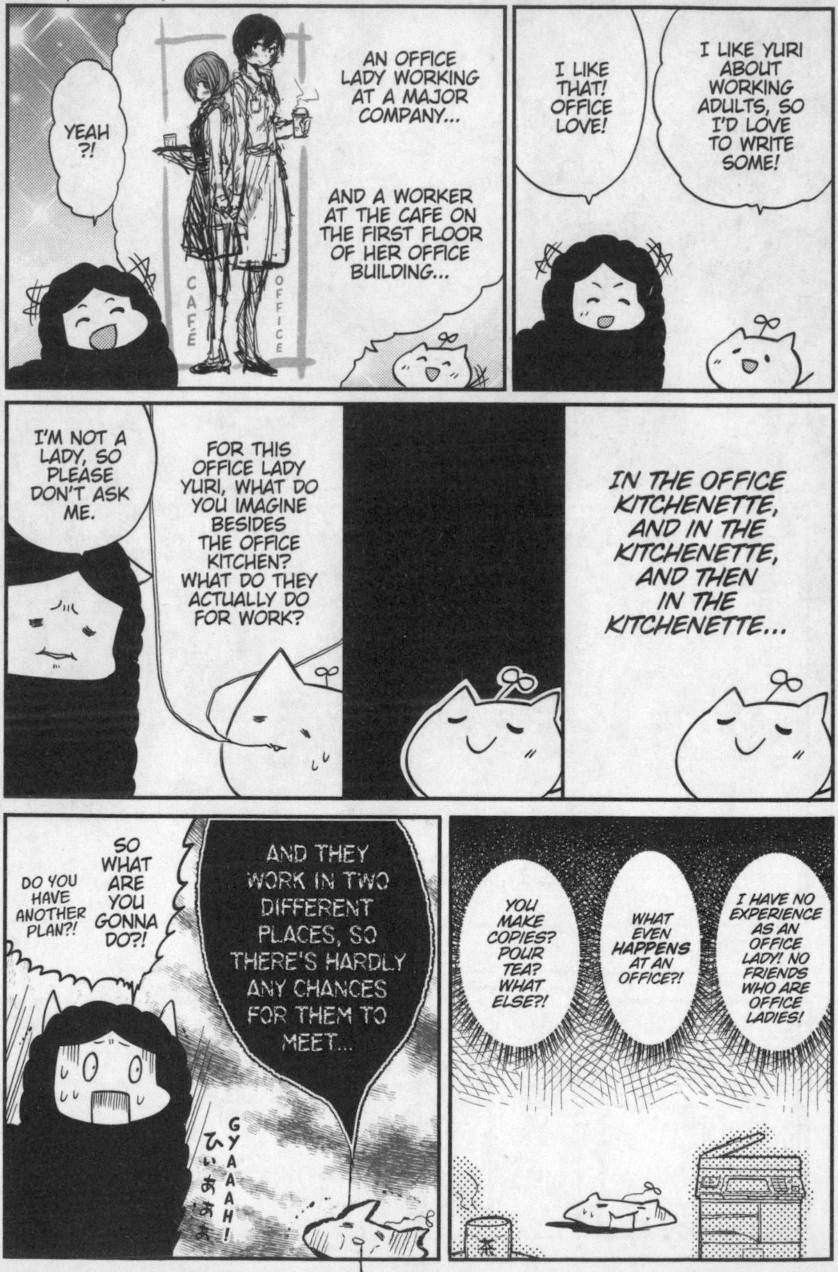
I LIKE YURI ABOUT WORKING ADULTS, SO I'D LOVE TO WRITE SOME!
I LIKE THAT! OFFICE LOVE!
AN OFFICE LADY WORKING AT A MAJOR COMPANY...
AND A WORKER AT THE CAFE ON THE FIRST FLOOR OF HER OFFICE BUILDING...
OFFICE
CAFÉ
YEAH?!
IN THE OFFICE KITCHENETTE, AND IN THE KITCHENETTE, AND THEN IN THE KITCHENETTE...
FOR THIS OFFICE LADY YURI, WHAT DO YOU IMAGINE BESIDES THE OFFICE KITCHEN? WHAT DO THEY ACTUALLY DO FOR WORK?
I'M NOT A LADY, SO PLEASE DON'T ASK ME.
I HAVE NO EXPERIENCE AS AN OFFICE LADY! NO FRIENDS WHO ARE OFFICE LADIES!
WHAT EVEN HAPPENS AT AN OFFICE?!
YOU MAKE COPIES? POUR TEA? WHAT ELSE?!
茶
AND THEY WORK IN TWO DIFFERENT PLACES, SO THERE'S HARDLY ANY CHANCES FOR THEM TO MEET...
SO WHAT ARE YOU GONNA DO?!
DO YOU HAVE ANOTHER PLAN?!
GYAAAH!
ひいあああ

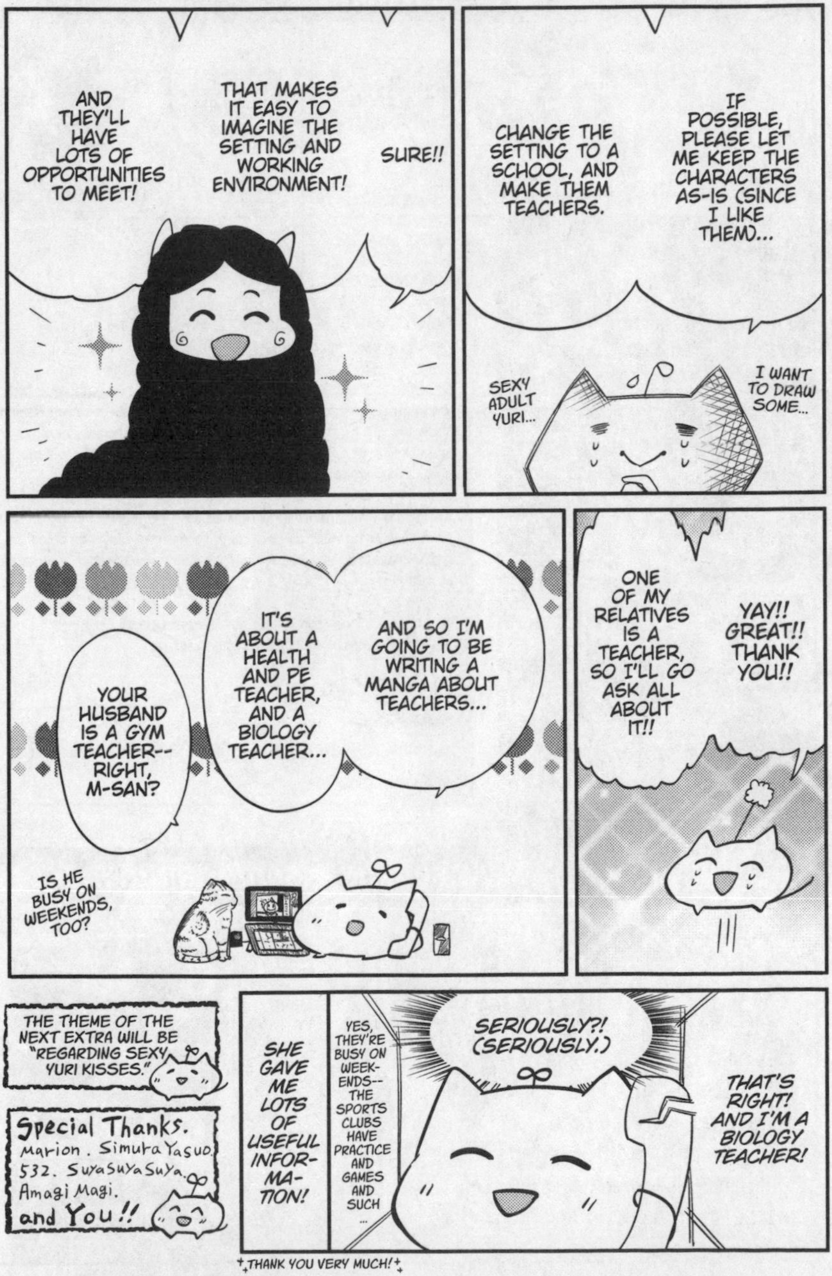
IF POSSIBLE, PLEASE LET ME KEEP THE CHARACTERS AS-IS (SINCE I LIKE THEM)...
CHANGE THE SETTING TO A SCHOOL, AND MAKE THEM TEACHERS.
I WANT TO DRAW SOME...
SEXY ADULT YURI...
SURE!!
THAT MAKES IT EASY TO IMAGINE THE SETTING AND WORKING ENVIRONMENT!
AND THEY'LL HAVE LOTS OF OPPORTUNITIES TO MEET!
YAY!! GREAT!! THANK YOU!!
ONE OF MY RELATIVES IS A TEACHER, SO I'LL GO ASK ALL ABOUT IT!!
AND SO I'M GOING TO BE WRITING A MANGA ABOUT TEACHERS...
IT'S ABOUT A HEALTH AND PE TEACHER, AND A BIOLOGY TEACHER...
YOUR HUSBAND IS A GYM TEACHER--RIGHT, M-SAN?
IS HE BUSY ON WEEKENDS, TOO?
THAT'S RIGHT! AND I'M A BIOLOGY TEACHER!
SERIOUSLY?! (SERIOUSLY.)
YES, THEY'RE BUSY ON WEEK-ENDS--THE SPORTS CLUBS HAVE PRACTICE AND GAMES AND SUCH...
SHE GAVE ME LOTS OF USEFUL INFOR-MA-TION!
THE THEME OF THE NEXT EXTRA WILL BE "REGARDING SEXY YURI KISSES."
Special Thanks.
Marion. Simura Yasuo. 532. SuyaSuyaSuya. Amagi Magi.
and You!!
THANK YOU VERY MUCH!

SEVEN SEAS ENTERTAINMENT PRESENTS

Our Teachers are Dating!

story and art by PIKACHI OHI

VOLUME 1

TRANSLATION
Jennifer Ward

ADAPTATION
Rebecca Scoble

LETTERING AND RETOUCH
Erika Terriquez

COVER DESIGN
Nicky Lim

PROOFREADER
Cae Hawksmoor

EDITOR
Jenn Grunigen

PREPRESS TECHNICIAN
Rhiannon Rasmussen-Silverstein

PRODUCTION MANAGER
Lissa Pattillo

MANAGING EDITOR
Julie Davis

ASSOCIATE PUBLISHER
Adam Arnold

PUBLISHER
Jason DeAngelis

OUR TEACHERS ARE DATING VOL. 1
© Pikachi Ohi 2019
First published in Japan in 2019 by ICHIJINSHA Inc., Tokyo.
English translation rights arranged with KODANSHA.

Seven Seas press and purchase enquiries can be sent to Marketing Manager
Lianne Sentar at press@gomanga.com. Information regarding the distribution
and purchase of digital editions is available from Digital Manager CK Russell
at digital@gomanga.com.

Seven Seas and the Seven Seas logo are trademarks of
Seven Seas Entertainment, LLC. All rights reserved.

ISBN: 978-1-64505-834-2

Printed in Canada

First Printing: September 2020

10 9 8 7 6 5 4 3 2 1

FOLLOW US ONLINE: *www.sevenseasentertainment.com*

READING DIRECTIONS

This book reads from *right to left*, Japanese style.
If this is your first time reading manga, you start
reading from the top right panel on each page and
take it from there. If you get lost, just follow the
numbered diagram here. It may seem backwards at
first, but you'll get the hang of it! Have fun!!

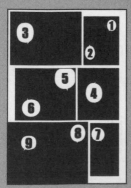

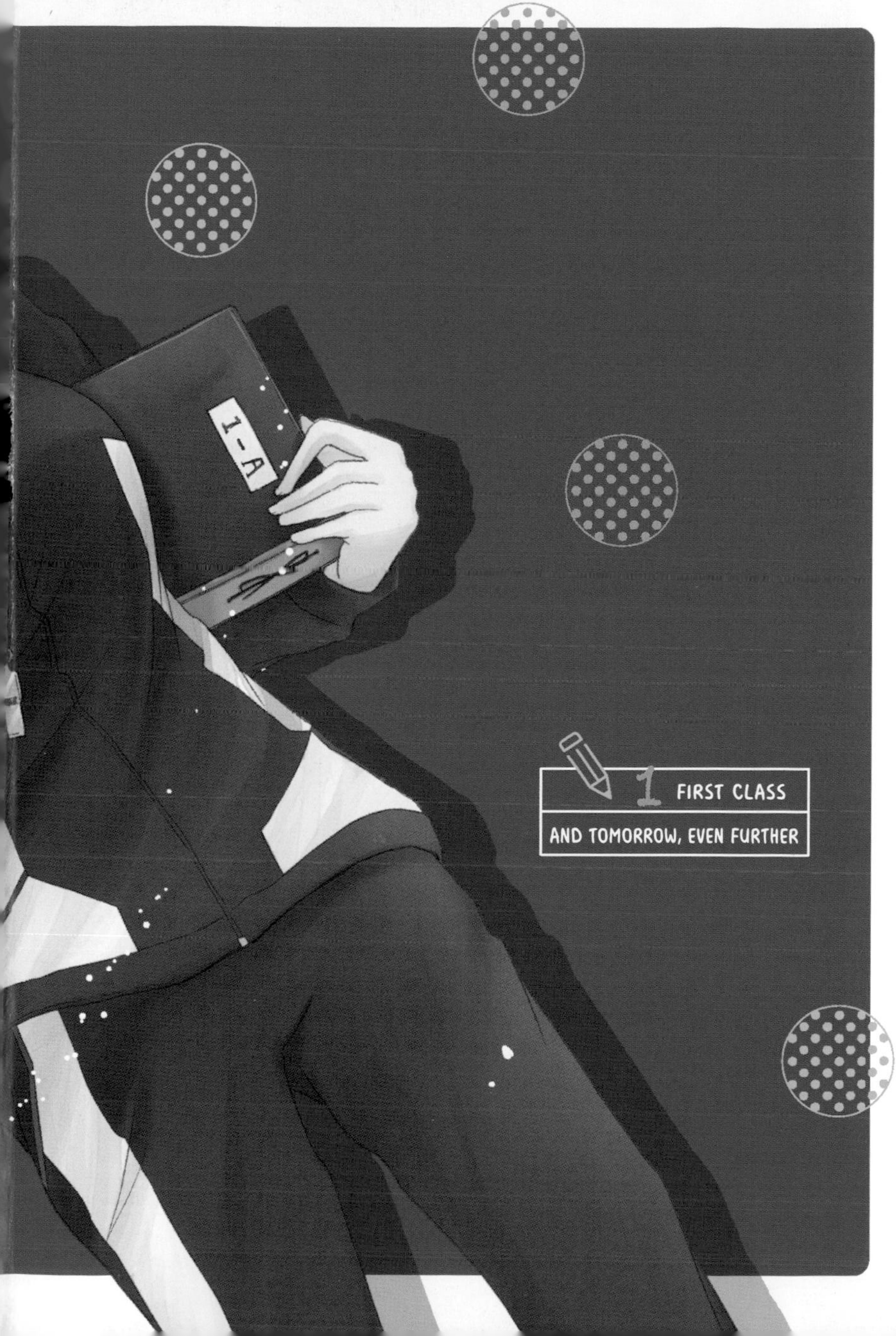
1-A
1 FIRST CLASS
AND TOMORROW, EVEN FURTHER

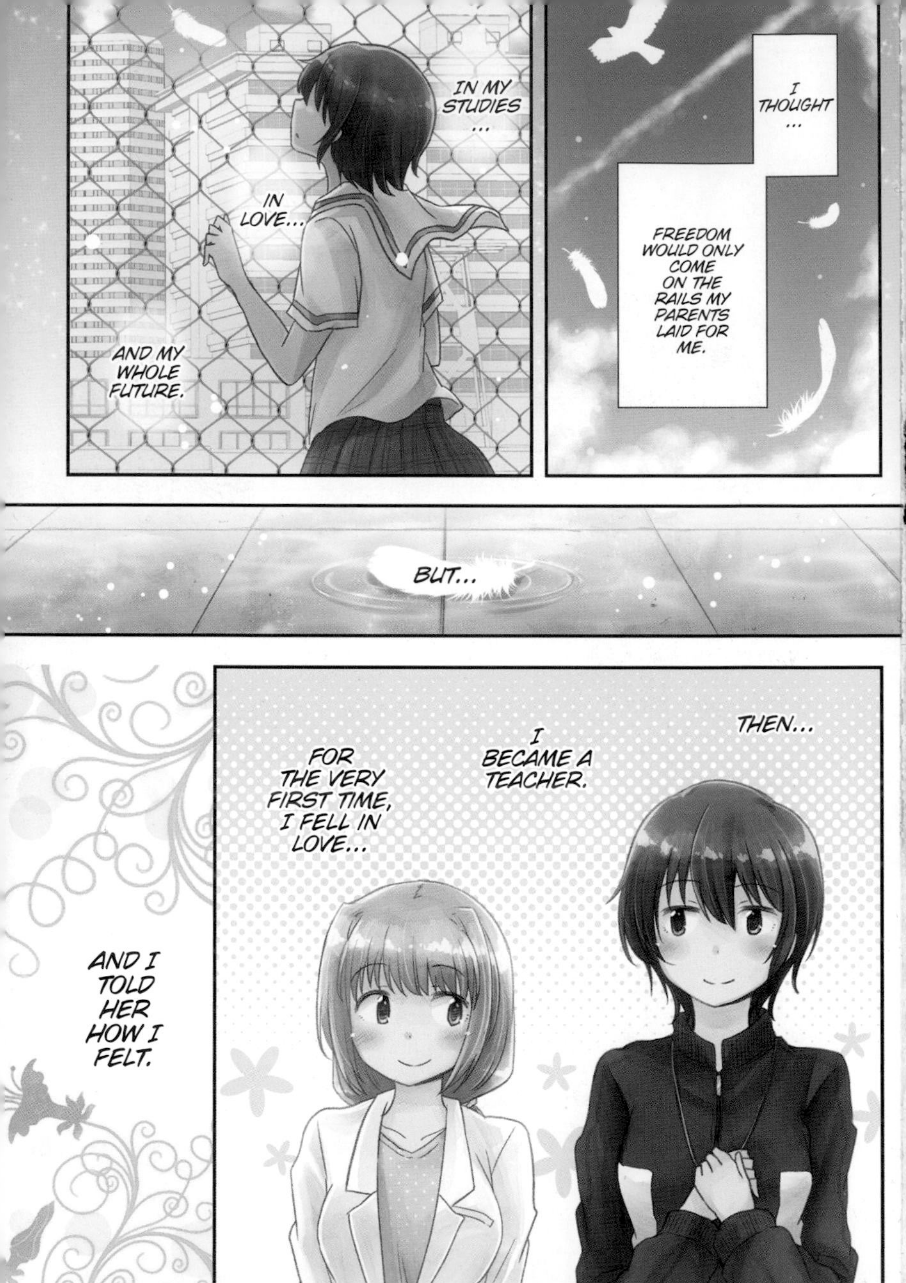
I THOUGHT ...
FREEDOM WOULD ONLY COME ON THE RAILS MY PARENTS LAID FOR ME.
IN MY STUDIES ...
IN LOVE...
AND MY WHOLE FUTURE.
BUT...
THEN...
I BECAME A TEACHER.
FOR THE VERY FIRST TIME, I FELL IN LOVE...
AND I TOLD HER HOW I FELT.